HARD AGROUND

HARD AGROUND

HARD AGROUND

The Wreck of the USS *Tennessee* and the Rise of the US Navy

ANDREW C. A. JAMPOLER

THE UNIVERSITY OF ALABAMA PRESS

Tuscaloosa

The University of Alabama Press
Tuscaloosa, Alabama 35487-0380
uapress.ua.edu

Inquiries about reproducing material from this work should
be addressed to the University of Alabama Press.

Typeface: Garamond Premier Pro

Cover image: "U.S.S. *Memphis* aground off Santo Domingo," 1916; National Archives
and Record Administration, NARA Records Group 80, Box 828 (2-365-21379)
Cover design: Lori Lynch

Cataloging-in-Publication data is available from the Library of Congress.
ISBN: 978-0-8173-2139-0 (cloth)
ISBN: 978-0-8173-6108-2 (paper)
E-ISBN: 978-0-8173-9421-9

Contents

Note on the Cover

"USS *Memphis* aground off Santo Domingo"

After christening in 1904 and until mid-1916 the armored cruiser *Memphis* had been the USS *Tennessee* (ACR-10). Changing her name to "Memphis" that May freed up "Tennessee" for BB-43, the lead ship of the small *Tennessee*-class of battleships scheduled to be laid down at the New York Naval Shipyard in 1917, reserving the names of the states for the navy's new capital ships.

Late in the afternoon of August 29, 1916, a typical, balmy late summer's day in the Caribbean, ranks of enormous waves suddenly pushed from the south into the open anchorage of the Dominican Republic's capital city, where *Memphis* lay at anchor. Dragging her anchors and unable to get under way, *Memphis* was quickly driven up onto the sloping foreshore by the waves. Once aground, the big cruiser was swiftly destroyed.

Forty-three members of *Memphis*'s crew died or were lost at sea that afternoon, including twenty-five men who drowned when one of the cruiser's motor sailers, imprudently returning a recreation party to the ship, capsized in the seas on its way from the capital. Eight were lost from several of *Memphis*'s other boats, afloat briefly between ship and shore late in the day. Not all the dead drowned off ship's boats. Several were scalded to death in a fire room during their desperate efforts to get steam to the main engines to get the ship under way. A further 204 crew members were injured, many seriously.

This unattributed photograph of *Memphis* aground and seemingly abandoned, with a swing bridge rigged to allow easy movement between the wreck and the shore, and still flying her navy jack and the American flag, is from the collection of the National Archives. The vacant lot adjacent to the wreck abutted one of Santo Domingo's baseball fields. Ball games soon resumed there with the imposing hulk as a backdrop beyond left field.

———

Illustrations

CHARTS

ACKNOWLEDGMENTS

I owe a special debt to Captain Todd Creekman, USN (Ret.), for many years the executive director of the Naval Historical Foundation, who was generous with his and the foundation's help in many ways throughout the nearly two decades that I have been researching and writing maritime history. I'm grateful, too, to Mark Mollan (then archivist, Old Navy Maritime Reference, NARA), who through several books has helped me plumb the vast collection of the National Archives to find what I sought, and unknown treasures besides; to Anita Barrett, of Loudoun County Virginia's public library system, a tireless and always willing manipulator of the national interlibrary loan system; and also to Captain Roger Ekman, USN (Ret.), whose generosity permitted the digitization of the *Proceedings* of the US Naval Institute, beginning with the 1874 volume.

I am grateful also to Ed Caylor (the senior surviving pilot of Navy AF 586, whose ditching off Kamchatka in October 1978 was the subject of my first book, *Adak*), Andrew Gordon (author of *The Rules of the Game: Jutland and British Naval Command* [Naval Institute Press, 2013]), Nick Jellicoe (author of *Jutland, The Unfinished Battle* [Seaforth Publishing, 2016]), Paul Pedisich (author of *Congress Buys a Navy* [Naval Institute Press, 2016], this while dealing with Hurricane Harvey), and Mike Pestorius (a fellow member of the navy's Strategic Studies Group III in 1983–84), all of whom read the manuscript in draft and shared their valuable comments with me. This is a better story and more accurate history thanks to their help. Its remaining flaws, of course, are sadly mine.

Others who have been generous with their assistance while I learned and wrote about the era of the Great War and armored cruiser USS *Tennessee*'s short life and swift death include Jeff Bridgers (reference section, Prints & Photographs Division, Library of Congress); Darla Brock (archivist, Tennessee State Library and Archives); Lisa Budreau (Tennessee State Museum); Tiffany

Cabrera and Evan Duncan (special projects division, Office of the Historian, US Department of State); Michael Crawford (senior historian, Naval History and Heritage Command); Laura Deal (digital products librarian, Woodrow Wilson International Center for Scholars); Jeff Giambrone (reference services, Mississippi Department of Archives and History); Glenn Gottschalk (director of Institutional Research, Planning, and Assessment, US Naval Academy); Tina Gutshall (conservation administrator, the Mariners' Museum); Megan Halsband (Library of Congress); Carly Houlahan (Stanford University, class of 2017); Alix Jefferson (curator, Map Collection, Free Library of Philadelphia); Michael Klein (senior reference librarian, Geography and Map Division, Library of Congress); Steven Lynch and Alexandra McCallen (Navy Department Library); Jessica Lyndon, (associate archivist, Special Collections Research Center, Temple University Libraries); Michael Macan (history reference librarian, Nimitz Library, US Naval Academy); Kelly McAnnaney (archivist, NARA, New York City); Adam Minakowski (reference and special collections librarian, Nimitz Library); Tim Nenninger, National Archives; Pam Overmann (curator, Navy Art Collection, Navy History and Heritage Command); Terry Potter (director of Archive & Library, Independence Seaport Museum); Scott Price and Beth Crumley (chief and assistant historian, US Coast Guard Office of External Outreach and Heritage); Anna Shaffer (regent, Old Glory Chapter, DAR, Franklin, Tennessee); Alec Smith (MLIS candidate, Drexel University); Ann Toplovich (executive director, Tennessee State Historical Society); and Kimberley Tully (curator of rare books, Paley Library, Temple University).

My thanks also go to Jeff Bridgers, Michael Crawford, Captain Todd Creekman, USN (Ret.), James McGlothlin, Gale Munroe, and Meghan Townes for their generous assistance in locating some illustrations.

I am also grateful to Dan Waterman, editor in chief of the University of Alabama Press—our extended dialogue brought this book to where it is today; to David Alcorn, of Alcorn Publication Design, for his very great technical assistance with this book and several of my previous titles; to Lys Weiss of Post Hoc Academic Publishing Services, who copyedited the manuscript and prepared the index; and to Carol Connell, project editor for this book at the University of Alabama Press.

And finally, now for the eighth time, my last "thank you" goes to my wife, Suzy, who among other assistance prepared the many illustrations for publication. For that, and for everything else during almost sixty happy years, Suzy, thank you.

HARD AGROUND

FIGURE 1.1. The Navy of the United States.

This illustration of seemingly all of the combatant ships of the US Navy under way at once, churning the ocean into foam, appeared as a double-page, fold-out centerfold in the June 19, 1897, edition of *Harper's Weekly* (vol. 41, no. 2113), about a year before the Spanish-American War began. Artist Louis Sonntag's drawing accompanied a three-page article describing "The American Fleet," by the prolific author and naval analyst, Lieutenant Commander J. D. Jerrold Kelley, USN. Kelley judged that the US Navy then ranked fifth in the world in combat power, behind the navies of Great Britain, France, Russia, and Italy. In the generation just past, the American navy ship count had gone from being inferior to Chile's to superior to Germany's. In the generation to come, the US Navy would climb to a precarious third, behind the fleets of Great Britain and Germany, now in furious competition against one another, and just ahead of those of France and fast-rising Japan.

Secretary of the Navy John Long's report to President William McKinley that same year said the navy's "effective fighting force" in November numbered 54 ships, with another 22 under construction. In time of need, Long wrote, combatant ships in commission could be augmented by 64 other naval vessels and by many merchant "auxiliaries" after the latter were armed according to contingency plans.

W. Louis Sonntag (1869–98), the artist, and son of a well-known landscape painter, was a gifted watercolorist, an able draftsman, and a model builder. Sonntag also drew

illustrations, especially "marine pictures," for newspapers and periodicals, often for *Collier's Weekly*, New York City's popular "illustrated journal of art, literature and current events." According to its editor, "the outbreak of the war against Spanish domination of Cuba roused [Sonntag] and stimulated his powers to their extreme limit," so wrote Robert Collier in the May 21, 1898, issue (vol. 21, no. 7) of the magazine, explaining Sonntag's premature death.

"Of slight figure and delicate physique," Sonntag had died in New York City ten days earlier at twenty-nine years of age because, Collier explained obscurely, "his vitality was not equal to the demands which his spirit, intensified by patriotic ardor, made upon him in the past few weeks." It's possible, but unproven, that Sonntag died of malaria, contracted in Cuba while on a sketching trip to that island.

Source: Naval Historical Foundation.

Chapter One

THE RECONSTRUCTION OF THE AMERICAN NAVY

In conclusion, we ask for the bill now reported fair and unprejudiced consideration. It is a subject to which the committee have given patient and laborious study and effort. It comes before the house with the sanction and approval of an entirely unanimous committee. During its preparation no question of politics or party interest has for a moment divided us. On this subject the doors of the committee room have been barred and bolted against such intrusions. We see the country which we love and honor with equal zeal, a country which ought even now to lead the world in commerce, and which, from its great promise may justly aspire to become the ruler of the seas, helpless on the ocean to defend itself against even the feebler naval powers, and without division of sentiment, seek to provide partial present remedy for so grave a misfortune, and the beginning of a policy which may lead up to the hoped for results.

—47th Cong., 1st Sess., HR 653, "Construction of
Vessels of War for the Navy," March 8, 1882

Her future, of course, was unknowable when, near the end of 1904, the new USS *Tennessee*, armored cruiser no. 10, was eased off the building ways into the Delaware River across from Camden, New Jersey, by her Philadelphia shipbuilders, William Cramp and Sons. Cramp's had competed for the contract against six other yards, all bidding to build one of two "first class armored cruisers" that Congress had described in July 1902 as "carrying the heaviest armor and most powerful armament," and capable of the "highest practicable speed" for vessels of their class.[1] Not until October 28, 1902, had the decision finally been made to prioritize power over speed as the majority of the Naval

Construction Board had recommended. This done, the navy judge advocate general, Captain Samuel Lemley, USN, released the navy's request for proposals for the construction of the first two *Tennessee*-class cruisers to industry the same day.[2]

The competition among the yards was very aggressive; the bids clustered within several percent of each other. Fore River of Quincy, Massachusetts, was the high bidder at $4,578,000, and William Cramp and Sons the low, at $4,200,000. The winner to build the second of the pair, USS *Washington*, was the misnamed New York Shipbuilding Corporation, actually located in Camden, New Jersey. Years earlier Cramp's had built the first two armored cruisers in the US Navy, the well-regarded *New York* and the slightly larger *Brooklyn*, so the *Tennessee* award would have appeared very low risk to both contracting parties.

Tennessee's home yard was likely somewhat better known to the general public than were its half-dozen competitors in the bidding. Cramp's, which had stood on the Delaware River waterfront in Philadelphia's Kensington district since 1830, had been one of the principal American exhibitors in the great Transportation Hall at the World's Columbian Exposition of 1893, a Chicago world's fair marking the four centuries of progress since Christopher Columbus had first set foot on the New World, believing to the end that he'd arrived in the Orient. The five-month-long exposition, the setting for Erik Larson's gripping *The Devil in the White City: Murder, Magic and Madness at the Fair That Changed America* (New York: Crown, 2003), would ultimately lure some 27 million fair-goers to its vast grounds on Chicago's lakefront Jackson Park, making it a brilliant financial success.

Cramp's was prominent among the dozens of international exhibitors in the fair's imposing transportation exhibit hall, with a display that featured a full size, 70-foot-long, 35-foot-wide slice of a ship's hull above the waterline, and included a funnel that soared 80 feet above the exhibit hall's floor. The model represented a cross section from one of the pair of identical steamers then under construction in Philadelphia for the American Line, the SS *St. Louis* (Cramp's hull no. 277) and SS *St. Paul* (Cramp's no. 278), each displacing 11,629 tons. The wonderfully detailed, life-sized exhibit revealed portions of four interior decks, and included a lifeboat atop the deckhouse, ready for launching. In all, the exhibit represented, as one industry observer reported, "a little more than half the beam and one-seventh the length of the ship itself."[3]

Later, SS *St. Louis* was chartered as a transport during the Spanish-American War, when—according to her former commanding officer, Captain Caspar Goodrich, USN, writing in the March 1899 *Proceedings of the U.S. Naval Institute*—she'd won "exceptional credit" for her four weeks of wartime service (at $2,500 per day). That was so in part, Captain Goodrich explained helpfully, because of "adequate water closet accommodations." He went on to elaborate in surplus detail: "Twenty men to one hole is a barely comfortable but not luxurious ratio. Over fifty men to one hole is a ratio bordering on the distressful. About a dozen extra seats were provided in the *St. Louis* to reach the former proportion." And through such thoughtful plumbing accommodations in the crew's heads was her exceptional credit won.

Renamed USS *Louisville*, the former *St. Louis* then sailed as a navy-crewed transport during the later years of World War I. Back in mufti after the war, she caught fire in early 1920 during a refit in Hoboken, New Jersey, and sank at the pier, never to go to sea under power again.[4]

SS *St. Louis*'s sister ship, SS *St. Paul*, suffered an equally sudden end. Launched in March 1895, she hung up in the building ways at Cramp's, thus disappointing the huge crowd assembled at the yard expecting to watch her slide majestically into the Delaware River, there also to hear famed author and humorist Mark Twain's remarks lubricate her passage from the ways to the water. The delay meant that Twain never spoke at her rescheduled christening ceremony two weeks later. *St. Paul* then went on to a history very like her sister ship's, including six weeks under charter to the navy during the Spanish-American War, troop transport service during the Great War (occasionally sailing alone in a nod to her 22 knot speed), and a photogenic April 25, 1918, capsizing at Pier 61 on the Hudson River, killing two people. (Oddly, something similar happened six months later to the much larger troop transport USS *America*, formerly Hamburg America's liner SS *Amerika*. She also sank at her dock in New York.)

For the most part, Cramp's many other vessels—there were around 540 of them built between the sloop *Elizabeth* in 1830 and the *Balao*-class submarine USS *Tusk* in 1945, everything from dump barges to battleships for several countries, before the historic yard closed for the last time—enjoyed much longer and more successful service lives at sea than did the two *Saints*.

Not so the armored cruiser USS *Tennessee* (Cramp's no. 322).

Launched some ten years after the close of the World's Columbian Exposition, on the snowy morning of December 3, 1904, this *Tennessee* (the second ship of the US Navy to have that name; the first was a ship-rigged screw frigate) soon became the first of four imposing 14,500 ton, four-stack combatants that together constituted the US Navy's new armored cruiser squadron. (The others were *Washington*, *North Carolina*, and *Montana*.) *Tennessee* was the fifteenth ship Cramp's had built for the navy since its first in 1888, the notably ugly and much smaller protected cruiser USS *Baltimore* (Cramp's no. 254).

Two years after that, following fitting out and trials, USS *Tennessee* was commissioned at the Philadelphia Navy Yard under the command of Captain Albert Berry, USN, a fifty-eight-year-old Naval Academy graduate from—appropriately—Nashville, Tennessee. The story is that in 1865 young Berry had been granted an appointment to the US Naval Academy, when the school had just returned to Maryland from Rhode Island, by President Andrew Johnson (governor, senator, and later military governor of Tennessee between 1862 and 1865), reportedly as Johnson's first official act on taking office after the assassination of Lincoln.[5] Berry graduated in 1869, fourth from the bottom of his class. Many years later, Captain Berry (1848–1938) became the first of *Tennessee*'s thirteen commanding officers during her short ten years afloat.

The big (504 feet long with a complement of 44 officers and 930 men), fast (22 knots), powerful (23,000 horsepower), and heavily gunned (four 10 inch and thirty-eight 6 inch and 3 inch guns) ship had gone from contract award to commissioning in just three years and five months, saving Cramp's the fine for late delivery that after the first month's delay would have ratcheted up from $300 to $800 per day.

Tennessee in the water marked a further step two decades or so into the navy's revitalization after a collapse following the Civil War so profound that on November 28, 1881, then secretary of the navy William Hunt's annual report to newly inaugurated president Chester Arthur lamented:

The condition of the Navy imperatively demands the prompt and earnest attention of Congress. Unless some action be had in its behalf it must soon dwindle into insignificance. From such a state it would be difficult to revive it into efficiency without dangerous delay and enormous expense. Emergencies may at any moment arise which would render its aid indispensible to the protection of the lives and property of our citizens abroad and at home, and even to our existence as a nation.

We have been unable to make such an appropriate display of our naval power abroad as will cause us to be respected. . . . It is a source of mortification to our officers and fellow countrymen generally, that our vessels of war should stand in such mean contrast alongside those of other and inferior powers.[6]

"These things ought not to be . . . ," Secretary Hunt allowed, in calm understatement.

Admiral David Porter's annual report to Secretary Hunt, enclosure no. 4 to Hunt's own report to Arthur (in office only two months), was no less grim. "Our Navy has for some years past," Porter, a veteran of the Civil War battles for control of the Mississippi River and the nation's senior serving naval officer, told the secretary, "been in rather an inefficient condition, not altogether useless in time of peace where it is only necessary to have well-kept vessels to visit foreign countries, but for war purposes it is nearly worthless, reminding one of the ancient Chinese forts on which dragons were painted to frighten away the enemy." Dismissing the "simply useless" vessels of the iron-clad navy, in June 1881 Porter counted only twenty-six ships that could go to sea in case of war, of which only eighteen had sufficient speed either to pursue or to escape from an enemy combatant.

Circumstances were no better in the American merchant marine, which had collapsed early in the Civil War as ship owners rushed to escape the depredations of the Confederate States Navy's commerce raiders—most built in the United Kingdom—by registering their ships under foreign flags. That flight, the successful CSN attack on the Union's whaling fleet, and a generally hard life at sea thinned American merchant seamen from the ubiquitous presence they had once been in foreign ports to infrequent sightings, to be replaced beginning in the 1870s with American tourists, thick on the ground overseas by the 1910s. The beginnings of the merchant marine's recovery were still forty years away.

Even outsiders might have considered Secretary Hunt's (and Porter's) description of the 1881 US Navy to be generous. Certainly, nothing in the American press about the tragic, failed Arctic cruise of USS *Jeannette* that overlapped the end of the decade suggested that as the 1880s began the US Navy was capable of planning and accomplishing great deeds on salt water.

Jeannette's exciting mission—a transit of the Bering Sea through what turned out to be an entirely imaginary "thermometric gateway" and then via the "supposed open sea" surrounding the North Pole to the Pole itself (the quotations are from the title of a map published in 1872 by American oceanographer Silas Bent)—had begun brightly enough the midafternoon of July 8, 1879, when the handsome, former British gunboat HMS *Pandora*, now commissioned, renamed, and under the command of Lieutenant Commander George Washington De Long, USN, steamed from San Francisco for the distant Arctic Ocean.[7] Accompanied by a collier, the schooner *Fannie A. Hyde*, the heavily laden USS *Jeannette* slowly moved toward the open sea, escorted through the harbor by a flotilla of tugs and yachts "amid," the *New York Times* reported, a celebratory "dipping of flags, screaming of steam whistles, and a salute of 10 guns from Fort Point."

Perfect success would have included not only reaching the Pole, but also finding clues to solving the Arctic's great mystery: the fate of Sir John Franklin's vanished, two-ship Royal Navy expedition of 1845 in search of the undiscovered middle segment of the Northwest Passage. As it happened, *Jeannette* was instead caught fast in sea ice off Wrangel Island in the Chukchi Sea and then crushed there on June 12, 1881, forcing her crew of thirty-three onto the ice and into a heroic trek, hauling small boats as sleds, south toward distant Siberia and salvation. Only thirteen of the men survived. The details of the catastrophe, when reported to the public later in 1881, marked the nadir of the navy's post–Civil War reputation.

Puck, the acerbic American humor magazine, described the navy in its September 14 issue later that year (vol. 10, no. 236) unkindly as comprising "three mud scows supplemented by a superannuated canal boat." Months later, in 1882, the *Judge*, the year-old satirical magazine staffed originally by *Puck*'s malcontents, seemed to share *Puck*'s judgment and that of the general public.

Secretary Hunt, whose resemblance to Colonel Harlan Sanders of Kentucky Fried Chicken fame is striking, lasted only a year in this office, from March 1881 to April 1882—notably, that was four times as long as his immediate

FIGURE 1.2. "Before Alexandria."

In James Albert Wales's cover illustration for the August 12, 1882, issue of *Judge* magazine (vol. 2, no. 42), the US Navy is represented as a tiny, tattered gaff-rigged skiff manned by an anorexic Uncle Sam sailing past the towering stern of Her Majesty's Navy at anchor off Alexandria, Egypt. A plump Royal Navy gunner beams down on the skinny American.

The Royal Navy's shelling of the Egyptian port's forts the month before preserved Muhammed Tewfik Pasha, Great Britain's favorite, on the throne of Egypt in the face of a revolt by Ahmed Urabi. With this help, Tewfik Pasha managed to keep his seat, but under increasingly intrusive British tutelage. The bombardment set the stage for imposition three decades later, on December 18, 1914, of a formal British protectorate over what had been a province of the Ottoman empire since the 1517 defeat of the Mamluks. The ensuing British occupation of Egypt lasted until 1936.

The French, refusing to participate, had relocated their fleet east to Port Said. Not so the Americans, whose part in this bit of bullying by Britain's Mediterranean Squadron would, two days later, put some 160 sailors and marines ashore in Alexandria from US European Squadron ships *Lancaster*, *Quinnebaug*, *Nipsic*, and *Galena*—the first foreign troops ashore—to protect the American consulate and other city real estate from rioters and looters. Urged along by a fascinating adventurer, Charles Chaillé-Long, some in the landing party remained in the battered city for several days, all earning back-dated expeditionary medals. Four days later the British came ashore.

James Albert Wales (1852–86) was one of the breakaway artists from *Puck* who started up the *Judge* in 1881, only to return to *Puck* in 1885 after *Judge* was taken over by Republican investors, looking for a counter to *Puck*'s Democratic voice after the defeat of their presidential candidate, Blaine. Cover political cartoons eventually became unusual for the magazine, which went on to great success, often behind covers that featured a pretty young woman posed winsomely in what was for the day scanty clothing. The *Judge*, confronted by increasing competition after the turn of the century, finally shut down in 1947.

Source: Enoch Pratt Free Library, Baltimore.

predecessor, Nathan Goff of West Virginia—not long enough to preside over the tangible start of navy revitalization two years later under the successor to the assassinated president James Garfield, Chester Arthur. Thanks, however, to Hunt's establishment in June 1881 of the first Naval Advisory Board (chaired by Rear Admiral John Rodgers), which earlier that same November had put the idea of steel ships on the national legislative agenda, there's some reason to credit Hunt with metaphorically "having laid the keel of the new navy."

William Hunt's son and biographer, Thomas, did just that, and so apparently did Senator Henry Anthony of Rhode Island, chairman of the Senate Committee on Naval Affairs until his death in 1884. This is remarkable recognition for an unlikely person to stand at the helm of the US Navy, however briefly: a South Carolina–born graduate of Yale who had spent his adult life as a lawyer in Louisiana; who'd managed to evade active service with his regiment during the Civil War despite holding a lieutenant colonel's commission; who'd served as a judge on the US Court of Claims, and from that place was appointed to Garfield's cabinet representing the rarest of citizens from the American South in that century, white Republicans. There's no evidence that Hunt had ever been afloat on salt water before 1881 when he became navy secretary, or even seen much of it. Then again, neither had Goff. Nor would most of his successors.

If some credited Hunt with even more than having "laid the keel," with having been the proverbial father of the new navy, then its conception occurred during a long evening meeting in his office in the navy secretariat on February 15, 1882, attended by both chairmen of the congressional naval affairs committees and several of their members; by Admirals Porter, Ammen, and the two Rodgers, along with six other commissioned officers; and by several senior civilian engineers and naval constructors.[8] The men, sitting members of Congress, and members of the Naval Advisory Board, met to discuss candidly the complex choices that would define the new navy they all sought. They took as their point of departure the Advisory Board's November 7, 1881, report (delivered four months after President Garfield was shot and two months after he died) that had recommended a $30 million ship construction program. That far-seeing and wildly optimistic proposal encompassed twenty-one armored ships and nearly seventy more unarmored ones. In response, the next year Congress approved construction of two steel warships, but deliberately neglected to appropriate any money for them. A year later, in March 1883, a more generous Congress appropriated $1.3 million to fund the construction of four, and the first bits of a more modern navy finally and slowly moved to the drawing boards: a 4,500 ton cruiser, two 3,000 ton cruisers, and a single 1,485 ton patrol gunboat.

The merit of Hunt's claim for paternity entirely aside—a decade later President Harrison's navy secretary, General Benjamin Franklin Tracy, claimed the same distinction, as had Secretaries William Chandler and William Whitney before Tracy, and Hilary Hebert and others after him—Hunt wasn't present for much that followed that seminal mid-February meeting of minds in his office.[9] On April 16, 1882, Hunt was pushed out of the navy secretariat and from his cabinet by President Arthur. Offered his choice of posting as minister (ambassador) leading the American legation at either the Russian or Austrian imperial court, Hunt reluctantly selected the better paid post at St. Petersburg, where far from home at age sixty he died on February 1884, miserably from a diseased liver.

His death came two months before the first of the navy's initial four steel ships, the schooner-rigged, three-masted dispatch boat USS *Dolphin*, was launched after a troubled construction history from the Delaware River Iron Ship Building and Engine Works, at Chester, Pennsylvania. At 1,485 tons the little *Dolphin* was designed to provide "rapid communications from the seat of government to any point on the coast or to the West India islands, or . . . to act as a fleet dispatch boat or flag-ship."[10] Reflecting an oddly benign view of possible threats to her mission, the unarmored (and barely armed) USS *Dolphin* had been built to merchant ship specifications, and was capable of only 15 knots.

Dolphin's home works, usually called John Roach and Sons, was the largest shipyard on the Delaware River around the turn of the century. Competing against seven other yards, Roach's won the construction contract for all four of the pioneering steel combatant ships funded by the Naval Appropriations Act of 1883, with a bid of $2.44 million. At the time, award of the entire contract to low-bidder Roach must have seemed reasonable, perhaps even cautious. A few years earlier the yard had successfully delivered SS *Columbia*, its hull no. 193, to the Oregon Railroad and Navigation Company. Ordered in July 1879, the iron-hulled, single-stack, steam-powered, 2,700 ton *Columbia* went into mixed passenger and freight service the following May with Thomas Edison's incandescent light system on board, making *Columbia* the first ship to go to sea with electrical power. Her other state-of-the-art features included a large refrigerated space for food storage and four ostensibly watertight compartments in her hull. (Alas, her compartmentation was insufficient to save the ship, when early on July 21, 1907, she collided in the fog with SS *San Pedro* between San Francisco and Portland. *Columbia* quickly sank, putting out her lights and drowning eighty-eight of her passengers and crew, but evidently not dimming Roach and Sons' reputation. That eclipse came later.)

The other three ships in Roach's navy contract were the protected cruisers *Atlanta*, *Boston*, and *Chicago*. All four were steam powered, but each prudently carried a full sailing rig for economy and for use in the event of engine failure or fuel exhaustion. (As had SS *Columbia*; she was rigged as a brigantine.) The twins *Atlanta* and *Boston* were rigged as brigs with 10,400 square feet of sail; the much larger *Chicago* as a bark with nearly 15,000 square feet.

Even before *Dolphin* was launched in April 1884, however, that contract was becoming a disaster, both for Roach and Sons and for the navy, which refused to accept her delivery after sea trials. The result was that Roach and Sons went bankrupt. After complex litigation by both parties, the navy took over the yard and managed completion of the four vessels.

In the early 1880s USS *Dolphin*, *Atlanta*, *Boston*, and *Chicago*, one after the other, introduced something new to the US Navy—steel hulls, to replace familiar wood and recently wrought iron—while retaining until after World War I something very old, full rigs for sail. Interestingly, the decision to move from iron to steel was made not by Hunt's Naval Advisory Board, whose fifteen members in their November 1881 report had been unable to agree on adopting the new materials technology (or on another question of the eight posed by Secretary Hunt, the utility of spar decks), but by the Naval Affairs Committee of the House of Representatives. On March 8, 1882, in HR 653 ("Construction of Vessels of War for the Navy") the eleven members of the committee unanimously recommended to the full House that "steel should be used instead of iron."

The House report, signed by the committee's chairman, Benjamin Harris of Massachusetts, was slow to get to this conclusion. It began with a pages-long commentary on the material condition of the 140 vessels then on the navy register, identifying fully 42—approaching one-third—by name and home port that represented "not only no naval power whatever, but which can hereafter serve no useful purpose, and which are, moreover, a constant drain on the appropriations for the support of the Navy, and a consequent loss to the government to the extent of their cost of protection, which aggregates annually no small sum." Further eliminating tugboats, sailing ships, single-turret monitors, and other ships unsuitable for the open sea from the remaining 98 on the register, left only 38. And among those 38 survivors, the committee concluded dolefully, "many . . . are old and nearly worn out, slow in speed, feeble in offensive power, and utterly deficient in defensive power, even in the power of running away from danger." Nowhere in this much reduced fleet, the committee noted, was there even a single high-power, long-range, rifled breech-loading cannon.

On its way to an assessment that confirmed Secretary Hunt's observations of a few months earlier about the navy's impotence (and similar conclusions in committee reports of the 45th and 46th Congresses), Harris's committee report sharpened the pain by strewing about descriptive phrases like "rotten and utterly worthless," "shameless folly," and "unpardonable extravagance." Tables enumerating ships in the navies of Great Britain and of ten other powers (including Japan) further pressed home the point.

Not until two-thirds of the way through its thirty-page report (plus two hundred pages of testimony by thirty-six witnesses) did Harris's committee get to the question whether iron or steel should be used in the construction of the eighteen first- and second-rate, unarmored cruisers that members recommended be built, the chief parts of a proposed sixty-eight-ship, $29.6 million new building program meant to bring an anemic navy up to date and up to strength. The committee's answer was open-hearth steel, "the only proper material for the construction of vessels of war. . . . The difference between steel as at present manufactured in this country, adapted for shipbuilding purposes, and iron, commonly used, is so great and so much in favor of steel that we would commit a great wrong should we leave the question open." (Interestingly, that wasn't the unanimous answer of the shipbuilding industry executives who testified before the committee. Roach chose steel, but Cramp chose iron when he appeared before the committee on February 3, and had to be bullied by Rep. Leopold Morse, of Massachusetts, into reluctantly endorsing steel.)

FIGURE 1.3. "The Cruel Secretary and the Patriotic Contractor" (*Puck* 17, no. 421).

The collapse of John Roach and Sons under the weight of its July 1883 contract with the US Navy was a scandal of such proportions, and such an attractive opportunity to score political points, that satirical cartoons featuring John Roach appeared four times in *Puck*, the popular satirical magazine published in New York City, during early 1885. These covers from the April 1 and May 20, 1885, issues are two of those four appearances.

The magazine's suspicion that navy ship construction and repair contracts under Republicans had been designed chiefly to funnel money to the party's business supporters and not to fund fleet modernization was the subject in the June 24 issue of yet another, scathing full-page color cartoon, "There's a New Policeman on the Beat." That cover openly identified Roach as a crook being stalked by Secretary of the Navy Whitney in police uniform. Democrat Whitney's rejection of *Dolphin* in mid-1885 (and likely problems with the future three deliveries) prompted the aging and ailing Roach to turn his shipyard over to the government.

FIGURE 1.4. "John Roach's Little Miscalculation" (*Puck* 17, no. 428).

Puck's political orientation favored Democrats, so savage criticism of shipbuilder Roach and Secretaries of the Navy George Robeson (in service 1869–77) and William Chandler (who succeeded Hunt in 1882) came naturally. The magazine gleefully compared the three, Republicans all, by name to one Charles Buddenseik, a notorious builder of a row of flimsy New York City tenement houses that collapsed on top of their tenants in April 1885 and ultimately caused the model malefactor to be sent to jail.

Cover art done jointly by Eugene Zimmerman (1862–1935) and Joseph Keppler (1838–94). After two years at *Puck*, the Swiss-born and self-taught Zimmerman went to the *Judge* in 1886, where he spent the next twenty-six years until retirement drawing cartoons. Keppler, an immigrant from Austria, founded the German-language *Puck* twice, the second time in New York City after a stint drawing for *Frank Leslie's Illustrated Newspaper*. Published in English beginning in 1877, *Puck* went on to great success.

Source: Library of Congress, Prints and Photographs Division.

At 4:00 p.m. on August 1, 1884, USS *Thetis*, USS *Bear*, and USS *Alert* arrived from St. John's, Newfoundland, at the Portsmouth, New Hampshire, inner harbor, where the US Navy's North Atlantic Squadron (including flagship USS *Tennessee* [the first *Tennessee*] with Secretary of the Navy Chandler embarked, *Vandalia*, *Swatara*, *Yantic*, and *Alliance*, together with the training vessels USS *Portsmouth* and *Jamestown* from Annapolis) at anchor awaited them, ships dressed and rigging manned. As the three entered the harbor, *Tennessee*'s band struck up "Home Again." Later, the new arrivals would be serenaded by a song written especially for the occasion, "Home from the Frozen Seas." Here is a sample of the lyrics by Earl Marble, stanza 2:

> Sing the immortal seven / Saved from the Polar blast,
> One winging off to heaven / Crying they're saved at last.
> Honor, renown and fame / Theirs for all coming time,
> Ice has enkindled a flame / Shooting in tongues of rhyme.

"Tongues of rhyme" aside, the hoopla that followed in Portsmouth, repeated a week later in New York City, marked the return of six survivors of the US Army Signal Corps twenty-five-man, three-year-long scientific encampment at Camp Conger, on the shore of Lady Franklin Bay in the Canadian Arctic. Among the six was their chief, Lieutenant Adolphus Washington Greely, USA. (A seventh survivor had "winged off to heaven," meaning died, three days after rescue following emergency surgery to amputate his frostbitten hands and feet.) Commander Winfield S. Schley, USN, commanding the all-navy rescue expedition, had reported its success to Secretary Chandler in a long telegram from St. John's two weeks earlier, providing ample time for arranging the tumultuous welcome afloat and on shore.

The survival and recovery of any of the men was astonishing. Two years of high-level lack of interest in Washington, coupled to the failure of annual scheduled resupply expeditions during the summers of 1881 and 1882 to reach their base camp (at 81°43′N, 64°43′W), or to leave adequate replenishment stocks at planned caches on the shore of Davis Strait, had threatened all twenty-five with miserable death from exposure and starvation. That any were alive the evening of June 22, when their wretched campsite between Cape Sabine and Cocked Hat

Island was discovered by a search party from USS *Bear*, was marvelous. They'd been holed up there, languishing and dying quietly, for the past seven months.

That good news marked the beginning of the return of the US Navy to public confidence and admiration following several decades of post–Civil War decline—a decline that in retrospect appears to have finally bottomed out a few years earlier with the loss of USS *Jeannette* and most of her crew in the midst of what was for their mission's civilian impresario, *New York Herald* publisher James Gordon Bennett, Jr., a circulation-building exercise akin to journalist Henry Morton Stanley's search for Dr. David Livingston in Central Africa (an earlier, highly successful Bennett business promotion).

The greetings in Portsmouth were lavish, among them a several-thousand-man-strong, three-mile-long parade through the city, and a gala reception featuring speeches by Secretary of the Navy Chandler, Governor Hale of New Hampshire, and many other worthies, all of them eager to commiserate with the survivors, to honor the sacrifices of the dead, and to congratulate the rescuers in public, often at great length.

Soon after the three ships reached New York City's Governors Island on August 8 (where the ceremonial delivery of the bodies to the hospital was attended by Secretary of War Lincoln, the Army Signal Corps chief, General William Hazen, and the US 5th Artillery Regiment in formation), the greetings took on a darker cast, as revelations of the cannibalization of the dead, and charges about Greely's "incapacity and arbitrary conduct" drawn from the dead Lieutenant Kislingbury's diary, begun after the camp on Lady Franklin Bay was abandoned, leaked and then flowed into public commentary. But the navy continued to enjoy a very good press, with admiring treatment heightened by contrast to general criticism of the army, and especially of General Hazen, for his command's grotesque mismanagement of the Greely Expedition's logistic support.

On December 1, 1884, President Chester Arthur sent his fourth and last state of the union message to Congress. (The coming March Arthur would be succeeded by Grover Cleveland.) Roughly midway through its text Arthur mentioned the return—finally—on February 20 of the bodies of Lieutenant Commander De Long and others of USS *Jeannette*'s crew from Siberia's Lena River Delta, and immediately went on to congratulate Schley and the crews of *Thetis*, *Bear*, and *Alert* for their rescue of Greely that summer. "The organization and conduct of this relief expedition," the departing president wrote, "reflects great credit on all who contributed to its success."

After that prologue, Arthur went on again to urge the strengthening of the navy, as he had in a special message to Congress the previous March that proposed $4.3 million of new construction, representing three new cruisers and four additional gunboats, and $3.8 million to complete the four double-turreted monitors still under construction. "I can not too strongly urge," he wrote in December, "[upon Congress' attention] the duty of restoring our navy as rapidly as possible to the high state of efficiency which formerly characterized it."[11]

The rosy glow that illuminated the navy after Greely's rescue continued well beyond the end of the year, and long past the publication the following March of Schley's book, *The Rescue of Greely* (Charles Scribner's Sons, 1884). Twenty years later he'd retell the story in the near obligatory admiral's memoir, *Forty-five Years under the Flag* (D. Appleton, 1904).

FIGURE 2.1. "The Sphinx of the Period. An Unknown Quantity in Modern Warfare."

Puck's April 27, 1898, issue came out two months and two weeks after USS *Maine* blew up at her mooring in Havana harbor, in a close-coupled pair of explosions on the evening of February 15 that instantly sank the ship, killed 266 of her 355-man crew, and injured 80 others. The magazine's cover mused about the role America's new capital ships would play in the future. The answer came on the cover of the June 1 issue: an outsized sailor holds an equally outsized American flag as his ship, guns still smoking, steams triumphantly through the wreckage of the Spanish fleet at Manila.

The stunning American victories at sea in Manila Bay and off Santiago, Cuba, shaped the Treaty of Paris of December 1898, which saw Spain cede Porto Rico, Guam, and for $20 million the Philippines, to the United States, and the United States join the ranks of

European imperial powers in Spain's place. (A really perceptive observer might have forecast that exchange in roles years earlier, perhaps as long ago as 1800, when Spain returned Louisiana to France, or when Spain terminated the Acapulco-Manila galleon route in 1815, or four years after that, in 1819, when Spain yielded what remained of La Florida to the Americans. All three show evidence of a Spanish eclipse after three centuries as the world's first truly global power.)

Chromolithographs by cover artists Udo Keppler (1872–1956) and Louis Dalrymple (1866–1905) who were, with Samuel Ehrhart (1862–1937) and Frederick Opper (1857–1937), among the half-dozen or so superb political cartoonists, the inheritors of Thomas Nast, who illustrated the periodicals of the Gilded Age.

Source: *Puck*, April 27, 1898 (vol. 43, no. 1103) and June 1, 1898 (vol. 43, no. 1108).

FIGURE 2.2. "The Modern Sphinx Has Spoken. The American Battleship is no Longer an Unknown Quantity."

Chapter Two

THE NEW NAVY AND SPAIN

The individual courage of the men ranks high, but Spanish officers throughout their whole history have shown marvelous capacity for doing the wrong thing at the wrong time. They are wretched engineers and depend almost wholly on the Scotch and French to fill these positions. Their gunnery does not enjoy a high reputation for accuracy, and the poverty of their resources has prevented target practice.

—J. B. Crabtree, *The Passing of Spain and the Ascendency of America* (Springfield, MA: King-Richardson Publishing Co., 1898), 51

to the History Makers of the United States,
The President, The Cabinet, The Congress
And the
Officers and Enlisted Men
of the
American Army and Navy,
Whose Deeds Officially Written
In Action
Are Recorded in These Pages,
Edited by the Author;
A War for Humanity in the
Name of Liberty
Became One of Beneficent Conquest,
Imposing Duties of Emancipation and Dominion,
Adding to the Broad Lands of the free,
Spanning the Continent,
The Islands of the Southern Seas,
While the Energy of the Conquerors

Was Merciful to the Vanquished

For the Startling Strokes of Conclusive Victory

Brought the Swift Return

Of the Security of

Peace

—Murat Halstead, *Full Official History of the War with Spain*
(Chicago: J. H. Moore and Co., 1899), dedication

USS *Maine* (ACR-1) arrived from Key West at Havana January 25, 1898—the first US Navy ship to visit the port in three years—and swung quietly at buoy no. 4 in the harbor for the next three weeks. She'd been unwelcome on arrival, local Spanish authorities having asked the American consul in Havana, Fitzhugh Lee, the portly former Confederate general, to postpone her impending "friendly" visit, once they learned of it, until they could get instructions from Madrid. They feared, they told Lee, that the visit would "obstruct autonomy, produce excitement, and . . . a demonstration."

Lee, described at the time by *Collier's Weekly* as filling "the most trying position which any American consular official ever occupied," tried on January 24 to get the port call delayed six or seven days, but *Maine* steamed into the harbor the next day at 11:00 a.m. anyway. By the end of the month advocates had reversed positions: the navy then wanted to sail *Maine* away, fearing a "sanitary danger" (exposure to tropical disease) to the crew; Lee, discounting any such threats to health until later in spring, argued that *Maine* should stay or be replaced by a first-class battleship, to preserve "peaceful control" of the unsettled situation on shore.

Maine's public mission was to show the flag at the Spanish island colony's capital, a further expression of American interest as Cuba passed through yet another troubled episode in its seemingly permanent political crisis, this one triggered by rioting in Havana on January 12. Her private mission, implementing a decision made during a cabinet meeting in Washington on January 24, was to serve as a floating refuge for expatriates, should turmoil in the city escalate to threaten resident Americans with business interests on the island.

Only sixteen of *Maine*'s crew, among them her commanding officer, Captain Charles Sigsbee, USN, survived unhurt the explosion that sank the ship the night of February 15. *Maine* had been Captain Sigsbee's fourth command.

Sigsbee's remarkably composed telegram to the secretary of the navy reporting the catastrophe, scribbled in draft that night on board SS *City of Washington*, on the handsome letterhead of the steamer's parent New York and Cuba Mail Steamship Company, said "many wounded and doubtless more killed or drowned," and went on to urge fruitlessly, "Public opinion should be suspended until further report." He soon published a richly illustrated "personal narrative of the great disaster," *The "Maine": An Account of Her Destruction in Havana Harbor* (Century Co., 1899).

Two officers and two hundred fifty enlisted men died in the blast, and fourteen of the injured died later. Not yet three years old when she sank, *Maine* had been a disappointment throughout her brief career: expensive and slow, and short-legged because of limited coal bunker capacity; her odd main gun arrangement—a pair of 10″/30 caliber guns mounted in each of two "sponsoned" outboard turrets—permitted all four big guns to fire forward in the unlikely event of a ramming attack (dangerous to do with a steel ship), but made her twitchy in high seas.

The next Saturday, February 19, all of the stories on the front page of the *Kansas City Journal* reported news about the blast or about Spanish-American relations more generally—still, and for weeks to come through the war and after, the chief news stories in central Kansas and everywhere else in the country. The *Journal*'s headlines included: "Nothing Kept Back, Public has all Available News on the Maine Disaster"; "Says Torpedo Couldn't Do It"; "A Maine Sailor's Story"; "Purely an Accident"; and, "*Vizcaya* has Come," the last a reference to a Spanish cruiser's day-old port visit to the chief American city.

Anxieties were great and tempers hot. A short story, one paragraph, below the fold reported without comment on the murder of Alander Alexandrior, a Spanish miner of uncertain citizenship, slain in Ohio's coal country by a pick driven through his brain as punishment for "boasting that Spain would make short work of the United States in case of a naval war."

The *Journal* was representative of a newly potent force on the American political scene. The last years of the 1800s marked the beginning of what would be the golden century for print journalism, newspapers and periodicals, in the United States. (Hints that was coming had been apparent during the Civil War, when the telegraph, high-speed rotary presses, a well-developed national mail system, and loose notions of what constituted proprietary reporting, began to bring real news quickly to readers everywhere.) In 1898, for two cents a day, each of the literate citizens of Kansas City (total population at the turn of the century 51,400) could have their own window on the larger world.

From the Spanish-American War on through the next century and the development of cheap color-printing technology, print media established the national agenda, defined what the "facts" were, and fixed the vocabulary used in public discussion of current events. The press managed to hang on to control of both its readers and its advertisers even through the introduction of radio and television, but with the arrival of the internet, both readership and advertising revenues collapsed, threatening not only the traditional press business model but soon even the core idea that facts existed to be discovered and described, and were not malleable.

A navy board of inquiry chaired by Captain William Sampson, USN, exonerated Sigsbee and concluded unanimously on March 28 that *Maine* had been destroyed by a mine. (Five weeks earlier, on February 17 and just two days after the sinking, the board's finding had been preempted by a piece in William Randolph Hearst's *New York Journal* that had ascribed the deadly event to "an enemy's infernal machine.") Sampson's conclusion was reaffirmed by a second analysis in 1911 led by Rear Admiral Charles Vreeland, USN, one that included inspection of the exposed hull, but beginning in 1974 some of the several subsequent investigations—one notably by the late Admiral Hyman Rickover, USN, in 1976— pointed instead not to hostile action but to spontaneous combustion of "fire damp" gas in a bituminous coal bunker and the subsequent explosion of ammunition stowed in a magazine on the opposite side of the steel bulkhead that separated the two spaces. Several such spontaneous explosions occurred on board combatant ships in the early twentieth century, suggesting *Maine*'s could well have been innocent. A 1998 analysis by Advanced Maritime Enterprises, commissioned by the National Geographic Society, came to a more ambiguous conclusion, however, and the cause of the fatal explosion on board *Maine* is still debated today.

At the end of May 1913 the National Maine Memorial Monument was dedicated in New York City, on Columbus Circle at the southern entrance to Central Park (today adjacent to the Trump International Hotel and the park's Merchants Gate). Designed by architect Harold Magonigle and including the obligatory allegorical sculptures (nine of them, by the superb Attilio Piccirilli), and built for $185,000, the handsome, nearly sixty-foot-high monument stood capped by a gilded, bronze female figure of "Columbia Triumphant," riding in a seashell chariot drawn by three plunging horses.

The monument's gala, two-day dedication ceremony began on May 29 with sixteen ships of the Atlantic Fleet, behind flagship USS *Wyoming*, steaming up the Hudson to drop anchor between 72nd and 120th Streets. A day later, Memorial Day, five thousand fleet sailors paraded to the ceremony, joined on the march by additional thousands of soldiers, National Guardsmen, and war veterans. The distinguished reviewing party, including now-Admiral Sigsbee, took their salute, standing on a small podium surrounded by massed bands. Former president Taft, Secretary of the Navy Daniels, the governors of New York and Maine, and four lesser titans then spoke. All this to honor "the Valiant Seamen who Perished in the Maine . . . by Fate Unwarned, in Death Unafraid." (*Maine's* salvaged main mast was dedicated as a memorial at Arlington National Cemetery by President Wilson two years after that.)

The theoretical threat *Vizcaya's* batteries of two 11 inch and ten 5 inch guns posed to the undefended port of New York led to lurid, circulation-building speculation in the press. Thus the *Kansas City Journal's* front page on February 19 reported glumly:

Naval men say the Vizcaya could demolish the greater part of the Greater New York in less than two hours.

There are no warships in the Brooklyn navy yard which could be made ready for service in less than two months. The cruisers Atlanta and Chicago are there, but they are at present nothing more than useless hulks. Their engines, funnels and boilers are stripped and in a sea fight they would not be as serviceable as a ferry boat. The dispatch boat Dolphin, the presidential yacht, is also in the navy yard, in the stone dry dock being refitted with new boilers. She could not be made ready for a sea trip inside of two months. In an engagement with a vessel of the Vizcaya's type she would be as impotent as a baby against a [circus strong man].

. . . With the nearest warship hundreds of miles away and the rest of the North Atlantic squadron off the Dry Tortugas—three days distant—New York could have to pay the richest tribute in the history of the world to escape destruction.

Two days later the Los Angeles *Herald* played to the same fears on its front page, above a line drawing of Spain's year-old, sole battleship, the French-built, 9,700 ton *Pelayo*, "Spain's most effective warship," and quoting for authority a

FIGURE 2.3. *Vizcaya* under way.

Three days after USS *Maine* broke in half and sank in Havana, the Spanish armored cruiser *Vizcaya* made a reciprocal visit to New York City, arriving on February 18 directly from Las Palmas, in the Canary Islands, and surprising everyone when she materialized unannounced off New Jersey to await a harbor pilot.

Vizcaya had been expected in New York on February 15, but via a stop in Cuba. USS *Brooklyn* had been sent to Hampton Roads to intercept and accompany the Spanish cruiser as she steamed up the American coast on her presumed track from Havana to New York. What might have been simply a hospitable gesture had an important side benefit: reassuring goosey Americans, worried about the vulnerability of their coastal cities to shore bombardment, that *Vizcaya* would not be under way in gun range unsupervised.

This 1898 newspaper photograph of *Vizcaya* at sea was captioned: "The Vizcaya is one of the most effective fighting machines in the Spanish Navy. In her armament she even approaches the dignity of a battleship for she carries two guns of eleven inch caliber which can hurl a 500 pound steel conical projectile for a distance of twelve miles. She is also equipped with five inch rapid fire rifles. When it is considered that *New York, Brooklyn* and *Minneapolis*, our best cruisers carry nothing heavier than 8-inch rifles, it can be seen that the *Vizcaya* would prove an extremely dangerous antagonist to either of these vessels. Her presence [in New York harbor] so soon after the destruction of the *Maine* created great excitement..."

Source: Naval History and Heritage Command (NH 45325).

certain Lieutenant Palmo of the Spanish Navy, who was then allegedly passing through Mexico City. The story was headlined "The Vizcaya Is Relied On to Be Able to Effect the Destruction of New York City and Other American Ports Will Be Taken Care Of." Speaking of New York, "you must be aware," Palmo reportedly continued blithely, "we have a powerful 7,000 ton cruiser there, and we can well afford to lose it if the Yankees can afford to have their largest city in ruins."

Vizcaya had been at sea for twelve days, with no radio on board, and so, when she arrived at New York, Captain Antonio Eulate, her commanding officer, was entirely ignorant of *Maine's* sudden death in Spanish waters days before.

The timing of armored cruiser *Vizcaya's* New York City port call a week after USS *Maine* suddenly sank in Havana harbor—"undoubtedly destroyed by design," the *San Francisco Call* had concluded—was awkward, at best. But there were no incidents during the days *Vizcaya* spent at a deliberately isolated anchorage off Tompkinsville, Staten Island, a visit highlighted by the traditional courtesy calls on his hosts expected of any visiting foreign naval vessel's commanding officer.

So it was that on Monday, February 21, Captain Antonio Eulate y Frery called first on Commodore Francis Bunce, USN, commander of the Brooklyn Navy Yard, and then at his last duty station before retirement. Eulate's next courtesy call was on Major General Wesley Merritt, chief of the army's Department of the East at Governors Island. Later Eulate also called, very briefly, on the new mayor of New York City, Robert Van Wyck, at City Hall. According to the *New York Times* Van Wyck forced a grim smile when Eulate visited him, but apparently couldn't bring himself actually to speak to the Spaniard, who was hustled out the door.

Captain Eulate had declined to attend memorial services on Tuesday for battleship *Maine's* dead at the Church of the Sacred Heart, understanding the rites to be unofficial, but in a gesture to acknowledge February 22 as George Washington's birthday, he had *Vizcaya* dressed in flags and fired a gun salute at noon.

Everyone, including the crews of the six American "guard tugs" that constituted *Vizcaya's* security detail, must have been relieved when the Spanish cruiser departed—at high speed, newspapers reported inaccurately—on the afternoon of Friday, February 25, directly for Cuban waters.

Maine's sudden destruction pushed the American press (notably Joseph Pulitzer's *World* and William Randolph Hearst's *New York Journal*), the public,

FIGURE 2.4. "Unlucky '13.'"

The Spanish Navy suffered a horrible year in 1895, losing between March and September four second- and third-class cruisers to heavy weather, groundings, and collision. (Among the four was the *Reina Regente*, named in honor of Queen Maria Christina, regent after the death of her husband Alfonso XII in 1885 until her son was crowned in 1902. It fell to Maria Christina on March 17, 1899, to sign for Spain the peace treaty that ended the war.) The year 1898 would prove to be much worse.

In this *Judge* back cover illustration by Victor Gillam (1858?–1920), Spain's King Alfonso XIII, in April 1898 not yet twelve years old and here playing with toy boats in Cuba, is about to suffer humiliating American retribution for the sinking of USS *Maine*.

The Republican-leaning *Judge* was aggressively expansionist in this period, running several covers extolling American expansion and pressing for the construction of a canal linking the Pacific to the Atlantic through Nicaragua. *Judge*'s rival, the Democratic-leaning *Puck*, was no less expansionist at first but became less so over time. Its June 29, 1904, cover by Udo Keppler (vol. 55, no. 1426) showed an American spread eagle casting its shadow from Porto Rico to the Philippines, over the uneasy caption, "Gee, but this is an awful stretch."

Source: *Judge*, April 23, 1898 (vol. 34, no. 862). The P. J.
Mode Collection, Cornell University Library.

and Congress beyond increasingly overt sympathy for the revolutionaries on the island to an ultimatum on March 29 (the day after Sampson's report) to Spain to leave Cuba. The pressure for revenge had swiftly become irresistible, even as some voices argued for restraint, at least until Spain's guilt for the sinking had been established persuasively.

On April 19 a joint resolution for war passed easily in Congress, 42 to 35 in the Senate and 311 to 6 in the House of Representatives. The formal American declaration of war against Spain followed on April 25.

Despite some sympathy for Spain on the Continent, perhaps driven by European investments in Spanish government securities, the expectation in the United States was that the combatants would fight alone, each without allies. *Collier's Weekly* considered the impending contest on March 12, 1898 (vol. 20, no. 23), and in a column headed "If Spain Fights, She Will Have No Ally" concluded that France would not join the Spanish cause in the face of the certain opposition of Imperial Russia ("the best friend that we possess in Europe. . . . The friendship of the Czar is to us a tower of strength, and so long as we retain it, we need not apprehend a demonstration on behalf of Spain by any of the Continental powers.")[1] Moreover, following Germany's lead (Berlin was reported to be distracted by events in China), neither would Italy and Austria join with Spain; nor would England, an outspoken opponent of Spanish colonialism in the Western Hemisphere.

The outcome, *Collier's* concluded, thinking about the bottom line, was certain: "In ships, men and money . . . Spain would be too greatly overmatched, and she would be fortunate if she escaped the loss not only of Cuba and Porto Rico, but also of the Canaries and of the Philippines. Of course we should not wish to keep the two insular groups last named, but we could easily sell the Canaries to England and the Philippines to Japan."

The Philippines prediction aside, not all of *Collier's* pieces aged as well as this anonymous one. Example: Edgar Saltus's "Our Note Book" column in the issue of June 3, 1897, reported that Professor Percival Lowell's recent astronomical observations had confirmed that Mars was inhabited. "The famous canals, he says, form a system of irrigation of such ingenuity that it is impossible to attribute them to natural forces. With time and the development of the telescope it is not extravagant to prophesy that we shall be able to behold the Martians, to view their cities, and to promenade the eye along their streets." After much delirious speculation, Saltus concluded that interplanetary communication might lead to interplanetary travel . . . and coupling: "that we will visit Mars, that the Martians will visit us, that there will be elopements, marriages."

In the same April 28, 1899, edition of the newspaper that announced breathlessly, "Filipinos Will Surrender: Hostilities Are Suspended," Philadelphia's *Evening Bulletin* also reported that President McKinley and Secretary of the Navy John Long had that morning in Philadelphia visited the "gallant little cruiser" USS *Raleigh*, the ship credited with having fired the first shot of the Battle of Manila Bay. (After joining the European Squadron in mid-1897 *Raleigh* left the Mediterranean that December, passed through Suez Canal, and arrived in Hong Kong February 18 to reinforce Dewey's Asiatic Squadron.)

Almost exactly a year earlier, less than a week after the American declaration of war against Spain on April 25 (backdated to April 21), *Raleigh* had steamed on May 1 with Dewey into Manila Bay through its southern entrance, hunting the squadron's Spanish counterpart. Late the day before, the Americans had ducked into Subic ("Subig" then in navy reports) Bay. Finding it empty, the squadron had then sailed for Manila, thirty miles away, expecting to find their enemy there.

Around midnight Dewey's squadron churned past tiny El Fraile (The Friar) Island, at the mouth of Manila Bay's Boca Grande Channel. *Raleigh* was fourth in line, behind Commodore Dewey's flagship, USS *Olympia*, USS *Baltimore* (the Cramp shipyard's ugly duckling, its hull no. 254), and USS *Petrel*, and ahead of USS *Concord* and USS *Boston*. "At about 12:10 a.m. of May 1, when passing in column, natural order, abreast of El Fraile Island, at the entrance to the bay," *Raleigh*'s captain, Joseph Coghlan, formally reported to the commodore three days later, "I observed a flash, as of a signal thereon, and at about 12:15 a.m. a shot was fired from El Fraile, passing, as I think, diagonally between the *Petrel* and this vessel. A shot was fired in return, but without effect, by the starboard after 5-inch gun of this vessel." That 50 pound, 5 inch shell became the legendary first shot of a decisive American victory at sea in the Pacific Ocean that had no rival until the Battle of Midway forty-four years later.

Partway through the battle Admiral Montojo abandoned his mortally wounded flagship, the *Alfonso XII*–class unprotected cruiser *Reina Cristina* (the victim of four gunnery passes by the American fleet), and shifted his flag to the small cruiser *Isla de Cuba*. She, too, was soon sunk. (Later, raised, repaired, and commissioned as the gunboat USS *Isla de Cuba*, she served in the US Navy and with Maryland's naval militia before being sold to Venezuela in 1912.) After the American squadron famously paused over midmorning to feed its crews, and to inventory its remaining big gun ammunition, the action ended at 1:30 p.m., with *Raleigh* "in as good condition" as when the shooting began, and no one on board killed or even wounded. Coghlan's after-action report to Dewey described *Raleigh*'s particular contribution that morning as having sunk the Spanish cruiser *Don Antonio de Ulloa* at the cost to *Raleigh* of slight damage to one of her whaleboats, soon repaired.

When the carnage was over, Montojo wrote in his report to the Spanish admiralty, 381 of his men had been killed or wounded and all his ships sunk by enemy fire or scuttled in a cataclysm that had seen his vessels, he claimed, outgunned three to one by those of the Americans.

Even while Dewey's squadron was moving against Manila, on the east side of the International Date Line editors of the *San Francisco Call* were preparing their Sunday edition of the paper. Below its arresting front-page headline ("What Might Happen to San Francisco in the War—If Commodore Dewey Did Not Have the Spanish Fleet in Check in the Philippine Islands") was a lurid, half-page illustration of the "great center of California commerce" being shelled by several Spanish cruisers at sea outside the Golden Gate, just off Ocean Beach. Plumes of smoke rising above the city represented what would happen if defenseless San Francisco failed to pay ransom to "the dons." Helpfully, the *Call* tabulated a possible basis for the levy calculation to lend some scale to the threat, nearly a half-billion dollars, the sum of everything from private bank deposits and the holdings of the US subtreasury to the value of city real estate.

Dewey's own short, triumphant report to Secretary Long, telegraphed to Washington from Hong Kong on May 7, reported the destruction at Manila of *Reina Cristina* and ten other Spanish ships, as well as a shore battery on Cavite Island. A follow-on report advised the secretary of the capture of Cavite's naval station and the destruction of its fortifications. In response to this thrilling news, Dewey was promptly, but belatedly, promoted to rear admiral. He'd been denied the usual promotion to rear admiral on assuming squadron command by Secretary Long, as punishment for his and Assistant Secretary Theodore Roosevelt's politicking. The new admiral would be treated to a hero's welcome in New York City in September 1899, complete with a parade beneath a

FIGURE 2.5. "Battle of Manila."

Like its American counterpart, the Spanish Navy entered the 1880s with a small, obsolescent fleet, soon enlarged and modernized through a construction program launched in 1884 that eventually saw combatant ship contracts placed with domestic shipyards and others in France, Great Britain, and Italy. The losses of 1895 aside, the 1898 edition of *The Statesman's Year-book* credited Spain with a "capable navy," to become a "formidable force" following the delivery of 21 ships and boats under construction.

As depicted here by an unknown artist, during the morning of May 1, 1898, an outclassed and poorly led Spanish squadron in the Pacific, consisting of six cruisers (one, *Castilla*, sixteen years old, with a wooden hull, and under tow; the others marginally more modern with unarmored iron hulls) and a dispatch boat, under the command of Admiral Patricio Montojo y Pasarón, was quickly destroyed in an action that saw the American combatants shuttle largely uncontested back and forth in the bay along the 5 fathom curve on their charts, shelling the Spaniards, passing one after the other under the squadron's guns first to port and then to starboard.

Oscar Williams, the American consul in Manila, whose intelligence collection had prepared Dewey for his mission, rode USS *Baltimore* and then USS *Olympia* during the day, concluding his dispatch to the State Department on May 4, "our Commodore will officially inform you of events which will rival in American history the exploits of Paul Jones."

John Muller and Jacques Luchsinger, publishers of prints, lithographs, and chromo-lithographs, including this one, were in business at several New York City addresses from the mid-1880s through the 1920s. The relatively low cost of these reproduction technologies opened a large market for decorative art on popular subjects.

Source: Library of Congress, Prints and Photographs Division.

mockup at Madison Square of an enormous arch commemorating his triumph, never realized in marble and in 1900 quietly disassembled and forgotten. In 1973 an easily overlooked plaque on a four-foot-high plinth was erected in New York's Battery Park to honor the service of the officers and men in Dewey's squadron. For his part, Montojo was court-martialed in Madrid the following March and convicted, but later spared serving his sentence.

Often neglected in accounts of the excitement in Manila Bay soon after Montojo's shattering defeat is the confusing confrontation between Dewey and his triumphant squadron, and ships of the German East Asia Squadron under the command of Vice Admiral Otto von Diederichs.

Germany, at first after unification bereft of the colonies that confirmed great power status because of Bismarck's lack of interest, had begun eyeing some of the Philippine islands as candidate additions to the new Deutsches Kolonialreich (possessions and protectorates scattered throughout Africa and elsewhere in the Pacific) even before the outbreak of their revolution against Spain in midsummer 1896. By early 1897 the mercurial Kaiser was already anticipating Spain's ejection from the place, telling his inner circle of his determination to buy or otherwise absorb the archipelago or some of its parts.

Pursuit of Wilhelm II's ambitions had sent the first of von Diederichs's ships, the cruisers SMS *Irene* and *Cormoran* into Manila Bay early in May, followed a month later by the transport SMS *Darmstad* with 1,400 infantry on board. In June the three were joined by SMS *Prinzess Wilhelm* (*Irene*'s classmate) and von Diederichs's aging flagship, the British-built cruiser SMS *Kaiser*. Absent an obvious innocent explanation for the presence of this now sizable force, Dewey was appropriately unsettled.

A shouting match between Dewey and von Diederichs on June 12, 1898, and an encounter at sea two weeks later that might have seen the nearly new revenue cutter *McCulloch* (Cramp's no. 288) fire a warning shot past SMS *Irene*, raised the temperature dangerously. Tensions soon calmed, however, and nothing came of this particular face-off. But before the Kaiser (and his naval advisor, Admiral Alfred von Tirpitz) turned his attention in the new century to construction of the powerful blue-water fleet that would soon enough catastrophically heighten tensions with Great Britain, Wilhelm had his naval staff semiseriously explore several options for a German presence in the Caribbean and draft plans (Nos. I, II, and III), also semi-seriously, for operations against the US East Coast from Cuba or Porto Rico.[2]

Suspicions of German ambitions in the Caribbean were among the great drivers powering the US Navy's capital ship construction program.

Two months after Dewey's victory in Manila Bay, *Vizcaya* was part of Admiral Pascual Cervera y Topete's squadron with her class-mates, *Infanta Maria Teresa* and *Almirante Oquendo*, and three other ships. On Sunday, July 3, after thirty-four days trapped inside the bay, Cervera very reluctantly challenged the American blockade of Santiago de Cuba—everything about Cervera's participation in this war had been reluctant. *Vizcaya* was second in line to attempt the escape behind *Infanta Maria Teresa*, and despite her fouled bottom (thus encumbered, she was so slow that Cervera once called her a "buoy" and later "a boil on the body of the fleet"), Cervera decided he couldn't leave her behind during the escape attempt. In the event, she managed to steam some fifteen miles west before she was deliberately run ashore on Aserraderos Beach at 11:00 a.m. By then only the cruiser *Cristobal Colon* was still afloat, and she not for long. It might have been some consolation to Captain Eulate that his ship managed to get farther from Santiago de Cuba than all but one of Cervera's ships.

The next night, with much of her engineering plant out of commission, *Reina Mercedes*, a class-mate of Montojo's *Reina Cristina*, was scuttled near the channel (not closing it, which had been the Spanish plan) under furious American gunfire. Contemporary photographs of her wreck show her resting on the bottom, twin stacks still standing, heeling to port with her main deck awash and her upper works shot to pieces.

Reina Mercedes was recovered, refitted, and commissioned in 1905 as USS *Reina Mercedes*. She spent her remaining fifty-plus years afloat, first as the receiving ship in Newport, later as the station ship at Annapolis, next as a disciplinary barracks for midshipmen, and—marred only by her utilitarian but dreadfully ugly lines—finally, until 1957, as flag quarters for the commander of the Severn River Naval Command.

Some had thought any contest at the end of the century between the two navies could be close, ranking the US Navy sixth and the Spanish Navy eighth among the principal fleets of the world (spanning Japan's at number seven). Still, the one-sided battle swiftly fulfilled the dour expectations its commander, Admiral Pascual Cervera y Topete, had had when he'd sailed from the Cape

Verde Islands on April 29 for Cuba with four armored cruisers towing three torpedo-boat destroyers (to save coal). Cervera, freed with hundreds of his sailors from confinement in New Hampshire in September, was also court-martialed on arrival home but, unlike Montojo, he was acquitted.

On November 5, 1898, the Madrid newspaper *La Epoca* printed extracts from a series of private, posterity letters written by Admiral Cervera beginning that January and extending for some months, until just before his squadron had knowingly sailed to its destruction. The letters to friends and relatives were about the state of the Spanish Navy and in particular how his squadron compared to its American counterpart, about the prospects of keeping Cuba Spanish, and about the importance of defending home waters against a possible American raid across the Atlantic to the Iberian coast. The December 1898 issue of the US Naval Institute's *Proceedings* (vol. 24, no. 4) quoted *La Epoca*'s month-old story at length.

Long before he sailed, Cervera deeply regretted every aspect of the certain failure he anticipated, certain thanks to "the stupidity of some, the cupidity of others, and the incapability of all." Cervera's census of the rival fleets in late February, "counting only modern vessels capable of active service," showed that the Americans' combatant tonnage was double that of Spain's (an easy calculation) and the offensive power of American guns nearly three times that of Spain's (a much more difficult one). The outcome was never in doubt. More discouraging still was the purpose of the sacrifice to come: "to defend an island which was ours but belongs to us no more, because even if we should not lose it by right of war, we have lost it in fact, and with it all our wealth and an enormous number of young men, victims of the climate and bullets, in the defense of what is now no more than a romantic ideal."

In essence, the admiral was proposing to his ministry and government a trade: Cuba lost, in exchange for a remnant of Spain's navy and its prestige preserved. His argument, repeated through much of the year, had no traction in Madrid, but probably accounts for the relatively sympathetic treatment of his case by contemporary American navy officers and the navy's off-line think tank, the US Naval Institute.

Only months after a piece titled "The Navy of the United States" (written by Louis Sonntag) appeared as a centerfold in the June 19, 1897, issue of *Harper's*

Weekly, a handsome pamphlet by W. J. Lawrence, *The United States Navy Illustrated* (subtitled "A New Series of Over Fifty Reproductions from Original Photographs"), was published in New York. Lawrence's timing was impeccable. *The United States Navy Illustrated* appeared in the marketplace just as the Spanish-American War focused enthusiastic popular attention on the US Navy—the easy victor in short, decisive, and virtually painless sea battles half the world apart—in a way not seen in the decades since the Civil War.

In the seventeen years following Secretary Hunt's despairing assessment of the state of the US Navy in 1881, the navy had grown from a fleet of perhaps two dozen barely deployable combatant ships to one several times as large, including twenty-four battleships and cruisers.

For his citizen's guide to the fleet, Lawrence assembled photographs of the navy's combatant ships, and drawings by artist C. McKnight Smith of those six not yet in the water. Lawrence described each with a single line of specifications including length, beam ("breadth"), mean draft, displacement, speed (in knots to an improbable three decimal points), complement, and contract cost. Curiously, for a roster of what were, after all, warships, nothing was said about any ship's weapons, about her main and secondary gun battery; about the number, diameter, and caliber of the turreted great guns; or about the size and number of the smaller, rapid-fire defensive weapons usually found in blisters jutting out from both sides of the hull.

Lawrence's inventory of ships in service began with USS *Indiana* (Cramp's no. 270), commissioned in 1895 as the navy's first "sea-going coast line battle ship of first class" and an embarrassing failure during the fight off Cuba. It followed with the navy's three others of the type: *Indiana*'s classmate *Oregon*, famous for her 16,000 mile sprint around South America to join the squadron heading for Cuba; *Massachusetts* (Cramp's no. 271); and *Iowa* (Cramp's no. 276). USS *Maine*, commissioned originally as the first armored cruiser, appeared next in a posthumous listing; until that February 15 she'd been one of the navy's two second-class armored battleships. The other was *Texas*. (Cramp's pretty three-stacked battleship *Maine*, the yard's hull no. 302, was commissioned almost five years after the first *Maine* sank.)

Lawrence went on to depict a dozen armored, unarmored protected, and unarmored cruisers, the three types together very loosely forming the largest fraction of the fleet ("cruiser" here spanning lengths between 412 and 271 feet, and displacements ranging from a porky 9,215 tons to a svelte 2,089) and many of them, like USS *Atlanta*, exhibiting the familiar masts, spars, and stays of already obsolescent sailing rigs.[3]

Other examples of error and obsolescence afloat followed without comment or apology. The first was the bargain-priced ($350,000 in 1886) unarmored dynamite gunboat USS *Vesuvius* (Cramp's no. 256), later converted to a floating torpedo test-bed. She was a one-of-a-kind ship whose three fixed-elevation (+18°), 51 foot long, 15 inch bow guns were aimed by steering the ship, and used compressed air to launch projectiles filled with gun cotton against targets inside of a few miles away. Assessing in 1899 "The American Fleet" in *Harper's Pictorial History of the War with Spain*, Lieutenant Commander Jerrold Kelley, USN, delicately described the "dynamite cruiser" *Vesuvius* as having "not yet achieved the place so loudly heralded" by enthusiasts for the type. That place was never achieved.

Next came the harbor defense armored ram *Katahdin* (a pure ram, the only combatant ship in the navy's register with no offensive weapons whatever on board), followed by the twin-turret, coast defense monitors *Puritan*, *Amphitrite*, *Terror*, and *Miantonomah*. The last three were class-mates. The four monitors' near-twenty-year-long gestation period, from orders placed by Grant's navy secretary, George Robeson, with shipbuilders in 1874 to the dates of commissioning and entry into service some two decades later, set an astonishing record, viciously lampooned by magazines of the day. *Amphitrite*'s galling fate—she was named after the sea god Neptune's mythical consort—was to end up as an unsuccessful waterfront hotel in several East Coast ports successively.

The monitors were bad ideas and bad designs slowly brought to misshapen life, in part because the navy had misread the lessons of the historic Battle of Hampton Roads (March 1862), of the assault on Drewry's Bluff (May 1862), and of *Monitor*'s sudden demise in December 1862—while under tow by USS *Rhode Island* in high seas off Cape Hatteras. The navy had imagined special virtue in a design that was providential one time, but inherently unsafe at sea and flawed in combat, and, like the next century's gas-inflated dirigibles, a technological dead end. In 1862 it fell to USS *Monitor*'s second commanding officer, Lieutenant William Jeffers, USN, on May 2, and again on June 16, to point out his ship's half-dozen serious design, performance, and habitability defects to the commander of the North Atlantic Blockading Squadron, Flag Officer Louis Goldsborough, USN, and to Secretary of the Navy Welles.[4]

European navies made the same mistake as did the American. Monitors appeared briefly, for example, in the navies of Sweden, Norway, Finland, and for somewhat longer service lives in that of Great Britain, in which fleet the type managed several times during the next two generations to eke out creditable service. HMS *Mersey* and *Severn*, two of three Scottish-built monitors diverted at the outbreak of World War I from the Brazilian to the Royal Navy, after seeing action off Belgium went on in mid-1915 to winkle out and help destroy the German light cruiser SMS *Königsberg*, then deep in her hideout up German East Africa's Rufiji River (in Tanzania today).[5] One war later, *Erebus*-class monitors' big guns helpfully bombarded the shore, supporting landings in several important battles, including at Normandy.

Next in Lawrence's photo inventory came eight single-stacked gunboats and four torpedo boats, three of the latter—*Ericsson*, *Porter*, and *Cushing*—boasting steel hulls. Finally, looking toward the future, he included sketches of five first-class battleships then under construction (four of which, all but *Wisconsin*, would sail as part of the Great White Fleet in 1907–9), and a radically new, steam-powered submarine torpedo boat, USS *Plunger*, that progressed from contract award in 1895 to cancellation in 1900.

What looked like a complete roster of the fleet in fact wasn't. Secretary of the Navy John Long's November 15, 1898, report to the president included a wartime census of the US Navy by class. It numbered 59 modern ships altogether. At the top of his list were 5 first- and second-class battleships, followed by 17 cruisers (and the single "dynamite cruiser"), 6 coast defense monitors, an armored ram, and 29 gunboats and torpedo boats. The list went on to include 14 more vessels of the "old navy" and 123 fleet auxiliaries.

More significant than Long's fleet census, however, was his opening appraisal. "Years of patient, persistent training and development," Long wrote, sounding nothing like Secretary Hunt, had brought the navy to "a point of high efficiency, which resulted in the unparalleled victories at Manila and Santiago—victories which have given the names of our naval commanders world-wide fame, and added an additional page to the glorious naval history of our country."

The two lopsided victories over Spanish Navy squadrons seemingly changed everything. What had begun little more than a century ago under the short-lived Articles of Confederation as a squabbling fraternity of newly independent states, clutching the side of a presumably nearly empty continent, had suddenly become, almost inadvertently, a proud global imperial power. The scope of this change was captured in the title of Jerome Crabtree's *The Passing of Spain and the Ascendency of America* (King-Richardson Publishing Co., 1898), and illustrated by a popular political cartoon of the period in the *Philadelphia Press* that showed the American Eagle with its wings spread, spanning ten thousand miles from tip to tip, a reach that encompassed much of the Atlantic, the North American continent, and the Pacific Ocean past Manila.

Looking back on that triumph, Captain James Oliver, USN (soon Rear Admiral Oliver, and one of the giants of navy strategic planning), began his illustrated essay, "Shall We Control the Pacific?" in the May 1914 issue of the monthly the *World's Work*—his answer was yes—with a prideful and overblown description of the great reach of now-imperial America.[6]

In all the world's history no country other than our own has ever claimed anything like so great an extent of the world's surface for a charge to keep, as guardian or sole possessor. The entire continent of America, North and South, the Caribbean Sea and the islands that encompass it, and almost the entire surface of the vast Pacific Ocean—over all this our arm is stretched.... The line which outlines all this vast extent of the world's surface must then be regarded as the boundary of the great fortress we must protect.[7]

Oliver's prescription was a strategy anchored on a few island bases, Hawaii, Guam, Tutuila, Kiska, and Samoa, "irremovable obstacles to possible enemies and . . . firm foundations for aggressive action by ourselves." Without such a base structure, Oliver warned, "the value of a fleet must always be greatly diminished and in certain circumstances easily conceivable, that value might decline to nothing."

Rear Admiral Oliver (1857–1928) was another navalist who seemed to speak with special authority, despite a career that included a November 1904 collision at sea while in command of the British-built refrigerated supply ship USS *Culgoa*, followed by a general court-martial, acquittal, his subsequent furious resignation, and later reinstatement of his commission by President Theodore Roosevelt. Oliver served before the war on the Naval War College staff, then as chief of naval intelligence, as governor of the US Virgin Islands 1917–19, and later on the Board of Naval Strategy. He was a particular favorite of the *World's Work*, lauded in its August 1915 issue as one of "the war chiefs of the Navy."

To the persistent question in the capital and on the hustings, "What do we need a navy for?" the answer had come at Manila and Santiago de Cuba: to grasp and preserve an empire. But domestic enthusiasm for America's new status as an imperial power wasn't universal. Months after the battle of Santiago and just a month before the December 1898 signing of the Treaty of Paris, a group of notable and other American citizens formed the Anti-imperialist League. At first under the presidency of President Grant's aging former treasury secretary, George Boutwell, then eighty, and including in its leadership industrialist Andrew Carnegie, labor leader Samuel Gompers, Stanford University president David Jordan, and Harvard professor William James, during its nearly twenty-year history the league spoke and lobbied for the conscience of America.

The league's best known officer was probably Mark Twain, who between 1897 and 1905, following his 1895 world speaking tour of English-speaking capitals and colonies, was approaching a period of intense introspection and cynicism. No longer an entertainer, he would have an increasingly shrill voice in the domestic debate about empire triggered by the Spanish-American War. That debate placed Twain (and his allies from the abolition, women's suffrage, and labor movements) against imperialism's leading spokesman, Teddy Roosevelt, in a contest described most recently by Stephen Kinzer in *The True Flag: Theodore Roosevelt, Mark Twain, and the Birth of American Empire* (Henry Holt & Co., 2017).

Between 1897 and 1905 Twain wrote extensively against imperialism, colonialism, and the chest-thumping patriotism that propelled the American ambitions in the Pacific that Captain Oliver would soon celebrate. Twain's last piece on this general subject was his brilliant, imagined *King Leopold's Soliloquy* (P. R. Warren Co., 1905), published in pamphlet form by the American Congo Reform Association, of which he was also an officer. Only some of his work during this period was published in his lifetime.

"It gives me great pleasure," President McKinley was quoted as saying to Captain Joseph Coghlan, USN, and the crew of USS *Raleigh*, "to bid you welcome

FIGURE 2.6. Aerial view of the William Cramp and Sons Ship and
Engine Building Company in Kensington, Philadelphia.

During the second decade of the twentieth century, when this photo was taken, William Cramp and Sons Ship and Engine Building Co.'s shipyard filled some 50 acres along 2,000 feet of Delaware River waterfront almost directly across from Patty's Island and the city of Camden, New Jersey. Immediately upriver from Cramp's lay the huge railyard and many wharves of the Philadelphia and Reading Railroad, through which moved mountains of anthracite coal—some on colliers built next door—from Pennsylvania's mines to ports everywhere along the coast.

Cramp's principal structure, a nearly quarter-mile-long building on Beach Street behind (west of) the yard's eight shipbuilding slips, housed a variety of sheds, workshops, and lofts on nearly half a million square feet of covered floor space. Nearby stood the other offices, shops, and industrial facilities that, rising together over the past ninety years, had made Cramp's a strong rival of the Irish, Scottish, and English shipyards that had given Great Britain command of the oceans and control of world trade. Perspective drawings of the yard and its buildings, as Cramp's grew toward the end of the nineteenth century, appear in Ernest Hexamer's handsome general survey fire insurance maps for Philadelphia.

By December 1904, when USS *Tennessee*'s hull slid into the Delaware, propelled by a bottle of christening champagne swung by the teenaged daughter of the state's governor, Cramp and Sons had already built around three hundred cargo vessels, passenger liners, and combatant ships, including the *Pennsylvania*-class cruisers USS *Colorado* and USS *Pennsylvania*, as well as men of war for four foreign navies. During the next twenty years, Cramp's built another seventy or so ships for the US Navy, most of them destroyers.

Source: The Library Company of Philadelphia.

home and to congratulate you, and each one of you, upon the heroic part you bore in the great battle on the 1st of May at Manila, which was a most glorious triumph to American arms and made a new and glorious page in American history."

The president's quick visit to *Raleigh* on April 28, 1899, was welcome attention for Captain Coghlan (1844–1908, USNA '63), whose ship was at Philadelphia to represent the navy at McKinley's dedication of a handsome equestrian statue to the late U. S. Grant (Civil War general and US president) the day before. So too, a year or two later, would be the issue of one in a series of fifty "Heroes of the Spanish War" trading cards by Sweet Caporal cigarettes, featuring the captain standing on *Raleigh*'s afterdeck and leaning possessively against his ship's emergency manual wheel, an image lifted from his carte de visite.

President McKinley, Secretary Long, and the rest of the visiting presidential party departed USS *Raleigh* at 11:15 a.m., leaving behind them the glow of mutual admiration and accompanied on their way upriver by the cheers of the crew, and the usual quarterdeck bells and twenty-one-gun salute prescribed by ceremony. They went in a cutter directly to the Cramp and Sons Ship and Engine Building Company's shipyard, where the men disembarked to tour the *Illinois*-class battleship USS *Alabama* (BB-8), fitting out at Cramp's after having been launched there the previous May. That work finally done and sea and acceptance trials completed eighteen months later, *Alabama* would be commissioned in October 1900.

Thanks in part to the odd arrangement of her twin stacks, athwartships like a Mississippi riverboat's rather than fore and aft like those of a blue-water ship, *Alabama* was always regarded as funny-looking but serviceable, "like one of those girls," as one (politically incorrect by today's standards) Cramp's executive was quoted as saying as she approached commissioning, "that never would shine in the butterfly circles of society, but who knows how to look after her home."[8] *Alabama*'s last mission was ignominious: off the Virginia Capes as an inert, undefended target for Billy Mitchell's bombers in September 1921, demonstrating not much more than the vulnerability of such pinioned ships to air attack.

USS *Alabama* was Cramp's hull no. 290, which suggests incorrectly that approaching the turn of the century the yard had sent nearly 300 vessels to sea. The correct number, allowing for skipped and nonconsecutive numbers was likely some thirty fewer. USS *Tennessee*, launched in 1904 and commissioned in

1906, went into the water six years and some thirty-two hull numbers after *Alabama*. By that time William Cramp had been dead twenty-five years. The "and Sons" in the yard's name referred to Charles and William Cramp (who joined the company in 1857) and to Samuel, Jacob, and Theodore Cramp (who joined it in 1863). When Charles, the eldest, died in 1913 at eighty-five, the *New York Times* obituary reported that the yard's workforce of eight thousand men could build seven ships simultaneously.

Seven yards representing seven states tendered bids on January 6, 1903, to build the first two *Tennessee*-class armored cruisers, *Tennessee* and *Washington*. Just twenty years earlier, as Secretary William Hunt's committee met to ponder the future, one of the uncertainties it addressed was whether or not there was an American yard capable of working in steel. Now, a generation later, there were at least seven, including two on the West Coast.

Cramp's had recently finished the first two of the six *Pennsylvania*-class cruisers, *Colorado* and *Pennsylvania* (hull nos. 316 and 317), when it got the contract in 1903 for the slightly larger, more heavily gunned (10 inch guns versus the 8 inch guns of the *Pennsylvania*-class's main battery), and more heavily armored *Tennessee*. With this experience, it wasn't surprising that *Tennessee* passed her acceptance trials in early 1906 and was delivered on schedule to the navy that July, in exchange for the final few of the fifty progress payments meted out to the builder since contract award.

As Captain Edward L. Beach, Jr., USN, described in 1966, *Tennessee* and her sister ships were products of a lesson learned in the Spanish-American War, that a big and heavily armed cruiser could outrun anything it couldn't outfight, including the battleships of her day. Pushed along by her twin 26 foot screws, driven by 2 triple-expansion steam engines fed by 16 Babcock and Wilcox boilers, producing 23,000 horsepower, *Tennessee* was a seemingly ideal combatant for an antiquated navy on the cusp of a renaissance, with big plans but not yet a big budget.

Taking away lessons from that war was a high-risk proposition, however, given the condition of the Spanish Navy in the Caribbean and the Pacific at the end of the century, and so this particular lesson was true only until HMS *Dreadnought* put to sea in 1906. The new British all-big-gun (12 inch), 21 knot, steam-turbine-powered battleship seemingly made all other capital ship de-signs obsolete, specifically those of the French but also including the American *Tennessee*-class armored cruisers, although it took ten years for their demotion to take full effect. The proud American armored cruiser squadron had been caught in the same kind of sharp technology shift that had pushed aside over-land canals (slowly, by the railroad) and the pony express (quickly, by the tele-graph), and in time would displace Viscount and Electra turboprop passenger aircraft (also quickly, by Boeing's 707 and Douglas's DC-8 turbojets). *Dread-nought*, too, would be obsolescent in short order, replaced by *Invincible*, a re-flection of the furious pace of propulsion, protection, and combat systems de-velopment in the early years of the twentieth century.

But even in gray war paint in 1914, replacing the elegant white, buff, and black paint scheme and the handsome bow scrolls that had also ornamented the Great White Fleet of American battleships on its 'round-the-world cruise in 1906, and beneath her towering masts and four stacks, *Tennessee* looked im-posing . . . never mind that her last assignment had been as the receiving ship in Brooklyn, Purgatory, with not much more than a skeleton crew on board.

FIGURE 2.7. "Columbia's Easter Bonnet."

Reflecting its New York City reading public's interest in the navy, *Puck* often featured cover illustrations of ships and sailors, the incumbent navy secretary, and his cronies in Congress and industry. The magazine's April 27, 1898, issue (dated just two days after the United States declared war on Spain and four before the American triumph at Manila) had cautiously described the navy's new, heavily armed, steel-hulled combatant ships as "an unknown quantity in modern warfare." Five weeks later, with its cover now showing an American cruiser steaming assertively through waters artistically littered with Spanish wreckage, *Puck* acknowledged that any earlier uncertainty had been decisively dispelled.

Propelled by those triumphs against an enemy that had been in decline for most of the previous century, the US Navy grew rapidly through the next two decades. In his annual report of 1919, Secretary of the Navy Josephus Daniels described how a fleet that had numbered 124 serviceable combatant ships (counting everything from battleships to gunboats) afloat in 1900 had grown to one that could boast fully 441 just two decades later.

The weekly satire magazine (its motto was "What Fools These Mortals Be") was twenty-four years old when on April 6, 1901, it published this cover cartoon of a star-spangled, wasp-waisted and flat-chested "Columbia," representing the United States, proudly donning a ship-shaped bonnet bristling with guns, labeled "World Power," and pinning it into place with a miniature naval officer's dress sword. Written in the smoke spewing from the ship's stack is the word "Expansion." This issue (vol. 49, no. 1357) was published several weeks before the third anniversary of the start of the Spanish-American War and of the US Navy's crushing victories off Manila and Santiago, Cuba, that followed in May and July. The cartoon, signaling public recognition of the renaissance of the US Navy at the end of the nineteenth century, was created by Samuel Ehrhart (1862–1937) and Louis Dalrymple (1866–1905).

Source: Library of Congress, Prints & Photographs Division.

FIGURE 3.1. The new armored cruiser USS *Tennessee*.

Scientific American's issue of March 17, 1906 (vol. 94, no. 11), featured on its cover USS *Tennessee* at sea, above a two-line summary of her principal features and a quick census of the US Navy's soon-to-be ten armored cruisers (omitting the "somewhat obsolete" *New York* and *Brooklyn* [Cramp's nos. 268 and 275] from the count), including four in her class and six of the contemporary, more lightly gunned and armored *Pennsylvania*-class ships. The magazine was already sixty years old when this issue was published, and it often covered naval subjects. Three years later, in its February 20, 1909, issue (vol. 100, no. 8),

Scientific American devoted its cover and much of its content to the global cruise of the Great White Fleet and a comparison of the navies of the world.

At sea before 1909 in her original paint scheme, with a white hull and buff upperworks, beneath pole masts (the forward one was eventually replaced by a cage mast, a structure less likely to fail when hit by gunfire), and behind her elegant bow wreath, USS *Tennessee* was beautiful, a mighty demonstration of American prowess and resolve.

Tennessee's and her sister ship *Washington*'s procurements had been authorized by Congress on July 1, 1902. A purchase contract for $4,035,000 was signed for *Tennessee*, the class leader, on February 9 the next year with Cramp's. Keel laying, launching, and formal acceptance came on schedule during the following thirty-seven months. *Tennessee* was commissioned at the Navy's League Island shipyard, down the Delaware River from Cramp's, in the mid-morning of Tuesday, July 17, 1906. She wasn't ready to go to sea for several months.

The occasion of this *Scientific American* cover by C. McKnight Smith was *Tennessee*'s successful completion of her sea trials in mid-February, when she'd demonstrated a speed just over 22 knots on an 80 mile course off the coast of Maine. The short, anonymous article that followed on pages 230–31 of the magazine compared *Tennessee* favorably to the nine-year-old battleship *Iowa* (BB-4, built at Cramp and Sons shipyard as hull no. 276, the yard's third battleship in three years) and to the six *Pennsylvania*-class (*California*-class) cruisers, commissioned in 1905–8.

Tennessee was five knots faster than was *Iowa*; her four 10″/40 main battery guns had greater penetrating power than did *Iowa*'s larger 12 inchers; her sixteen, rapid fire 6″/50s were together more powerful than *Iowa*'s mix of 8 inch and 4 inch guns; and her 2,190 tons of armor protection was superior to *Iowa*'s throughout. *Tennessee* also boasted twenty-two 3″/50 guns and four 21 inch torpedo tubes in the bow below her waterline. In 1911 her forward military mast was replaced by the cage mast that appears in most photographs of the cruiser. Some bridge design errors that increased watch vulnerability were corrected at the same time.

By the 1880s Charles McKnight Smith, a maritime artist from central New Jersey, was drawing for New York's evening *Daily Graphic* and other illustrated newspapers. His drawings also appeared in books (his own *Drift from the Sea of Life* [Frederick A. Stokes, 1891] and W. J. Lawrence's *The United States Navy Illustrated* [Continent Publishing Co., 1898]), and often in *Scientific American*. Among these was an illustration in the issue of December 17, 1904 (vol. 91, no. 25), that paired battleship *Louisiana* with Farragut's Civil War flagship *Hartford*, to dramatize forty years of American progress in capital ship design and construction. Smith continued to draw and paint marine subjects for another twenty-five years at least.

Source: *Scientific American* 94, no. 11 (March 17, 1906).

Chapter Three

USS *Tennessee* Afloat, 1906–14

The Armored Cruiser Squadron

Here's to the cruisers of the fleet,
So gol-durn fast they're hard to beat,
The battleships they may be fine,
But for me a cruiser every time.

(*Chorus*: Away, away with sword and drum,
Here we come, full of rum,
Looking for someone to put on the bum,
The Armored Cruiser Squadron!)

They talk about the scores they make,
And all the records they will break,
But when the practice comes around,
The battleships cannot be found.

The *Washington* and the *Tennessee*,
The finest ships that sail the sea,
They came round the Horn to be
In the Armored Cruiser Squadron.

We are the boys who shoot six-inch,
Or anything else when we're in a pinch,
Gee but the battleships are a cinch
For the Armored Cruiser Squadron.

Sixteen battleships all in a line,

In Guantanamo Bay look mighty fine,

But for me a cruiser every time,

In the Armored Cruiser Squadron.

Here's to the cruiser days gone by,

With a bottle of scotch and a jug of rye,

We'll hope to meet again bye and bye

In the Armored Cruiser Squadron.

—*Book of Navy Songs*, US Naval Institute, 1926

Cramp's opened its shipyard gates on Saturday morning, December 3, 1904, for the christening of USS *Tennessee*, and, despite snow underfoot and occasional sleet and cold rain in the air, reportedly—very improbably—tens of thousands of people crowded onto its grounds to watch the traditional ceremony. Once inside, they perched on rooftops, atop scaffolding, and on lumber piles, anywhere with a line of sight to where pretty Annie Keith Frazier, the state governor's seventeen-year-old daughter, accompanied by five decorative "maids of honor" (all six teens were in Philadelphia for the weekend from the tony Miss Mason's School for Girls in Tarrytown, New York; all six garbed like the southern belles they were), and the other fifty or so people in her father's official party would christen the big ship. Annie, the governor's second of four children and his eldest daughter, had a big day that December 3: she christened *Tennessee* and, as later reported by the junior Captain Beach, also received her first marriage proposal. In 1908 and no longer a teen, at Washington's Willard Hotel she became one of fourteen founding members of the Society of Sponsors of the US Navy.

As for the ship, her bow wet with celebratory Möet & Chandon White Label champagne, her stub masts draped with a single line of flags, *Tennessee* splashed into the Delaware River accompanied by a celebratory din of "screeching whistles, clanging bells, and booming guns." So wrote the *Spokane* [Washington] *Press* and many other American newspapers over that weekend, all copying verbatim a news item from Philadelphia, and all including the same line drawing of young, comely Annie.

Tennessee now safely in the water, six hundred invited guests proceeded to a luncheon hosted by the shipyard in its cavernous mold loft. Out of consideration for its presumably abstemious southern guests, Cramp's had elected not to serve wine at lunch. That lapse prompted snarky commentary in local newspapers, whose readers apparently were used to a higher standard of fine dining, or thought that they were.

The following Tuesday, December 6, 1904, President Theodore Roosevelt (in high office since McKinley's assassination in September 1901, and elected in his own right just a month ago for what, beginning the coming March, would amount to his second term) delivered a short message to Congress. It started with a denial that would soon in Cuba, the Philippines, and elsewhere be proven false: "it is not true that the United States feels any land hunger or entertains any prospects as regards the other nations of the Western Hemisphere save such as are for their welfare." That said, Roosevelt went on to describe what would soon be called "the Roosevelt Corollary to the Monroe Doctrine." Its operative sentences were:

> Chronic wrongdoing, or an impotence which results in a general loosening of the ties of civilized society, may in America, as elsewhere, ultimately require intervention by some civilized nation, and in the Western Hemisphere the adherence of the United States to the Monroe Doctrine may force the United States, however reluctantly, in flagrant cases of such wrongdoing or impotence, to the exercise of an international police power . . . We would interfere with [our southern neighbors] only in the last resort, and then only if it became evident that their inability or unwillingness to do justice at home and abroad had violated the rights of the United States or had invited foreign aggression to the detriment of the entire body of American nations.

Roosevelt's message concluded: "In asserting the Monroe Doctrine, in taking such steps as we have taken in regard to Cuba, Venezuela, and Panama . . . we have acted in our own interests as well as in the interest of humanity at large." There was, at the beginning of December 1904, nothing really new in this text. Roosevelt had delivered essentially the same message via his old friend Elihu Root, then between cabinet posts, at the Cuba Society of New York's celebration dinner that previous May (the event had marked the second anniversary of the island's independence from Spain), but he waited until his reelection to speak it aloud for himself. An elaboration followed a year later, on December 5.

The Monroe Doctrine, to which Roosevelt referred, was originally an idea discussed several times in late summer 1823 by George Canning, the British foreign secretary, and Benjamin Rush, the American minister in London: a joint announcement of a common British-American perspective supportive of the revolt of Spanish colonies in South America that had begun in 1810. Such a statement would have been issued against the backdrop of increasingly authoritarian politics on the Continent after the fall of Napoleon, evidenced by the restoration of the Spanish and French royal houses, and in an alliance of the autocrats of Austria, Russia, and Prussia. Meeting in Troppeau in 1820 and at Laibach in 1821, these three in a "Holy Alliance," who ruled as they believed by divine right, had explicitly committed themselves to ending representative government where it existed, and to preventing its introduction in places where the form was unknown.

Monroe, after consulting with Jefferson, Madison, and John Quincy Adams (his secretary of state), elected not to join with the British in such a statement but chose instead to issue a unilateral declaration, and he did on December 2, 1823, in his seventh annual message to Congress, boldly announcing that the American Continents "are henceforth not to be considered as subjects for future colonization by any European Powers." He continued:

> We owe it therefore, to candor, and to the amicable relations existing between the United States and [the European Powers] to declare that we should consider any attempt on their part to extend their system to any portion of this hemisphere as dangerous to our peace and safety. . . .
>
> It is impossible that the allied Powers should extend their political system to any portion of either continent without endangering our peace and happiness; nor can anyone believe that our southern brethren, if left to themselves, would adopt it of their own accord. It is equally impossible, therefore, that we should behold such interposition, in any form, with indifference.[1]

The language was that of Adams, whose 1823–24 diary (vol. 34) reveals his worries about Russian, British, and French designs on assorted places in the Americas.[2] Remarkably, given the perfect inability of the United States until the end of the century to enforce the doctrine in the face of any serious foreign challenge, it remained intact and generally observed through the coming decades. The obvious, short-lived exception was France's installation in Mexico, three years after the start of the American Civil War, of a "fictitious emperor," a contemptuous American description of the ill-starred Austrian Archduke Maximilian, who died bravely in office in June 1867, shot by his own revolting subjects. The regicide was famously depicted soon after the fact in three paintings by Édouard Manet, *The Execution of Maximilian*, done between 1867 and 1869. The distinctly French-style uniforms of the firing squad in the last of the three paintings hinted broadly that Manet thought Napoleon III was ultimately responsible for Maximilian's deposition and murder.

Theodore Roosevelt's is the best known among the covey of "corollaries" to the Monroe Doctrine that followed its announcement. The others include texts drafted by Secretary of State Henry Clay (in 1825), by President Polk (also in the 1820s), by Secretary of State Richard Olney (in 1895), and, after Roosevelt, by Senator Henry Cabot Lodge (in 1912). Among these, Roosevelt's was notable because it put an interventionist cast on a doctrine that had begun eighty years earlier as fundamentally anti-interventionist, and especially because it justified the exercise of police powers by the United States in the Western Hemisphere; powers that could only be effectively exercised by a navy at sea, one capable of delivering marines ashore—as Roosevelt, the former activist assistant secretary of the navy and commander of a cavalry regiment in an expeditionary war, would have known better than anyone else in Washington.

Moreover, Roosevelt's velvety assurances in 1904 that the United States felt no land hunger for foreign places at best reflected a very recent conversion, one after the expansionists of 1848 had happily swallowed Texas, Oregon, California, and New Mexico, and not long after those of 1898 had celebrated the absorption of Hawaii, the Philippines, Porto Rico, and Guam. *Life* magazine's shocking May 22, 1902, cover (vol. 39, no. 1021) signaled this loss of innocence: three American soldiers are depicted water-boarding a barefoot Filipino guerrilla at pistol-point, while a cluster of five uniformed Europeans in the background gleefully choruses "Those pious Yankees can't throw stones at us any more."

Puck's June 29, 1904 cover, another by Udo Keppler, showed the American Eagle casting the shadow of its spread wings nearly halfway around the world, from the Philippines to the Eastern Caribbean, with the caption "Gee but this is an awful stretch," speaking for those others uncertain about where enthusiasm for imperialism might lead.[3]

FIGURE 3.2. "Peace."

In this centerfold illustration from *Puck* (vol. 57, no. 1465 [March 29, 1905]), a glowering Columbia in armor, saber in one hand and a sheaf of bayonets in the other, sits atop a US battleship under way, at the head of a fleet in formation so vast that it stretches to and across the distant horizon. The two helmeted doves flying beside her are also armed.

The grinning figurehead on Columbia's ship is President Teddy Roosevelt; three months before this image appeared, Roosevelt promulgated his corollary to the Monroe Doctrine, asserting an American right to intervene in sister republics to the south, in case of their "wrongdoing or impotence." The Monroe Doctrine had depended tacitly on the Royal Navy; Roosevelt's corollary depended explicitly on the American Navy that was giving him such evident satisfaction here.

The artist, John S. Pughe (1870–1909), an immigrant to the United States from Wales as a child, spent the last fourteen years of his short life as an illustrator for *Puck*, after first working for newspapers in New York and Brooklyn. *Puck* started publishing in English in 1877, after appearing for its first year in German, opening a competition for readers and influence with *Frank Leslie's Illustrated Newspaper*, with *Harper's Weekly*, and after the mid-1880s with the *Judge*, *Puck*'s new chief rival. The magazine finally folded in September 1918 after short periods publishing first twice and then only once a month.

Source: Library of Congress, Prints and Photographs Division.

In fact, as Steven Hahn describes in *A Nation without Borders* (Viking, 2016), territorial expansion was in the very DNA of the United States. The Articles of Confederation, ratified in March 1781 and the first expression of how the former colonies intended to govern themselves, offered Canada a unique opportunity to join the new country. Article XI read, "Canada, acceding to this confederation, and adjoining in the measures of the United States, shall be admitted into, and entitled to the advantages of this Union; but no other colony shall be admitted to the same, unless such admission be agreed to by nine states." That article quoted practically verbatim Article XX of a July 1776 draft of confederation articles, written at the dawn of the Revolution. These ultimately unsuccessful diplomatic initiatives were paralleled (and undercut) by several cross-border invasions of Canada, by revolutionaries fearful that the alternative to occupation would be "a nest of hornets on our backs that will sting us to the quick."[4]

Decades later, in August 1812, Thomas Jefferson, by then a former president, told Philadelphian William Duane that "the acquisition of Canada this year, as far as the neighborhood of Quebec, will be a mere matter of marching; & will give us the experience for the attack of Halifax the next, & the final expulsion of England from the American continent." In 1812 already "the American continent." As late as the 1860s, more than two generations after the War of 1812, some in the United States—among them Secretary of State Seward—were still eyeing Canada as a fit target for incorporation, perhaps in compensation for American shipping losses to the English-built Confederate commerce raider, CSS *Alabama*.

The enduring American appetite for Canada would be no secret. When war erupted in Europe in August 1914, Helmuth von Moltke the Younger (then chief of the German General Staff for the past eight years and no scholar of American history) thought it was possible to entice the United States into becoming Germany's ally in exchange for the promise of Canada, to be redeemed postwar. Not entirely fantastic: into the 1920s and 1930s, American contingency planning for a war against Great Britain (War Plan Red) included planning for an invasion of Canada.

Although Cuba and its neighbor to the east across the Windward Passage, Hispaniola, didn't get the same invitation as did Canada, it wasn't very long before American attention turned to their obvious attractions: excellent harbors (the deep-water one at Samaná Bay on Hispaniola's northeastern corner was especially appealing) and rich lands superbly suitable for plantation agriculture, all an easy sail from the American mainland at a time when travel over water was much more certain, faster, and cheaper than over land.

The strategic arguments behind the American interest in absorbing Cuba into the union in the nineteenth century can be found in summary form in a proposal to buy—or failing that, to take—the island, written in October 1854 to then secretary of state William Marcy by three senior US diplomats in Europe, James Buchanan, John Mason (a former secretary of the navy), and Pierre Soulé, responding to his request in mid-August for their ideas about the island. Their views, contained in a think piece that came to be called the "Ostend Manifesto," weren't entirely new to official Washington: Jefferson and Monroe had an exchange about acquiring Cuba in 1823; secretaries of state Henry Clay, Martin Van Buren, Daniel Webster, and John Clayton had all thought about it, too. What *was* new was the diplomatic trio's aggressive tone and conclusion, shaped largely, Sidney Webster (President Pierce's secretary) thought, by Soulé, a French-born attorney, former senator from Louisiana, and slavery supporter. The three began their letter to the secretary:

> We . . . are thoroughly convinced that an immediate and earnest effort ought to be made by the government of the United States to purchase Cuba from Spain at any price [later defined as $120 million, upping an 1848 offer by $20 million] for which it can be obtained. . . .
>
> It must be clear to any reflecting mind that, from the peculiarity of its geographical position, and the considerations attendant on it, Cuba is as necessary to the North American Republic as any of its present members, and that it belongs naturally to that great family of states of which the Union is the providential nursery. From its locality it commands the mouth of the Mississippi and the immense and annually increasing trade which must seek this avenue to the ocean . . .
>
> Indeed the Union can never enjoy repose, nor possess reliable security, as long as Cuba is not embraced within its boundaries. Its immediate acquisition by our government is of paramount importance.

And then continued somewhat ominously:

> Our past history forbids that we should acquire the island of Cuba without the consent of Spain, unless justified by the great law of self-preservation.

We must, in any event, preserve our conscious rectitude and our own self-respect.

Whilst pursuing this course we can afford to disregard the censures of the world, to which we have been so often and so unjustly exposed.

After we shall have offered Spain a price for Cuba far beyond its present value, and this shall have been refused, it will then be time to consider the question: does Cuba, in the possession of Spain, seriously endanger our internal peace and the existence of our cherished union?

Should this question be answered in the affirmative, then, by every law, human and divine, we shall be justified in wresting it from Spain, if we possess the power . . . Under such circumstances we ought neither to count the cost nor regard the odds which Spain might enlist against us. We forebear to enter into the question, whether the present condition of the island would justify such a measure? We should, however, be recant to our duty, be unworthy of our gallant forefathers, and commit base treason against our posterity, should we permit Cuba to be Africanized and become a second St. Domingo, with its attendant horrors to the white race, and suffer the flames to extend to our own neighboring shores, seriously to endanger or actually to consume the fair fabric of our Union.[5]

Unsaid in the manifesto's text was the expectation that, were Cuba to join the Union, it would be as a slave state. The Civil War eliminated that possibility, as well as the more expansive prewar fantasy that American slave-owning states might eventually multiply and extend so far south as to cross the Caribbean and even encompass Brazil. But the appetite for Cuba wasn't yet sated.

The other focal point of American interest in the Caribbean through the nineteenth and into the twentieth century was the arable eastern, Spanish-speaking two-thirds of the island of Hispaniola, Santo Domingo, separated in 1844 from French-speaking "Hayti" to its west by a revolution, and scarred by near continuous revolutions of its own into the next century.

Santo Domingo was attractive to Americans for many of the same reasons as was Cuba, and especially because of enormous, beautiful Samaná Bay on its northeastern coast. The great rectangular bay opened on the Mona Channel between Santo Domingo and Porto Rico, described by Grant's secretary of state, Hamilton Fish, as "the gate to the Caribbean Sea and the Isthmus of Panama."[6] (Until the United States developed naval bases on Cuba and Porto Rico,

Samaná Bay was one of two perennial, powerful lures—sugar was the other—to attract Americans to the table for negotiations with Dominicans.)

After independence Santo Domingo's shifting political leadership shopped the perennially bankrupt infant state around, inviting France, Great Britain, Spain, and the United States to establish a protectorate. Spain bit, briefly, in 1861, but by 1865 (after the end of a short-lived Spanish occupation) Santo Domingo was back on the auction block, where in the aftermath of the American Civil War, it drew the attention of President Ulysses S. Grant.

In 1869, under Grant's aegis, a treaty and a "convention" were negotiated by the resident American commercial agent, Raymond Perry, and the Dominican Republic's secretary of state for foreign affairs, Manuel Maria Gautier, and signed on November 29. Grant then presented both the "Treaty Celebrated between the United States of America and the Dominican Republic, for the Incorporation of the Second into the First," and a convention between the two parties "for a lease on the Bay and Peninsula of Samana" for fifty years at $150,000 in gold per year, to the Senate on January 10, 1870. (The convention anticipated the possibility that the treaty would fail to get the Senate's consent to ratification.)[7]

The essence of the treaty lay in its first two articles. "I. The Dominican Republic renounces all right of sovereignty . . . and cedes these rights to the United States to be incorporated by them as an integral portion of the Union . . . II. The citizens of the Dominican Republic shall be incorporated into the United States as citizens thereof, inhabiting one of its Territories . . . and may be admitted in the Union as a State, upon such terms and conditions and at such time as Congress shall provide by law."

The treaty and the backup convention both died in the Senate on June 29, 1870, victims of ferocious opposition led by Republican senators Charles Sumner of Massachusetts (who later lost his Foreign Relations Committee chairmanship as fallout from the issue) and Carl Schurz of Missouri, in a 28–28 vote with eighteen senators absent or abstaining. The failure came despite the fact that Republicans, Grant's party, held more than three-quarters of the seats in the Senate. The president didn't give up easily, but his efforts to revitalize the initiative during the coming year also failed.

Years after that, Grant relitigated the case, twice: once in his eighth and last State of the Union message to Congress (December 5, 1876), and again in his personal memoirs, published posthumously in 1886 by his old friend, Mark Twain, where Grant explained:

> The colored man . . . was brought to our shores by compulsion, and he
> now should be considered as having as good a right to remain here as any
> other class of our citizens. It was looking to a settlement of this question that
> led me to urge the annexation of Santo Domingo during the time I was Pres-
> ident of the United States.
>
> Santo Domingo was freely offered to us, not only by the administration,
> but by all the people, almost without price. The island is upon our shores, is
> very fertile, and is capable of supporting fifteen millions of people . . . I took
> it that the colored people would go there in great numbers, so as to have in-
> dependent states governed by their own race. They would still be States of
> the Union, and under the protection of the General Government; but the
> citizens would be almost wholly colored.[8]

American and Caribbean history would have been unimaginably different had
Grant succeeded in what resolved into a personal crusade to absorb the Dominican Republic into the Union, but his campaign triggered resistance in his own
party that the president lacked the political skills to defeat. American interest in
the Caribbean, specifically in Cuba and in Santo Domingo, however didn't di-
minish after the Civil War as the prospects for either a new slave state or for an
off-shore island home state for Black Americans evaporated. Buttressed instead
by powerful economic interests—Grant had gotten that right, the country's
sugar, coffee, mahogany, tropical fruits, tobacco, and yellow, blue, and black
dyewoods, held the lure of great wealth—and by an expansive vision of America's rightful place in a world of empires, that interest only sharpened with the
passage of time, this despite chronic indebtedness and instability.

The republic's catastrophic finances (by 1904 Europeans held $32 million
in Santo Domingo's largely uncollectible debt), and continuing government
turbulence (more than twenty presidents, including a few repeat offenders, and
several juntas had sat uneasily atop the government between 1870 and 1904),
eventually prompted US intervention. That intervention was reluctant, if you
believe Teddy Roosevelt, who in February 1904 compared the option of annexation (Grant redux) to swallowing a porcupine tail first, or avid, if you believe
critics of his activism. The appointment of the first resident American minister
to the island, and an increased level of naval deployments in Dominican waters,
typified by the cruiser USS *Detroit*'s eighteen months off the island between
January 1904 and June 1905, followed.

Next, after two years of arm wrestling between Roosevelt and the Senate, in 1907 came a takeover by Americans of Dominican custom house receipts under the terms of a bilateral convention signed on February 8 that was finally proclaimed in Washington July 25, after more than five months of partisan procedural massage on Capitol Hill. Although the convention nominally provided only for "the assistance of the United States in the collection and application of the customs revenues of the Dominican Republic," in fact, it represented an American takeover of much of the essential business of any government: raising money and expending it on selected programs, a prequel to a much greater intervention.

In that same July, USS *Tennessee* finished her first eighteen months of commissioned service. During the next decade she would play a central role in the increasingly intrusive American naval presence off shore of the Dominican Republic. She was there in May 1916, when US Marines landed on the island, beginning what would become a decades-long occupation, and also there—renamed, aground, abandoned, and broken—six months later, on December 1, when Rear Admiral Harry Knapp, USN, became the first American governor of Santo Domingo.

Scientific American in its March 1906 cover story quantified *Tennessee's* warfighting virtues in suitably technical terms, using the familiar *Pennsylvania*-class cruiser *Iowa* as a standard of comparison: "The total muzzle energy of a single discharge of all the guns of the 'Tennessee' amounts to 202,224 foottons, whereas the total muzzle energy of a single discharge of all the 'Iowa's' guns amounts to only 169,904 foot-tons. Furthermore, the great superiority of speed possessed by the cruiser (22½ knots as against 17 knots) and the higher velocity and flatter trajectory of her projectiles would enable her to choose a fighting range and bearing with relation to the battleship, which would put the low velocity guns of the 'Iowa' to a disadvantage and enable the 'Tennessee' to deliver her fire with telling effect." What the author did not explain was that *Tennessee* was explicitly designed to correct the many deficiencies of the predecessor *Pennsylvania*-class cruisers.

Despite that flattering comparison against the best of the already obsolescent "coast line" battleships, *Tennessee* in the water was a compromise. She'd been built to a US Navy design that was, at least, in its fifth full iteration at the Naval Construction Board when the final plans were delivered in 1903 to Cramp's, the yard that had built the navy's first two armored cruisers (*New York* [Cramp's no. 268] and *Brooklyn* [Cramp's no. 275]); Cramp's had also built *Iowa* (its no. 276). As it developed, the yard would now build one of the last four armored cruisers before the state of the art rapidly moved on to turbine-powered, heavily armored, all-big-gun battle cruisers.

Like the design of every modern combatant ship, *Tennessee*'s design traded the competing virtues of speed, range, firepower, and armor protection off against each other, in the hope that the ensuing balance would be optimized for war at sea in her era, in whatever form that war might take. These trade-offs, difficult at any time, made it especially hard for the US Navy—traditionally focused on port protection and commerce raiding, and anyway poorly organized around the turn of the century to manage the business of ship design and procurement—to define a new type of ship in a time of great change in materials science.

Sharp debates took place within the navy's board of construction between the chief engineer, Rear Admiral George Melville (an advocate for greater speed, and a survivor of the USS *Jeannette*'s catastrophic Arctic expedition), and the chief constructor, Rear Admiral Francis Bowles (one for greater weight of armor and guns), as the type was being defined, and the disagreements soon became public. Bowles advocated armor over speed throughout his career. Describing "Our New Cruisers" at length in the September 1883 issue of the *Proceedings of the United States Naval Institute*, he dismissed the advantage of "tremendous speed" as being "in great measure fictitious." Bowles retired unexpectedly in October 1903 after three years as chief constructor, to become president of the Fore River Shipbuilding Company, one of Cramp's competitors.

These fundamental differences continued even after *Tennessee* was in the water, with those focused on performance arguing at this late date that the ship's torpedo tubes should be removed and replaced by additional bunkering space for coal.

In the end, the *Tennessee*-class design was a significant improvement over that of the preceding *Pennsylvania* class (whose undersized main battery of 8 inch guns and relatively thin-skinned 6 inch belt of armor protection would likely have proved lethal in a fight during the coming war, like those in November and December 1914 off Coronel and the Falklands), but it was still compromised by focus on the special combat virtue thought to be found in high speed.

The world's principal naval powers all faced the same definition problems while each raced to build its own version of a ship that could protect trade, attack commerce, and join in a fight with equal facility. Thus, the Japanese—in 1906–7 still new to the status of major naval power—opted for weight and range of broadside over speed and armor protection, as evidenced by their choice of 12 inch and 8 inch guns for the main battery of the cruisers *Kurama* and *Ibuki*. The two each displaced about as much as *Tennessee*, whose main battery consisted of guns firing only 10 inch and 6 inch shells.

Tennessee's preliminary acceptance was finally reported to the secretary of the navy on July 13, 1906, five months after her all-important, four-hour speed trial run on the Owl's Head range off Rockland, Maine, in darkness and on smooth seas on February 12. Her sustained speed was then recorded as 22.16 knots, fractionally above the required 22. In the intervening months the six-member board had concluded that *Tennessee* was "sufficiently strong to carry the armor, armament, equipment, coal, stores, and machinery prescribed . . . well-built and well-performed, and in strict conformity with the contract, drawings, plans and specifications." Moreover, her steering qualities, steadiness, and seaworthiness were judged excellent. Payment of the balance in the contract was recommended.

But all this approbation followed seven paragraphs focused on the "glaring faults" of US Navy ship design in general, encompassing the design and interior arrangement of the armored conning tower, described as so cluttered that it would be impossible to handle the ship safely from inside its protection; a boat deck that in *Tennessee's* case was congested with nineteen cutters, launches, whale boats, and dinghies ranging in size from fifty to sixteen feet, plus life rafts and balsa floats; the generous use of "highly oiled and varnished woodwork" throughout, even in magazines, which once on fire would quickly force spaces to be abandoned; the great weight of "peace-time appurtenances"; excessive compartmentalization; awkward access to big gun ammunition storage, and even the design of the twenty-eight-berth sick bay.

The following Tuesday, July 17, just after ten in the morning, USS *Tennessee* was commissioned in a modest ceremony at Philadelphia's League Island Navy Yard. By the splendid standard of her christening ceremony twenty months ago, the cruiser's turnover to the fleet was almost surreptitious. The next day's *Washington Post* described the event mildly as "unostentatious."

The turnover was done in front of small, decorative formations of marines and sailors facing each other across the quarterdeck, and observed only by League Island's commandant, Rear Admiral Joseph Craig; Captain John Hyland, the yard's commanding officer; Colonel Randolph Dickins of the Marine Barracks; a small contingent of other officers, and a cluster of officers' wives looking down from the cruiser's bridge. With all hands at attention, the bugler sounded "colors"; the stars and stripes was raised aft, and a forty-five-star jack was raised forward. (Oklahoma would not become the forty-sixth state and add its star to both flags for another two years.) Next Captain Albert Berry, USN, read his orders, spoke briefly to the crew, and then withdrew with his guests to his great cabin aft for refreshment.

Heavy rain fell later in the day, but the morning was dry, and this modest event, recorded on the first page of *Tennessee*'s first deck log by her new navigator, Lieutenant Commander Samuel Robinson, USN, went almost without a hitch. "The ceremony, however, did not pass off without an incident that furnished food for gossip," the Wilmington, Delaware, *Morning News* revealed the next day. "When the captain's pennant was run up the military mast and was broken out its forty feet or more got tangled in the rigging. There it stuck, and was only released when a bluejacket climbed up the ratlines part way and then climbed up the rest of the mast and with a great deal of labor succeeded in getting the pennant free. For anything to happen to the captain's pennant is looked upon by old sea dogs as a bad omen," the paper explained to landlubbers.

Tennessee remained in the shipyard for the next fifteen weeks, until November 1, moored alongside the dock, first facing north and later south, while the rest of her enlisted crew dribbled on board, stores were loaded, and the yard's civilian shipfitters, joiners, and painters finished their work to make her ready for sea. The deck log for those fifteen weeks contains little more than a gloomy daily inventory of disciplinary infractions and punishments imposed.

Tennessee finally put to sea at 8:45 a.m. on November 1, 1906, for a first cruise that would keep her out of homeport until mid-December. President Theodore Roosevelt was going to Panama in the new *Connecticut*-class battleship USS *Louisiana*, lead ship in her class and just back from Cuba with Secretary of War Taft. Roosevelt's historic trip—the first time a sitting president would leave the United States—had been announced at the beginning of the summer; a high-speed, three-day pass through the muddy construction site, deliberately planned for the height of Panama's rainy season, that would keep him out of the country for three weeks altogether. The president had gloried in his role as the godfather of the canal, a project that *Judge* magazine had described in June 1904 as "the greatest achievement for trade in modern times." (Its cover showed an expressionless Roosevelt sporting an enormous gold crown, rakishly tipped to one side, decorated with miniature golden ships circling inside a finished canal.) This was the president's chance to bask in that bold project's early progress, seventeen years after the counterpart French project's costly collapse on the same site, and still with some eight years to go to completion.

Tennessee and her sister ship, USS *Washington*, sailed in *Louisiana*'s company to swell the procession, usually in "column natural order," at 14 knots, and separated one from the other by 500 yards. Roosevelt and his small staff of five (his physician, a secretary, and three Secret Service agents; future presidents would only travel abroad amid a small village of aides) were sailing in appropriate style, none of these three ships had been in commission for more than a few months, and *Louisiana*'s flag cabin aft had been specially enlarged for the president and his second wife, Edith. On November 14 the battleship and her escorts anchored in Panama's Limon Bay, near what would become in 1914 the north (Atlantic) end of the Panama Canal. In *The Path Between the Seas* David McCullough admiringly described Roosevelt's ensuing three breathless days ashore—marveling at the works and the giant equipment parked about, and barking questions at people—as "one of those small, luminous events that light up an era."[9] On December 17, the day before *Tennessee* returned to her berth at League Island (on the way home from Cuba on November 21 the little squadron had stopped for the day in Ponce, on the southern side of Porto Rico), Roosevelt released to Congress his long "Special Message concerning the Panama Canal."

Roosevelt clearly enjoyed his time on board. Five years later, in Hampton Roads welcoming the fleet home from its 'round-the-world cruise, the president made a point of telling the "Pelicans" of *Louisiana*'s crew, some among them his former shipmates: "I shall never forget the trip we made on the *Louisiana* and of all the things that happened to Mrs. Roosevelt and myself in the White house the one most cherished is when the crew of the ship presented to Mrs. Roosevelt the handsome loving cup which now stands in the White House dining room."

Tennessee's maiden cruise and first visit to Panama went off without incident—or perhaps it didn't. American and, eventually, some foreign newspapers reported that fifty or sixty stokers on board had mutinied during her return from Porto Rico, refusing to work in the ship's fire rooms under forced draft during a high-speed sprint on November 26, presumably laid on to show the president the performance his fleet was capable of. The story gained color as it passed from newspaper to newspaper and continent to continent. Allegedly beginning first as a complaint by some sailors ("Jackies" in the slang of the day) about the quality of food in *Tennessee*'s enlisted mess, then morphing into a walkout over oppressive conditions in the fire rooms during the maximum speed demonstration. By the time the mutiny story trickled across the globe to the *Times of India* the following March (via British papers), it had swelled colorfully to describe an entire mutinous crew under arrest, with order finally restored about the decks by armed marines. The reports were repeatedly denied by the navy, and as its novelty wore off, the mutiny story slowly disappeared. Oddly, a real and serious problem on board the cruiser, an engine breakdown on the way to Colon (eventually attributed to faulty lubricating oil) that required time in the League Island yard to repair, was never reported by the press.

Four years later, accompanied now by USS *Montana*, *Tennessee* was back in Panama on a second presidential visit, there for the third time. (Her second visit to the canal had been on its Pacific side during mid-December 1908, during the cruiser's long deployment in that ocean.) On this cruise *Tennessee* was actually carrying the president, no longer Roosevelt but William Taft. Taft's visit to Panama (his second also, he'd been there in January 1909 as president-elect) was, he said, to prepare to make various recommendations regarding the canal to Congress in its upcoming session. It's likely that President Taft was feeling badly bruised as he boarded *Tennessee*. His party had just been battered in the midterm elections, losing control both of the Senate (down twelve seats) and of the House (down fifty-eight), and turning Congress and its all-important committee chairmanships over to the Democrats for the first time in sixteen years. The losses in 1910 anticipated the presidential election two years later, when a Republican party cleft into conservative (Taft) and progressive (Roosevelt) wings was defeated by Woodrow Wilson and the Democrats. All three would easily push aside the Socialist Party's candidate, Eugene Debs, running for his fourth time and finishing fourth.

Tennessee sailed for the isthmus construction site at midday on November 10, 1910, out of Charleston, South Carolina, and returned Taft and his small party via a four-hour stop in Guantanamo, Cuba, to Fort Monroe, Virginia, twelve days later.

The short Cuba stop on the way home, another first by an American president but also not Taft's first (he'd been there as the provisional governor in 1906 while serving as secretary of war), was fraught. The president's purpose, the press explained, was to "inspect the port with a view to developing it into a permanent naval base for the United States." More than a century later, any route to a dignified withdrawal of the United States from Guantanamo, now chiefly a prison site, still eludes Washington.

The cruiser's passage home reportedly included a near-collision at sea, late on November 18, with SMS *Freya*, a German *Victoria Louise*–class protected cruiser half *Tennessee*'s size. Ten hours out of Cuba, *Freya*, eleven years old, already obsolete, and on a training cruise, was said by newspapers to have suddenly loomed out of the fog, passed within a quarter-mile, and then silently ghosted on. Sadly, there's nothing so dramatic in the watch officer's deck log entry for the eight-to-midnight watch that night. "At 11:30," Ensign James Parker wrote, "sighted and passed a foreign cruiser bound S.E., nationality unknown." The cruiser must have passed relatively close aboard *Tennessee* to make even that identification possible in darkness, but Parker makes no more of the fact of ships passing in the night than that, and the story seems to be another example of creative reporting. A brief period of turbulent seas later marked the only other excitement at sea reported during the dozen days Taft was away from the country. He, allegedly, enjoyed the experience.

No one has since described Taft's four days on the ground in Panama as "a small, luminous event that lit up an era." The president had a huge presence—Taft in presidential form equaled the displacement of an NFL lineman today, and the tropical white suit and big-brimmed hat he wore moving about *Tennessee* like a ship under sail made him loom larger still—but he was then and has been ever since in the shadow of the smaller, more effervescent, and charismatic Roosevelt.

Those four days on the canal site did form the basis for what Taft soon told Congress. Delivered to the lame-duck session a month after his inspection trip,

Taft's second annual message reported to members that the canal was on schedule (to open by January 11, 1915; it actually opened August 15, 1914) and also on budget ($375 million in construction costs). During the message he mentioned the canal fully fifty-four times.

The canal's inauguration three and a half years later was nothing like the gala ceremony that had been planned for the historic event before World War I broke out. The original plan had President Wilson riding the veteran battleship USS *Oregon* (with Captain Charles Clark, USN (Ret.), her commanding officer during the Spanish-American War and now, at seventy-one, a distinguished passenger) at the head of an international fleet just down from Hampton Roads. The whole assembly was to steam south in procession through the locks and lake from Cristobal to Balboa in mid-February 1915, aping Ferdinand de Lesseps's theatrical opening of the Suez Canal in 1869, after which the Americans would proceed to California, Wilson still on board *Oregon*, while the foreigners dispersed.

Instead, eleven days into the world war, the opening was marked by the sober, lone transit of SS *Ancon*, 9,600 tons and owned by the Panama Railroad Company, the full length of the canal with the two hundred or so embarked passing for notables. Among them was the president of Panama, but not the US president. Wilson cannot have minded the cancellation much. The canal was indelibly associated with Roosevelt and the Republicans, whom he'd defeated less than two years ago and would face down again in two years' time.

The first US Navy ship to transit the canal would be the nearly new collier USS *Jupiter* in October. En route from San Francisco to Philadelphia, she made the passage via the canal in twenty-three days. *Oregon* had required fully sixty-six to reach the Florida Keys from San Francisco.

The four intervening years, from 1907 nearly to the end of 1910, those between *Tennessee*'s high-visibility first and third cruises to the Panama Canal in company with or carrying the chief executive, were somewhat less substantial.

Back in December 1906 from the cruise with Roosevelt, *Tennessee* next left her home port on April 12, 1907, to participate in the gala international naval assembly and review that marked the opening of the Jamestown Exposition. The cruiser had spent part of March in dry dock at Boston, getting her hull cleaned and painted. (She'd be back in the dry dock again during the last week of May.) Now, handsome throughout, *Tennessee* steamed south to spend the next five weeks on display in Hampton Roads.

The event celebrated three centuries of English settlement in North America. *Tennessee* would be until May 16 part of a great, international fleet that materialized off until-then sleepy Sewell's Point, highlighting the start of the new exposition's seven-month run. A turgid illustrated record of the celebration, "the only authorized history," *The Official Blue Book of the Jamestown Ter-Centennial Exposition*, was printed in 1907 by the Colonial Publishing Company of Norfolk, Virginia. (Sample descriptive phrase: "[The exposition's] industrial features will be less amplitudinous than at several other expositions, but will be congregated with extreme care.")

Anchored in what became a huge arc of fifty or so combatant ships a mile and a half offshore from the barely finished fairgrounds, *Tennessee* was in impressive company. The assembled fleet included most of the Royal Navy's First Cruiser Division, flagship HMS *Good Hope*, together with *Antrim*, *Devonshire*, *Hampshire*, and *Roxburgh*. Even distant Japan was represented, by the cruisers *Chitose* and *Tsukuba*. *Chitose* had been built in the Union Iron Works in San Francisco (five years and thirty-three hulls after USS *Oregon*). *Tsukuba*, like *Kurama* and *Ubuki* powerfully armed with 12 inch guns in place of the 10 inch guns on *Tennessee*, was built entirely at the Kure Dockyard in Japan, the *Washington Post* noted portentously. Until then, Japan had bought most of the ships for its navy from Great Britain, the last of which would be the battle cruiser *Kongō*, delivered from Vickers in 1914. Navy ship construction in Japanese home yards was to foreign observers a new and disturbing development.

Chitose and *Tsukuba* sailed from Virginia to New York City and later to Bordeaux, France—where scrapes on shore with visiting US Navy crews on liberty were imagined by the local press—before continuing their eight-month, around-the-world cruise in mid-November. The pair's cruise was a pioneering demonstration in small scale of growing Japanese prowess on blue water that would be enlarged and repeated during World War I, to such effect that Japan would absorb at war's end Germany's former Pacific colonies.

In May 1907, at almost at the same time that the two Japanese cruisers joined the rest of the international fleet at anchor in Hampton Roads, in New York *Pearson's Magazine* published a long, scary piece of fiction spun out by

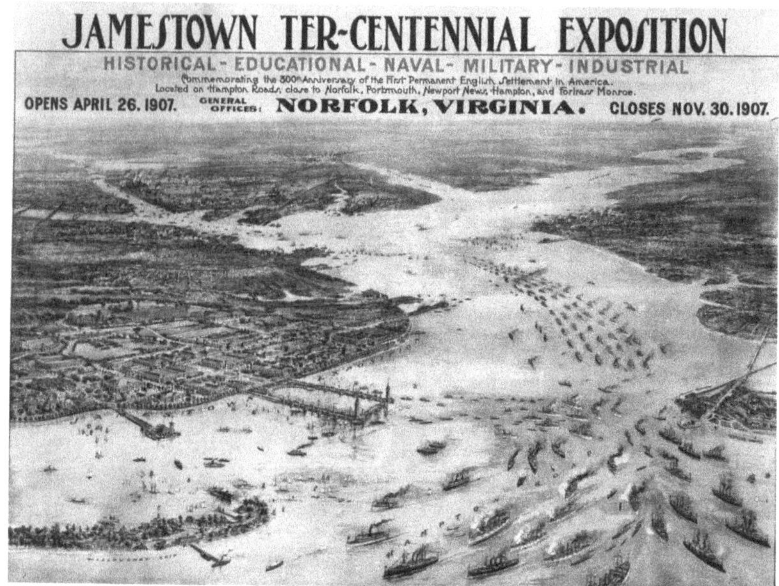

FIGURE 3.3. "Jamestown Ter-Centennial Exposition.
Historical—Educational—Naval—Military—Industrial."

The international naval review lay offshore from the exposition grounds, shown here at anchor above (west of) Willoughby Spit with other men o'war under way in the roads. Among the many foreign ships present was Norway's battleship *Harald Haarfagre*; Sweden's armored cruiser *Fylgia*, on her maiden voyage; the German cruiser *Bremen*; the Dutch cruiser *Gelderland*; and the French cruisers *Kleber* and *Victor Hugo*. Argentina's *Presidente Sarmiente* was also present, as were cruisers from Portugal, Austria, Italy, Brazil, Chile, and Mexico. None of several Russian capital ships thought by the American press to be candidates to appear at the review (the battleships *Czarevitvch* and *Slava* or the cruiser *Bogatyr*) showed up.

Such international naval assemblies were commonplace in this era, a form of host country chest-beating that supplemented world fairs, and in time would be replaced by hosting the quadrennial Olympic Games. None came even close to rivaling the Diamond Jubilee Naval Review, mounted in June 1897 in Queen Victoria's honor by the Royal Navy: 165 warships assembled at Spithead, all British.

A. Hoen and Co. was a Richmond branch of Baltimore's Edward Weber and Co. printing house, started in 1835 by German immigrants. The daughter company in Richmond, established during the Civil War, printed Confederate money but found a more durable business postwar printing exceptionally high-quality, five-color plate sheet music covers, maps, posters, cigar box labels, and other advertising art. It closed in the 1930s.

Source: Library of Virginia, Richmond.

Atherton Brownell, "Our War with Japan, A Brief History of Events Ending March 1917."[10]

In Brownell's imaginative telling—he dropped just enough names and descriptive technical details to make his story sound authoritative—the United States declared war on Japan on February 22, 1915, after battleship *Kentucky* and the cruisers *New York* and *Denver*, landing marines ashore near "Tokio" to quell violent anti-American riots prompted by the Exclusion Act, were attacked by a powerful Japanese squadron without warning, and sunk in "the Bay of Yeddo." With the US Navy outnumbered three combatant ships to one in the Pacific (and three to two in tonnage), any chance for the Atlantic Fleet to reinforce its overmatched western counterpart and respond to the attack vanished when *Kearsarge* and eight other ships heading there were trapped hard aground in the Panama Canal after the waters of Gatun Lake drained out by gravity through open, sabotaged locks at both ends of the waterway. Next, Oahu and Pearl Harbor quickly fell under a naval assault supported by tens of thousands of Japanese army veterans, cunningly infiltrated into Hawaii ostensibly as farmhands to work in the sugarcane fields of the islands. Without any chance of reinforcement, Subig Bay and Manila in the Philippines fell in turn.

At the end of six months, Brownell had the Japanese massing an amphibious force off Monterey Bay, California. They were beaten off, leaving the chastened United States confined behind its Pacific Coast shore defenses ruing its failures to arm adequately and to fortify its island possessions, and the Japanese as the masters of the entire Pacific.

An earlier, enormously popular British example of the same genre was Erskine Childers's book *The Riddle of the Sands: A Record of Secret Service* (Smith, Elder & Co., 1903), in which two intrepid amateur British agents come across proof in the Baltic of German preparations for an invasion of England across the North Sea. Another such, published a few years later, was a best seller by two of Childers's countrymen, William Le Queux and Herbert Wilson, *The Invasion of 1910; With a Full Account of the Siege of London* (Eveleigh Nash, 1906). First serialized in the *Daily Mail*, their story was eventually translated into twenty-seven languages and made into a movie, *If England Were Invaded*, released three months after the war began. (A bootleg German-language version featured a more congenial ending for its viewers than did the original English-language release.)

Such "invasion literature" was enormously popular in the years immediately before World War I, suggesting that ordinary citizens were thinking about the possibility of war, even if politicians were not. So, also, were extraordinary citizens (meaning here the authors of the genre), motivated to write by their fears about the democracies' evident lack of military preparedness.

Fabulists weren't the only ones thinking about how a war with Japan might play out. Another doing that much more seriously was an American named Homer Lea (1876–1912), a some time Chinese army general and author in 1909 of the prescient *The Valor of Ignorance, the Inevitable Japanese-American War* (Harper & Brothers). This, Lea's second book of three, foresaw war between the United States and Japan and Germany, and judged the American army and navy inadequate to resist invasion by either foe. Reviewed anonymously in March 1910 in the *North American Review* (vol. 191, no. 652), *The Valor of Ignorance* was described there as "a very vigorous and informing book . . . very disquieting." It was republished in 1942, a reviewer in that October's *Foreign Affairs* explained, "to indicate the author's prescience and firm grasp of strategy in foreshadowing some of the main lines of Japanese attack against the United States and its possessions."

At almost the same time that Brownell and Lea were drafting their stories, one fiction, the other explicitly meant to be warning, a few US Navy officers began a planning process that would extend over the next thirty-five years or so, looking with increasing specificity at how a war with Japan might unfold, and how it could best be fought and won. Their product (described superbly in 1991 by Edward Miller in *War Plan Orange: The U.S. Strategy to Defeat Japan, 1897–1945*), almost a script for the conflict to come—less its nuclear ending— would become a remarkable exception to the rule that "no battle plan survives contact with the enemy."

The *Post* described the great assembly of combatant ships off Sewell's Point hyperbolically and inaccurately as "a unique event in the history of the world," but it was truly a grand display. Spain's and Russia's absences—both nations still exhausted and embarrassed by their recent defeats at sea—merited little comment in the press, and everyone else who mattered was there.

The home team's presence at Jamestown, some two dozen bright white ships in an otherwise dark gray fleet, predictably exceeded that of the foreign navies combined. It included sixteen battleships (two not yet fully operational), four cruisers, and even five small torpedo boat destroyers, the latter painted dark green, glossy as alligators and distinctly out of place in the otherwise white and buff American lineup. Even the old, tired *Texas*, USS *Maine*'s sister ship, and *Brooklyn* were recommissioned to pad the line, with *Texas* lying just astern of *Tennessee*. All were under the command of Rear Admiral Robley Evans, USN, commander of the US Atlantic Fleet.

Evans's second memoir, *An Admiral's Log . . .* (New York: D. Appleton, 1910), included a scathing critique of exposition management, concluding: "the time finally came when the Exposition closed, and candour compels me to say that every officer and man in the American fleet was glad when the flags came down and the gates were closed. We felt that, while we had done all in our power for its success, we had been associated, from the opening day, with a failure."

At Jamestown, too, the Japanese ships attracted special attention, the *New York Times* devoting a full page with photographs on Sunday, May 19, to explain to its readers "the striking differences which the visitor observes between the ships of the Mikado's navy and our own." Putting aside the pay scale and rations of the crew, that difference seemed to be largely cosmetic, with the Japanese entirely free of any of the usual man o'war fancy ropework and other decoration except a small sun on the bow and "ideographs emblazoned on the stern, bits of gilt not unlike the Chinese laundry mark."

Difficult for visitors to get to, poorly planned, and badly managed, the Jamestown Exposition—held seven years after the brilliant Paris International Exposition, just five years after the Pan-American Exposition in Buffalo, New York (at which the famous elephant Jumbo was slated for public electrocution, and during which President McKinley was fatally shot), and only three after another expo in St. Louis, Missouri, celebrating the Louisiana Purchase—was a financial failure. Jamestown drew fewer than one-tenth as many people as had gone to the World's Columbian Exposition in Chicago in 1893, and fewer than half as many as had visited Buffalo. The day after the exposition closed at the end of November, the *New York Times*, which had deprecated the exposition for months, characterized it as having proved to be "the most colossal failure in the history of expositions," a description widely quoted in the months that followed.

Months earlier, on June 14, in company again with USS *Washington*, *Tennessee* had sailed on the first of what would become three cruises to Europe during the next seven years, punctuated by nearly three years deployed as part of the new Pacific Fleet.

Flying the flag of Rear Admiral Charles Stockton, USN, now commander of the newly designated, two-ship "special service squadron," *Tennessee* in mid-June headed across the Atlantic to France, to appear in another maritime extravaganza, the International Maritime Exhibition at Bordeaux, and then to call at several ports along the French Atlantic coast before returning home two months later. As Jean Jusserand, the long-serving French ambassador in Washington, had explained to Secretary of State Root the previous January, in a perfectly tuned solicitation to encourage American participation, this exposition's purpose was "to commemorate the centennial of steam navigation," "and consequently to do special honor to the genius of an illustrious American, Fulton, who operated his first practical steamboat on the Hudson in 1807. France will exert all the more zeal in doing homage to the great inventor, as it was in our country [on the Loire in 1803] he conducted his first experiments, fruitless to be sure, but significant enough to cause Napoleon to write . . . 'Citizen Fulton's proposition may change the face of the earth.'"[11] Honoring Fulton and much more: the exposition highlighted not only French shipbuilding (its centerpiece was the launch into the Garonne River on May 28 of the nearly complete, third *Liberté*-class battleship, *Vérité*), but also France's wine and automotive industries, and her colonial empire. This last through an "African village" on display that provided the opportunity for visitors to ogle "villagers," dragooned from four tribes of Francophone Africa, busily simulating daily life in an ersatz native habitat.

President Roosevelt—whose determined construction of closer ties among the American, British, and French navies had its source in his suspicions of German intentions in the Caribbean since the Venezuela Crisis—enthusiastically endorsed Ambassador Jusserand's appeal, and Congress in response thriftily appropriated $15,000 of the $25,000 requested.[12] The sum was barely enough for construction of a pavilion quayside on the Garonne to house an exhibit of Fulton artifacts and memorabilia managed by the Smithsonian Institution. (As built, the American pavilion resembled a small, oddly proportioned White House. The pavilion for the earlier Paris Expo had aped the design of the US Capitol.)

In parallel, Secretary of the Navy Metcalf approved the deployment of the cruisers, wresting them away in mid-June from Sewell's Point (after a loop through New York, Boston, and Newport) for France. There, at Brest on July 24, the two overlapped with the now-familiar IJN *Chitose* and IJN *Tsukuba*. The occasion prompted a deafening exchange of gun salutes between the ships of the several navies in port, in which the Japanese alone fired sixty-two guns, also a much quieter but no less formal exchange of officer calls, but not much else. With the senior Japanese officers in Paris to meet the French president, it fell to the Americans to entertain the remaining junior Japanese in *Tennessee's* wardroom. Neither navy had permitted its enlisted men time ashore on liberty that day.

While in port in Brest, *Tennessee's* first commanding officer, Albert Berry, still on board, took advantage of the lull in operations to remind the secretary of the navy of one of his ship's principal design flaws, her great topside weight, while revealing an unexpected aesthetic sense. "If pole masts could be installed in place of the present unsightly masts, heights of smoke pipes and ventilators lowered, and as many weights as possible removed, the load-waterline might be raised a few inches. At present the armor belt is almost submerged with all coal, stores and provisions on board, rendering the vessel's armor belt almost useless."

Back in New York on August 6 after a slow westbound Atlantic crossing, and after several weeks in the yard, *Tennessee* was soon back at sea. She sailed from Hampton Roads at midday on October 12 for the Pacific, where after port calls in the Caribbean, Brazil, and Uruguay on the way around, she was to operate for the next twenty-seven months, from November 1907 through February 1910.

Tennessee steamed into San Francisco Bay (in company again with USS *Washington*) February 20, 1908, having been delayed during a slow passage up the west coast of the Americas by several more port visits, including one that stretched over nearly seven weeks in Magdalena Bay, Mexico, to join the Pacific Fleet, newly assembled and reinforced generally to mirror the structure of the Atlantic Fleet, itself reorganized the year before. What had until reorganization been the Asiatic Fleet, based in the Philippines, and a single Pacific Squadron, based at San Francisco, after augmentation from the Atlantic became three squadrons of a new US Pacific Fleet, two squadrons based on the West Coast and one at Manila (a reinforcement that fiction author Atherton Brownell must have welcomed).

Secretary of the Navy Victor Metcalf's November 1907 annual report had explained this restructuring as "an important step for strategic reasons, since all operations in the Pacific as well as in the Atlantic should have one general direction and control. No proper development of naval efficiency could proceed without it, and it is important also as serving directly to bring about a general appreciation of the fact that geographical limits, such as our squadrons have hitherto had, were opposed to the idea of perfect mobility, by which a fleet, squadron, or division should be free of any local tie or dependence." No less significantly, the Pacific augmentation marked an easing of the power of Alfred Thayer Mahan's insistence on fleet concentration.

Metcalf (1853–1936), a three-term Republican congressional representative from California, served first as Roosevelt's secretary of commerce and labor (1904–6) and then for two years (1907–8) as his secretary of the navy. In 1905 he negotiated the agreement that admitted some young Japanese to San Francisco's public schools in exchange for self-imposed restrictions on the further immigration of Japanese laborers, which for a time cooled xenophobic tempers on the West Coast.

Metcalf had a son at the Naval Academy in 1902–6, but otherwise he knew little about the navy when he took office. His restructuring of his immediate office to include four flag officer "aides" (for operations, personnel, matériel, and inspections) was hailed by reformers in uniform who despaired of the navy's highly politicized system of eight bureaus.

The first of the West Coast squadrons, and by far its most powerful, was composed of two divisions of four cruisers each. Four *Pennsylvania*-class cruisers, *West Virginia*, *Colorado*, *Maryland*, and *Pennsylvania*, led by Rear Admiral James Dayton, USN, constituted the first division. *Tennessee* and *Washington*, together with *California* and *South Dakota*, under command of Rear Admiral Uriel Sebree, USN, made up the second.

The arrival in San Francisco of the first division of the new fleet the previous September had stimulated the *San Francisco Call* to an outburst of jingoism: "Before 9 o'clock the four big fighting machines were anchored in diamond formation in man o'war row," the newspaper exulted, "where in the bright sunshine they formed a picture that stirred in the souls of still sleepy commuters a desire to scream like eagles. The Japanese boys who work as waiters in the Southern Pacific ferry steamer restaurants were unusually polite, for every other customer wore a chip on his shoulder and a dare in his eyes ... It was easy to feel yesterday morning that licking creation would be a mere pastime for Uncle Samuel." For "creation" the *Call's* readers likely read "Japan."

The defense of America's new Pacific possessions was the driver behind this reposturing, challenged potentially by the rapid growth of the Imperial Japanese Navy, which soon after its humiliation of the Russian Baltic Fleet at the Battle of Tsushima boasted the fifth largest combatant fleet in the world (behind the United States and ahead of Italy), one supported by a capable shore establishment of five dockyards and arsenals. Capable enough that beginning after the battle cruiser *Kongō* in 1913, all combatant ships joining the IJN were built in home yards.

The IJN's growth had attracted excited attention in the United States, excitement inflamed by seemingly uncontrolled Japanese immigration to the United States, described during 1907 in the American press in near hysterical terms. "Hordes Come from Asia" was a front-page headline that year, followed by "Immigration of Japanese Is Menace . . . Coolie Laborers Enter from North and South . . . Government Appoints Additional Inspectors in Effort to Prevent Any Smuggling across Borders"[13]

American anxieties about Japanese ambitions were remarkably durable. Fully eight years later, in April 1914, an imaginative report in a Los Angeles newspaper of a major Japanese navy presence in Turtle Bay, Mexico—four Japanese cruisers, English and Japanese colliers, and four thousand Japanese marines and sailors allegedly ashore protected by a field of defensive mines—triggered real excitement on the West Coast. It took a dismissive statement by Rear Admiral Pond, then commanding the Pacific Reserve Fleet and not yet assigned to the Caribbean, to calm nerves. (A century later, in 2020, Americans' fear of hard-working refugees, speaking their own languages and practicing their religions while multiplying their children, and suspected to be contemplating who knew what violence, continued reliably to offer a handle where leverage could be applied to manipulate an anxious and uninformed electorate.)

In little more than thirty years, accumulated tensions between the two geopolitical rivals would explode at Pearl Harbor, but even as Jamestown was attracting small crowds to the exposition's waterfront in mid-1907, the *New York Times* and other newspapers were describing the "danger of an early clash" between the two young powers to a general public inclined toward being alarmed. "A Comparison of the Two Fleets Shows That This Country Commands a Larger and Better Equipped Navy Than That of Japan," the *Times* explained ungrammatically on July 7, before going on to report that "the vast majority of those in the naval service have long been of the opinion that sooner or later the Japanese situation would reach a crisis."[14]

That same summer, professional military journals were delivering to their more specialized readerships a similar alarming message, in much greater length and often less digestibly, about this impending collision. Thus, the June–July 1907 issue of the *Journal of the Military Service Institution of the United States* featured a long piece, "Military Conditions in the United States and Japan—A Comparison," by Captain Ignez Rodic of the general staff of the Austro-Hungarian Army, which in its original German had the more forthright title, "The Prospects of an American-Japanese War."[15]

To those likely prospects, he added an example of poorly disciplined Americans in uniform—he'd earlier reported how crew members had deserted "in crowds" from some ships in 1905—citing as fact the imaginary mutiny on board USS *Tennessee* when she escorted Roosevelt to Panama. "In the month of November," Rodic wrote, "during the presence of President Roosevelt with an Atlantic squadron, a strike of firemen occurred, this in itself throwing some light on the defective discipline and real worth of the American naval cruise."

Rodic was a myopic seer—there's no evidence that he foresaw that his own fragile Dual Monarchy had little more than a decade of life left—but his long analysis of Japan's "surplus population" and need for more land; of her feverish rearmament after Tsushima; of naval and military balances in the Pacific that favored Japan; of likely British support for the Japanese; of the spotty defenses of the American West Coast (not much more than four fortified points, among which only San Francisco "can be considered of any importance," and many unprotected harbors); and of an "insignificant" and ill-disciplined American army, led him to conclude: "it is the serious duty of America to lose no time in perfecting her defenses and guarding against a surprise."

Captain Rodic's prescription, including an immediate and extensive enlargement of the American standing army and expansion of West Coast fortifications, would have been congenial to the *Journal*'s readership, almost exclusively regular army officers, who would have read it as an argument for increased Army funding in austere times. But his views reached a much broader audience, reflecting and prompting widespread anxiety among Americans everywhere. In 1907–8 Rodic was quoted extensively in several dozen newspapers, among them some serving inland communities (for example, the Cheney, Kansas,

Sentinel; the Lincoln, Nebraska, *Commoner*; the Claire, Michigan, *Courier*; and the Minneapolis *Irish Standard*), places where a Japanese face would have been as rare as a giraffe's.

Tennessee and her counterparts weren't idle in the Pacific. August 24, 1908 (some three months after an accident in a fire room filled the space with steam, killing seven men and injuring six), she sailed from San Francisco via Honolulu for the Samoa Islands, visiting with the other seven cruisers of the new fleet's first and second divisions German-owned Apia and then backtracking to "Pango Pango" on American-owned Tutuila Island for ten days. Westbound, each cruiser had towed a destroyer "as a matter of practice and experiment."[16] *Tennessee*'s burden was the four-year-old *Truxtun*-class torpedo boat destroyer USS *Whipple* (Cramp's no. 483), 259 feet long, 430 tons, and a crew of 78. (Later and then under her own power, *Whipple* served respectably during the war. She was decommissioned and sold in 1920, and ended her time at sea ignominiously decades later as SS *Whipple*, having been reduced, together with several of her classmates, to carrying bananas for several fruit companies.)

The towing exercise might have been a demonstration to Japan of the American fleet's reach, even absent accompanying colliers (which in fact eventually joined and coaled both squadrons at Pago Pago for their return to Honolulu), but apparently it made little sense to *Tennessee*'s new commanding officer, Captain Bradley Fiske, USN. Fiske was skeptical about what the tow proved and rightly believed in 1919 that, since nothing like it had ever been done again, "our trip had little value for the future." (In fact, towing small combatants west was considered in some iterations of War Plan Orange, the contingency plan for war with Japan.)

Tennessee dragged little *Whipple* without incident more than five thousand miles west, all the way to Apia, at an average speed of 9½ knots. *Tennessee*, the other cruisers, and their covey of destroyers, now steaming on their own and unfettered by tows, passed eastbound back through Hawaii in October, eventually returning to San Francisco after spending the intervening winter operating off and visiting ports along the coast of Central and South America.

The division's next and *Tennessee*'s last cruise on the Asiatic Station began in August 1909 with an 18 knot sprint to Honolulu, almost twice the speed of the same passage hauling destroyers the year before. From Hawaii the cruisers sailed via the Admiralty Islands (Fiske: "We did not like the Admiralty Islands at all . . . The officers who did go ashore described the customs and costumes of

FIGURE 3.4. USS *Tennessee* coaling ship at Honolulu, Hawaii.

Coaling ship was inevitably an exhausting and messy evolution, despised by crews. With careful hand stowage, just over 2,000 tons of coal could be packed into *Tennessee*'s 30 coal bunkers, giving her a range of 7,300 miles at 10 knots.

Three other cruisers, likely *Washington*, *South Dakota*, and *California* (the other ships of the Pacific Fleet's Second Division), are visible on the horizon. This undated photograph was taken during one of the cruiser's three calls at Oahu between late 1908 and early 1910, while *Tennessee* was deployed to the Pacific Fleet.

Despite its many disadvantages—among them the large number of "coal passers" required to operate fire rooms, a thermal energy density half that of oil, and the difficulties of attempting to refill bunkers under way safely—coal, and later coal splashed with oil, remained the chief fuel for ships through World War I.

The US Navy put its first oil-fired ship, the destroyer USS *Paulding*, to sea in late 1910. (She operated out of Queenstown during the war.) Not until fifteen years later was the fleet's conversion from coal to oil essentially complete.

Source: Harry Gilfillan Collection, US Naval History and Heritage Command.

the natives as evidencing almost the lowest state of civilization a human being could live in."); to gunnery practice at Manila; then for Wusung, China, downriver from Shanghai, arriving just before Christmas; next for Yokohama, Japan, from where early in January 1910 the squadron's senior officers took a train to Tokyo for a call on the emperor. (Fiske thought that Emperor Meiji, two years from death when the Americans saw him, "did not look like a well man.") *Tennessee* reappeared in Honolulu for the last time in February 1910 on the way to the West Coast.

One month later, she cleared the navy yard at Puget Sound, heading south on her long passage around South America (after a stop at Panama to coal) via the Strait of Magellan for the Atlantic Ocean, to return to the Atlantic Fleet.

The cruiser's long transit—out of Bremerton, Washington, in mid-March, into Hampton Roads, Virginia, in late July—had two highlights. The first was a 16 knot passage east through the 330 mile-long Strait of Magellan during autumn in the Southern Hemisphere. With *Tennessee* in the van and *South Dakota* one-quarter mile astern, over the next several days the pair threaded its three infamous narrows, the first of them, in Crooked Reach, barely a half-mile wide, to arrive at its eastern exit on May 1.[17]

Captain Fiske was a romantic as well as a reformer and inventor (he'd later become one of the three senior officers leading the crusade against Secretary Daniels). Fiske wrote prettily about their arrival at the strait's western entrance the morning after he'd passed the night studying sailing directions avidly, "the day breaking behind a dim, rocky barrier that seemed to be in front of us, closing the way entirely, and covered with clouds that descended to the water's edge. When the sun rose these clouds took on various reddish tints dark and light . . . Then they retreated gradually at the bottom and disclosed a rocky shore and tremendous waves breaking on it. Finally they uncovered a narrow entrance that pierced those rocks." He saved his most expressive writing, however, for a decade later, when on March 23, 1921, the *New York Times* described his harsh denunciation of the just departed navy secretary as an "arraignment," a charge sheet.

Fiske had timed the entry into the strait at daylight on April 25 to ensure the two would get to "Sandy Point" (Punta Arenas, Chile) before sunset. *Tennessee* and *South Dakota* passed the next five days there, in a waterfront town of some 12,000 people all living on what they could sell to and buy from passing vessels. With Fiske's bemused cooperation, the American consul (seventy-two-year-old

John Rowen, in his last year of consular service) hosted a gala welcoming ball for the crews, all the props for which party were hauled ashore from his ship. With Rowen's imported ball *Tennessee* became the backdrop for a stream of events and entertainments until, with bunkers finally filled, she sailed away.

Out of the strait, and full of coal from Punta Arenas after nearly a week there at anchor, on May 9 the two reached Maldonado, Uruguay, where they joined company with *Montana* (the brilliant army chief of staff and sometime presidential candidate, Major General Leonard Wood, on board as special ambassador to the event), *North Carolina*, and the scout cruiser USS *Chester*. The five sailed for the fleet transfer's major event: a three-week exposition celebrating the centennial of Argentina's independence from Spain. American participation had been invited the previous June, acknowledging the fact that the United States had been the first country to recognize Argentine independence. Drawing too much water to steam upriver to Buenos Aires, the Americans remained near Bahia Blanca at Puerto Militar, there part of an international assembly at anchor that included the British cruisers *Argyll*, *Hermes*, and *Amethyst*.

The exposition was brilliant: a proud exhibition of a century of Argentine progress in the arts, industry, agriculture, and transportation, punctuated by "nautical festivities in port," congresses, and glittering events for high-level visitors from abroad that managed to go off uninterrupted by the eruptions of the labor unrest that had roiled Argentina for the previous two years. Fiske was dazzled by the Argentines' generosity, which in the case of the American commanding officers included ten days in a deluxe hotel in Buenos Aires gratis, and a gold commemorative medal. Tragically, Argentina's second century would not live up to the promise exhibited in Buenos Aires at the end of its first.

Little USRC *Unalga*, the Revenue Cutter Service's newest commissioned ship, left on her maiden voyage from Norfolk, Virginia, in the early afternoon of September 26, 1912, steaming east for her first duty station, Port Townsend, Washington, more than three-quarters of the globe around and three ocean crossings away. In her hold lay a little more than 300 tons of coal. Coal, rations, and fresh water (topped up, *Unalga* could carry 11,685 gallons for drinking and a further 4,896 gallons for boiler feed) set the limits of the small ship's endurance, notwithstanding the presence of a seemingly anachronistic full suite of sails on two masts.

The alternative route would have been a late spring passage through the Strait of Magellan westbound, better than a winter one around Cape Horn challenging the storms of the "furious fifties" head on, but still tough on a new ship and her new crew. Less than two hundred feet long and under twelve hundred tons, the homely single-stack, *Miami*-class cutter—armed with two, almost symbolic 6 pound deck guns—offered close quarters for her complement of seventy-one, including thirteen officers and fifty-eight petty officers and crew (among the least of the latter were several first- and second-class "boys," serving as mess men and stewards). She'd been built at Newport News for $250,000, and commissioned just four months earlier. In a few weeks, this small chip of a vessel would assume an outsized role, becoming most of the American naval presence in troubled waters.

At an economical 8–9 knots cruising speed—not very much faster than her nineteenth-century counterparts could have made good—her 21,000 mile voyage across the full width of the Atlantic, the Mediterranean, the Indian Ocean, and the Pacific should have taken *Unalga* nearly five months to complete—a long time for her crew packed snugly onboard. Instead, the cutter arrived at Washington near the end of March 1913, having lingered for six weeks during November and December 1912 at anchor in Port Said, Egypt, while the First Balkan War played out to the north. (A second war, fought during July 1913 between former allies Bulgaria, Serbia, and Greece over the spoils of the first, explains why the 1912 war is called "the First.")

On October 8, 1912 (while *Unalga* was in the Atlantic three days west of Gibraltar), Montenegro declared war on Turkey. Ten days later, with *Unalga* now approaching Naples, so did Serbia, Bulgaria, and Greece, their ultimatum to the Turks having since expired. Propelled by personal ambitions and historic ethnic and religious animosities, and taking advantage of Italy's two-year-old invasion and occupation of Tripolitania and Cyrenaica in North Africa, and also of the political turbulence in Constantinople that had demoted Sultan Mehmed V (r. 1909–18) from his usual status as "the shadow of God on earth" to a mere constitutional monarch, the four frequent rivals determined finally to force the expulsion of Turkey from Europe and to divide the imperial residue among themselves. Their invasion of Albania, and the threat to foreigners elsewhere in the Ottoman empire that any fighting between Muslims and Christians in the Balkans automatically raised, prompted embassies in the Turkish capital to consider emergency measures. On October 31 (with a Bulgarian army rumored to be rapidly approaching) Ambassador Rockhill in Constantinople wrote the secretary of state that at a meeting of the diplomatic corps in the capital, its members had agreed to recommend to their governments "the presence of foreign war vessels as the only measure, in their opinion, as likely to ensure the safety of life and property of foreigners."[18]

After an uneventful five-week passage from Virginia, and perfectly ignorant of the turmoil on shore, *Unalga* arrived at Port Said, at the head of the Suez Canal, the next day, November 1. Early November 7, now topped up with 73 tons of coal and 28 tons of water, and with the necessary pilot on board, the cutter got quietly under way for the canal's entrance, anticipating a port call in Aden followed by a passage eastbound through the Indian Ocean.

A day later, on November 8, in Washington, Acting Secretary of State Huntington Wilson asked Secretary of the Navy Meyer to "despatch two vessels with the least possible delay to the ports of Beirut and Smyrna to protect or give refuge to American citizens in case of antiforeign outbreaks there, subject, however, to any supplemental requests the American Embassy at Constantinople may make." And a day after that, November 9, the department informed the embassy in Constantinople that the armored cruisers *Tennessee* (detached from a stint in the Reserve Fleet after her Pacific deployment and put back in full commission for this cruise) and *Montana* (just out of an extended overhaul) would sail for the Mediterranean in the next few days, with *Tennessee* arriving in Smyrna on November 29 and *Montana* in Beirut on December 1. Washington's fears focused largely on the vulnerability of the substantial number of American missionaries and educators at work throughout the region; trade aside, these men and women and their service were the chief interests the United States had in the Levant.

American newspapers promptly gave their readers the same news. A headline in the *New York Times* on Saturday, November 9, announced "America Rushes Warships to Turkey. President Orders Tennessee and Montana to Prepare for Immediate Service." Several headlines in Saturday's *Washington Post* sounded much more excited, if not yet hysterical: "Powers Fear a Clash, Situation in Balkans Strains Diplomacy of Europe; Terror in Turkish Capital Grows with Massacre Tales," and "Proclaims Holy War, Head of Turkish Hierarchy

Calls Priests to Front." (Calmer headlines in the next day's *Post* read, "Ships Sent to Turkey . . . U.S. Cutter Unalga to Protect American Citizens . . . Montana and Tennessee Sailing from Philadelphia Tomorrow. Requires Two Weeks for the Voyage—Precautions against Outbreak of Antiforeign Feeling in Ottoman Empire." On the same page the *Post* helpfully included a sketch map titled—perhaps with tongue in cheek, considering the season of the year—"Plans for the Slicing Up of Turkey," illustrating how "a possible division of Turkey in Europe among the Balkan Allies" might be effected.)

Also on November 9 *Unalga*, now past the Daedalus Reef Light and near midway through her southbound transit of the Red Sea, abruptly reversed course and steamed at full speed on both boilers back to Port Said, responding to the first of two urgent radio cablegrams from Assistant Secretary of the Treasury Sherman Allen (this one relayed to the cutter by the Hamburg-America liner SS *Cleveland*) to remain at Suez. *Unalga* made good 289 miles during the following day's sprint back up track, and a little after noon on November 12 she was again moored in the Port Suez Basin, awaiting orders. She'd remain there until December 17, her crew doing by rote the usual ship's work and drills, pinned in place by instructions not from Ambassador Rockhill in Constantinople (who on November 12 had released her from any mission in Turkish waters) but from Washington, cautiously determined to keep her in local waters at least until an armored cruiser arrived in Beirut.

William Rockhill (1854–1914), the American ambassador in Constantinople between August 1911 and November 1913, was one of the state department's superstars. In 1911 Rockhill had moved to Constantinople from the American embassy in St. Petersburg, reportedly transferring at his own request to research a book about the Ottoman empire. His replacement at Constantinople two years later by Henry Morgenthau—a wealthy campaign contributor with an impressive but irrelevant résumé shouldering aside a professional, apolitical diplomat with nearly three decades of experience in Washington and at American legations abroad—was met with surprise and outrage in career foreign service circles and elsewhere in the American capital.

Rockhill died suddenly in Honolulu on December 8, 1914, while crossing the Pacific to take up an appointment as advisor to the Chinese president, Yuan Shih-K'ai. An obituary in the *New York Times*, published early in 1915, rightly called him, as a veteran of thirty years of government service and after 1897 of ambassadorial posts in six countries, "the dean of the diplomatic corps."

Rockhill had served as the American ambassador to China between June 1905 and June 1909. Decades later, in March 1959, the late diplomat was described in the *Journal of Modern History* as having been "Roosevelt's foremost advisor on Far Eastern affairs."

During the political crisis that spanned all of November, and until the cruisers *Montana* and *Tennessee* arrived in the Levant on November 30 and December 1, respectively, *Unalga* was the only (barely) armed American vessel afloat in the Eastern Mediterranean other than the schooner-rigged, former yacht USS *Scorpion*, station ship at Constantinople. The two, *Scorpion* with her four 6 pound guns and *Unalga* with her two 6 pounders, were what little the United States had afloat to rescue hundreds of American expatriates in the Turkish capital and in Ottoman Palestine, a situation that had Rockhill, under instructions from Washington, reluctantly seeking confirmation from his European counterparts in Constantinople that they would afford refuge to Americans aboard their ships if the worst came to pass.

Tennessee departed Philadelphia on November 12, the day after her hasty recommissioning, in company with *Montana* for Gibraltar. There the two separated: *Montana* headed for Beirut, *Tennessee* for Smyrna via Malta, arriving on December 1 at her destination, where she remained continuously at anchor in the Gulf of Smyrna for five long months, testing her crew's endurance. On May 3, 1913, the cruiser was finally released to steam home.

A third navy ship, the collier USS *Brutus* carrying 4,800 tons of Virginia coal for the two cruisers, sailed from Norfolk for Smyrna via Gibraltar some two weeks later, maximum speed 10 knots. *Brutus*, years earlier the British-built Norwegian cargo ship SS *Peter Jebsen* and now named after Caesar's assassin, Marcus Junius Brutus, finally arrived at Smyrna on December 28, four weeks after *Tennessee* had entered the roadstead.

Brutus wasn't uniquely honored by having a US Navy collier named after him. So was his victim, Caesar, and so were Nero, Pompey, and a pantheon of Roman gods. Fifteen colliers with these ancient names were among twenty merchant vessels that had been bought and commissioned by the navy in early 1898 as part of its hasty logistics buildup for the Spanish-American war. Among the twenty was USS *Merrimac*, ex-SS *Solveig* of Norwegian registry, which, when she was sunk by Spanish gunfire on June 2, 1898, after a failed attempt to scuttle her at the entrance to Santiago's harbor, became the only American ship lost in that war.[19]

The collier was more fortunate than the cruiser. *Brutus* visited Constanti-nople for a few days in February and during the next three months, while *Tennessee* remained fixed in place in the Gulf of Smyrna, called at Beirut twice and Malta once, before sailing from Smyrna with *Tennessee* on May 3 for Algiers and home. The much faster *Tennessee* got to Algiers four days ahead of *Brutus*, which left the North African port on May 17 and finally came dragging into Hampton Roads June 7.

An armistice in the Balkans months earlier, agreed December 3, 1912, had eased the fears of American expatriates in the meantime. A peace treaty was signed in London the following May (by everyone except the Turks). And one month after that—about the time that *Tennessee, Montana* and *Brutus* got home—the Second Balkan War erupted, with the former Balkan allies fighting like crows over roadkill to see who was to get which bit of Macedonia.

The modest American naval presence in the Mediterranean's troubled waters in 1912, and again in 1915—accomplished through urgent deployments from the US East Coast in both cases—was ahistoric. The US Navy had been more or less continuously afloat in the Mediterranean since 1801 and the Barbary Wars, with short absences in the nineteenth century only while fighting wars elsewhere: the War of 1812, the Mexican-American War, and the Civil War. From 1801 until 1905 the US Navy had otherwise supported a deployed Mediterranean or a European Squadron with responsibilities in the Mediterranean.

Explanations for this surprising neglect of the Mediterranean after 1905 are to be found in the American focus on the Caribbean (always distracting, but intense during, and for long after, the Spanish-American War), and also in the triumph of the strategic ideas of Captain Alfred Mahan, USN, which emphasized building a navy of capital ships, keeping them together rather than parceling them out, and building and defending an isthmian canal.

Eleven days out of Honolulu (Yokohama, Japan, had been the previous port), USRC *Unalga* anchored at 3:00 a.m., March 23, 1913, at Port Townsend, Washington, with 82 tons of coal and 391 rations remaining on board. (Unlike the practice in the US Navy, the cutter's watch officers didn't log fresh water consumption en route.) Along much of her track from Oahu to the American West Coast, *Unalga* had steadying sails aloft, a passage marked by two days of high winds, rain squalls, and big seas on March 20 and 21 that slowed the ship, pitching and rolling heavily enough to shatter crockery stowed below in the general mess, to as little as 2 knots.

Walter Frear, in his last year as governor of the Territory of Hawaii, had visited the cutter to see her off from the island, a visit marked by the usual ceremonies, but no high-level official greeted *Unalga* on arrival at the West Coast and no ceremony marked the cutter's quiet arrival in her new homeport.

When *Unalga* dropped anchor at home that third week in March, *Tennessee* and *Montana* still had several months to go in their hastily dispatched Mediterranean deployments, *Tennessee*'s first and *Montana*'s second. *Montana*'s first—a four-month deployment in April–August 1909 that had been triggered by the political tempest in Turkey that saw Sultan Abdul Abdulhamid deposed, forced out of the palace by proverbial "young Turks"—had been just after she'd escorted USS *North Carolina*, with President Taft on board, to the Panama Canal.

Tennessee finally left for home in early May 1913, arriving in Hampton Roads on May 25 after pausing for five days in the North African coastal city of Algiers on the way, and *Montana* returned in June, after showing the flag offshore of Smyrna, Beirut, Alexandretta, and Mersin, but doing little else.

Some anxious newspaper reporters fretted imaginatively that the return of the two from the Eastern Mediterranean was somehow related to the impending commissioning of the mighty, British-built, Japanese battle cruiser *Kongō* ("Indestructible").[20] (Not truly indestructible. By then rebuilt twice, *Kongō* was torpedoed by an American submarine and sank in November 1944 off Taiwan.) As delivered in 1913, with her speed, armor, and main battery of eight 14 inch guns, *Kongō* could have successfully challenged *Tennessee* and *Montana* at the same time. There was no connection.

After June 1913 until August a year later *Tennessee* was again on stage only once, when over Memorial Day 1914 she steamed up the Hudson River ("North River" then), pausing respectfully to fire salutes at the Union Soldiers' and Sailors' Monument and again a mile and a half upriver at President Grant's Tomb, both visible on the heights of the river's eastern shore and both generally neglected since dedication. The rest of those months she was either in the yard at Portsmouth, part of the Atlantic Reserve Fleet at Philadelphia, or tied up in the Brooklyn Navy Yard as the receiving ship for local recruits.

FIGURE 4.1. *The Atlantic Fleet in San Francisco Harbor* by Henry Reuterdahl.

The Great White Fleet called at San Francisco twice during the fleet's 'round-the-world cruise from December 16, 1907, through February 22, 1909, first coming to the city from Mexico and eventually departing it for the Philippines. On May 6, 1908, 14,400 miles out of Hampton Roads and passing beneath the Golden Gate Bridge and by Yerba Buena Island for the first time, the fleet, in two columns with USS *Connecticut* in the van, saluted Secretary of the Navy Victor Metcalf, in from Washington and on board the gunboat USS *Yorktown* for the occasion.

Henry Reuterdahl's oil painting shows *Connecticut*, flying for only another three days the two-star flag of the Atlantic Fleet's commander in chief, Rear Admiral Robley ("Fighting Bob") Evans, USN, proudly entering the harbor at the head of fifteen other battleships.

Unseen here, but welcoming the arriving parade of Atlantic Fleet ships, were two divisions of the Pacific Fleet's heavy combatants, among them the armored cruiser USS *Tennessee*, flagship of the second division, as well as the five ships of the Pacific Torpedo Flotilla. That force, the arriving divisions and the divisions welcoming them, included fully forty-two combatant ships. Their assembly constituted the largest American armada afloat in one place for the next three decades and more.

Tennessee had joined the Pacific Fleet in October 1907, and was to remain with it for three years, finally returning to the Atlantic in October 1910. Her long deployment was marred only by a boiler tube explosion during semi-annual speed trials off Hueneme Harbor near midday on June 5, 1908, that killed eight sailors and seriously injured six others, an accident described but studied inconclusively by Clem Copeland a few weeks later in San Francisco's *Journal of Electricity, Power and Gas.*

The American fleet's condition on its return home to the East Coast on February 22, 1909, from this extended demonstration of sea-keeping contrasted starkly with the tattered state of Tsarist Russia's imperial navy on arrival in Japanese waters having sailed half as far just a few years earlier.

Invited on board as an "artist correspondent," Swedish-born Reuterdahl (1871–1925) rode USS *Minnesota,* the *Connecticut*-class battleship leading the third division, on the cruise from Hampton Roads until Callo, Peru, the sixth port of call. He disembarked there in February 1908, either because of family problems or, more likely, because of the uproar that followed a critical article about "The Needs of Our Navy" that he'd published in *McClure's Weekly* a month earlier (vol. 30, no. 3). The piece identified eleven "chief reasons" why the US Navy was unprepared for war, including ship design flaws, the age of commanders, the inadequate number of destroyers, and ossified mismanagement by the Washington bureaus that managed the navy's work. His article prompted heated exchanges through the winter between critics of the navy in *McClure's* and its defenders, writing in *Scientific American.*

In 1917 Reuterdahl was commissioned a lieutenant in the Naval Reserve Force, this despite his continued overt criticism of navy ship construction practices and his politicized denunciations of Secretary of the Navy Daniels's leadership at meetings of the American Defense Society and of the National Security League the summer before. Eight years later, his obituaries reported without elaboration that Reuterdahl, promoted to lieutenant commander in 1918 and retired in 1921, had been admitted to Washington's St. Elizabeth's Government Hospital for the Insane in September 1925, one among the old institution's several thousand patients. He died there on December 21 and was buried with honors at Arlington National Cemetery two days later.

Source: *Collier's* 41, no. 14 (June 27, 1908): 14–15.

Chapter Four

The Great White Fleet, the US Navy before the Great War

What is more, we all knew that the great fleet would swing around the world, looking in at the Hawaiian Islands, the Philippines, into China and Japan, and back again without the slightest shade of doubt in the soul of any American that the fleet would always acquit itself well and achieve what it set out to do.

This, indeed, is the great thing that has been accomplished by the fleet. For the first time in history the Pacific ocean has been put into commission. This is a great fact, a great achievement, the results of which can never be changed or lost. Henceforth, in the world's history the Pacific ocean which first came into international prominence with Dewey's great victory in Manila bay and the Japanese victories in their own waters will loom up in historical importance as did the Mediterranean before Columbus' great cruise opened up the Atlantic.

—[Berea, Kentucky] *Citizen*, February 25, 1909, 3

Under the eyes of an obviously elated President Roosevelt, who watched the excitement from on board the presidential yacht, USS *Mayflower*, and in front of Secretary of the Navy Metcalf in USS *Dolphin*, battleship after battleship, sixteen in all, beginning with *Connecticut* and ending with *Kentucky*, steamed past the *Tail of the Horseshoe* lightship (LV-46) on December 16, 1907, heading out of Chesapeake Bay for the Atlantic Ocean and the world beyond. Saluting batteries of 3 inch guns boomed out passing honors to the commander in chief. In reply, the signal flags snapping in the wind above *Mayflower* spelled out the command: "Proceed on Duties Assigned."[1]

Unheralded, but essential to success, several auxiliaries also sailed off with the sixteen: the stores ships *Culgoa* and *Glacier*, the repair ship *Panther* (then-Lieutenant Benton Decker's old ship), and the tender *Yankton*. A water ship, SS *Arethusa* (later converted into a navy oiler and commissioned), had sailed with the lead destroyers. Unlike the combatant ships of the departing fleet, every one of these first auxiliaries had been at sea during the Spanish-American War. USS *Relief*, a hospital ship, would meet the fleet in Magdalena Bay, Mexico, and sail with it to Olongapo in the Philippines, on what became, unplanned, her last cruise. After being battered by a typhoon partway home, *Relief* reversed course and ended up as an immobile, floating hospital in Cavite.

In December 1907 Metcalf had been secretary of the navy for a year, the first of the two he'd serve, having relieved the previous December Baltimore lawyer Charles Bonaparte (a great-nephew of the first emperor Napoleon Bonaparte), who after nineteen months at the head of the navy had fleeted up to become Roosevelt's attorney general. Bonaparte's navy experience led him to conclude aloud a few years later that a secretary of the navy, "if unwilling to be merely a more or less ornamental appendage, must work hard, think for himself, keep his own counsel, and, while receiving outwardly military deference, count on many whispered maledictions." Behind that mild-sounding commentary were some lessons Bonaparte had learned during those months. He no longer believed that a commissioned officer should be the service's chief, because

> a body of permanent public servants [he's referring to the navy officer corps], educated in great part at the same institution, leading the same life, having the same interests and very largely the same sentiments and prejudices, connected with each other in many cases, moreover, by ties of early friendship, consanguinity, intermarriage, and hereditary association, will always display much of the strength and few of the weaknesses of a huge family; and history proves the wisdom of giving such a service an administrative head who is over it, but not of it.
>
> To do his duty, however, a Secretary of the Navy must belong to himself, not to any group or coterie within the service.[2]

Bonaparte was clearly on to something. Ian Toll began volume 2 of his Pacific War trilogy, *The Conquering Tide* (W. W. Norton, 2015): "during the past eras of peace, the navy had tended to become insular, inward-looking and parochial. Every flag officer (admiral) had passed through the same way stations . . . there was not an admiral in the navy who had not graduated from the Naval

Academy. Every senior naval commander had lived his entire adult life in the navy, beginning at the tender age of seventeen or eighteen . . . He had been taught to revere the heritage and traditions of the institution, to owe it fierce and undying allegiance."

During Josephus Daniels's term (1913–21) in Bonaparte's old office, these maledictions were no longer whispered but shouted in what became a small-scale clash of civilizations. The grievances of Daniels's senior uniformed critics (about which more later) had several sources. Daniels's overt pacifism aside—awkward given his position, but not inconsistent with the orientation of his chief and the country at large—his attack on officer perquisites (their wine messes aboard ships, in particular), and more generally on the class-based traditions of the navy, riled traditionalists who'd grown up with the status quo and saw merit in it. More generally, there was the tension between an officer corps determined to manage its own profession and to define its standards and procedures in changing times, and a civilian executive with constitutional authority over it, but no relevant experience and often little time to develop the necessary expertise. (There were fully five service secretaries between John Long, who left the job in April 1902, and George Meyer, who took it over in March 1909.)

The Royal Navy had solved this problem of melding professional expertise to political leadership through creation of what Nicholas Jellicoe in *Jutland: The Unfinished Battle* (Seaforth, 2017) describes as the "curious institution" of the British Admiralty. The Admiralty's naval professionals (four "Sea Lords," possibly the most dashing job title in government anywhere) were responsible for, respectively, operations, personnel, design and construction, and logistics. The four worked for the First Lord of the Admiralty, the navy's political chief, appointed by the government. By the first decade of the twentieth century the Admiralty had nearly three hundred years of history behind it. Not until the interwar years did the US Navy manage to construct a similarly successful blend of the political and professional.

The coming 'round-the-world cruise was a near perfect expression of President Roosevelt's personality and interests; he'd evidenced special interest in naval forces at least since he began research as a Harvard undergraduate for his first book, *The Naval War of 1812; or the History of the U.S. Navy during the Last War with Great Britain* (G. P. Putnam's Sons, 1882). As encapsulated by Edmund Morris in *Theodore Rex* (Random House, 2001), "the massive deployment appealed to Roosevelt as diplomacy, as preventative strategy, as technical training, and as a sheer pageant of power. There was also the enormity of the challenge." Once considered, the idea of the world cruise had to have been irresistible to a chief executive addicted to bold gestures.[3]

Heading for the open Atlantic in suddenly improved weather, the battleship division's first stop was Port of Spain, Trinidad, a week south in the British West Indies, where they passed a dull Christmas and coaled before getting under way for Rio de Janeiro and all that was still to come: 46,000 miles steaming during 305 days under way, 20 port visits on 6 continents, and the consumption en route by 14,000 sailors and marines of fully 19 million pounds of provisions. All assembled in just over five months of frantic staff work.

The impetus behind the extraordinary, fourteen-month battleship deployment had come at the end of June, when two officers representing the Joint Board of the Army and Navy, together with Secretary of the Navy Metcalf and Postmaster General George Meyer (filling what was a highly politicized cabinet post then) visited the president's summer White House on Oyster Bay. The four came to deliver a Joint Board contingency plan for responses to heightened friction between the United States and Japan. While dismissing the possibility of hostilities, Roosevelt nevertheless quickly approved the board's recommendation that the battle fleet should be deployed to the Orient. He soon shared with Senator Lodge an even bolder idea, that this deployment would in fact ease into "a practice cruise around the world."

Exiting the mouth of the Chesapeake Bay just two weeks after the Jamestown Ter-Centennial Exposition stumbled to its finale (and two weeks behind a flotilla of six torpedo boat destroyers and a stores ship also en route to the West Coast), the big ships were on their way to San Francisco and, as private instructions from the president to the commander, Rear Admiral Evans, soon leaked out to reveal, much farther than that. "The President authorizes the Commander-in-Chief to inform the officers and men," Evans signaled the other ships in his command over his flagship's new "wireless telephone" the first night underway, "that after a short stay on the Pacific Coast it is the President's intention to have the fleet return to the Atlantic Coast by way of the Mediterranean." An eavesdropping reporter on board promptly radioed the same exciting news to the press ashore, where it appeared in papers the next morning. Not until the spring, when the fleet reached Magdalena Bay, Mexico, was its intent to circumnavigate the globe officially confirmed to the public, apparently only for the second time in recorded history thrusting the Pacific Ocean into the consciousness of readers of the *Citizen* and the other good people of central Kentucky.

Fully seven different American shipyards were represented by the powerful—but to knowledgeable eyes, already edging on obsolescence—fleet now heading proudly toward the Atlantic Ocean and Cape Horn, and the broad Pacific beyond, the product of twenty-five years of navy expansion that had its origin in then-Secretary of the Navy Hunt's initiatives nearly three decades ago.

In his department's 1881 annual report to the president, if its recommendations were adopted by Congress, Secretary Hunt had foreseen two different navies going to sea near the end of the decade, replacing the unseaworthy, miscellaneous gaggle he'd inherited. One was "a peace navy of seventy cruisers, of which about twenty would have been fair commerce-destroyers in time of war." The other was a "war navy" for defense only, and was to consist of "five rams, five torpedo-gunboats, and twenty fast torpedo-boats."[4] The deployment in 1907 of the Great White Fleet explicitly signaled the end of any such idea of separate "peace" and "war" navies, and of the underlying rationale that the post–Civil War American navy had only two legitimate wartime missions: raiding enemy commerce and defending ports at home. Over the next fourteen months the Great White Fleet demonstrated the triumph of a profoundly different idea, Rear Admiral Alfred Mahan's conviction that sea power was the essential ingredient of empire and that the true purpose of a navy was to project offensive power across blue water.

Roosevelt's novella-length (27,000 words), seventh annual message to Congress, delivered in writing some ten days before the fleet sailed off, mentioned the navy more than thirty times, and included a long discourse on the importance of a navy focused on war at sea rather than on coastal defense, and one visible in both oceans. The message repeated Roosevelt's public rationale for the impending cruise to the Pacific, but it omitted an observation he'd shared privately with Albert Shaw, the editor of *Review of Reviews*, about "how useful the mere statement that [the fleet] was going there has already been in quieting the clamor for hostilities against us by the Japanese yellow press."[5]

Even with Shaw, a close friend, Roosevelt was being coy. He'd decided six months ago, at the end of June when Japanese-American tensions were higher, to send the Atlantic battleship fleet—"eighteen or twenty of the largest battleships," Secretary Metcalf had announced publicly on July 2, describing their deployment modestly as a "practice cruise"—west, to test and to demonstrate implicitly its ability to go the distance and arrive fit to fight.

The Japanese, victors in the First Sino-Japanese War (1894–95) and easily triumphant at sea ten years later during the Russo-Japanese War (1904–5)—for those paying attention, in the Imperial Japanese Navy's humiliation of Tsarist Russia's Eastern and then Baltic Fleets lay evidence of the terminally frail condition of Nicholas II's mismanaged Romanov empire—had become in the decades since the restoration of the emperor a powerful naval presence in the Western Pacific. The creation of a modern shipbuilding industry had been paralleled by, first, the opening of a Japanese naval academy in 1876, and then in 1888 (only four years behind the United States) the opening of a naval war college for the professional education of midcareer officers. This essential infrastructure, together with the Royal Navy's mentorship, practically guaranteed that when Admiral Tōgō put to sea in February 1904 against the Russians at Port Arthur, the contest would be an unequal one.

Japan's open unhappiness with American annexation of the Hawaiian Islands in 1898 and with American immigration policy's backhanded treatment of the Asian peoples hinted at serious problems in the future. On the back side of the Russo-Japanese War, those strains seem to have been resolved at least temporarily by midsummer 1905 in an atmosphere of quiet understanding and accommodation, but they reappeared just a few years later and would do so again and again through the first decades of the century.

In the meanwhile, both countries had agreed that trade with supine China should be on the basis of an "open door," and secretly also agreed on much more. Via the "Taft-Katsura Agreement," an accord privately agreed by Secretary of War Taft and Japanese premier Count Katsura in Tokyo on July 27, and confirmed by Roosevelt after his review a few days later, the two countries had also moved toward what looks now very like a three-party condominium in the Far East (the third party being absent Great Britain, Japan's naval mentor and treaty partner after 1902 and until 1923). Taft and Katsura, meeting just days before the beginning of the month-long negotiations in Portsmouth, New Hampshire, to end the Russo-Japanese War, took informal bilateral understanding into another level entirely: in exchange for Japanese recognition of US control of the Philippines, the United States acknowledged Japanese rule of Korea and condoned the three-year-old Anglo-Japanese alliance. Not until 1924 did the Taft-Katsura Agreement become public, but long before then, in November 1908, its substance had been formally confirmed by the Root-Takahira Agreement. Negotiated in Washington by Secretary of State Root and Japanese ambassador Takahira Kogorō, the new agreement was generally considered to be a byproduct of the improved bilateral relations that grew out of the fleet's visit to Japan the month before.

The logistical problems obstructing the path to the Atlantic Fleet's colorful departure for its historic cruise had been enormous. So, too, had been the domestic political problems, posed against a backdrop of sustained financial crisis on Wall Street dubbed by some "the Roosevelt Panic of 1907," and mirrored in a new Congress (the 60th) facing a president past the midpoint of what was presumably his last term in office, and resented by the conservatives in his party (led in the House of Representatives by Speaker Joseph Cannon from Illinois and in the Senate by Nelson Aldrich of Rhode Island). That opposition took one form in a threat from Senator Eugene Hale, of Maine (1836–1918), the Republican chairman of the Senate's Naval Affairs Committee, to deny funding for the president's naval adventure. (Hale had been a member of that committee since 1891, when the thirty-three-year-old Roosevelt was midway through serving on the US Civil Service Commission and still six years away from becoming the assistant secretary of the navy.)

Hale's roots in Maine went back to the 1630s, as ancient—if perhaps not quite as patrician—as those of the Roosevelts in New York. Lawyer, state representative, five-term congressional representative, and now fifth-term US senator who'd twice declined cabinet appointments, Hale briefly seemed ready to challenge Roosevelt, but the president stiff-armed the seventy-year-old senator aside, and citing his authority as commander in chief, ordered the fleet out anyway.

Much later, in January 1910, Secretary of the Navy George Meyer claimed that routine operations and maintenance of the fleet in home waters during the period of the cruise would have in any case cost $11.8 million, and that "the extra expense incurred by sending the Atlantic Fleet around the world" added only $1.6 million more, a total of $13.4 million. Meyer's "extra expense" tabulation, almost certainly understated, included only three items. The least of them was nearly $135,000 in Suez Canal tolls, payment for transit through the forty-year-old, ninety-mile-long canal by all twenty ships during the first few days of January 1909, a transit marred only by the temporary embarrassment of USS *Georgia* going aground on a mud bank near the Bitter Lakes.[6]

FIGURE 4.2. *"Le 'Petropavlo[v]sk' Torpillé, Mort de l'amiral Makharoff et de 600 marins russes."*

Other than triggering an exchange of formal declarations of war on February 9, 1904, the two surprise Japanese naval attacks against Russia's Far East Fleet at its base at Port Arthur, Manchuria, over February 7–8, first with destroyers and then with major combatants, produced inconclusive results. Subsequent engagements effectively bottled up the Russians in the harbor, and during the next year the Russians were beaten badly ashore and afloat.

On April 13, 1904, Russian vice admiral Stephan Makarov's flagship, *Petropavlovsk*, sank after hitting moored mines during a sortie outside of the port. Nearly 680 Russian officers and sailors went down with the ten-year-old battleship. Barely ten days later this colorful depiction of *Petropavlovsk*'s destruction appeared on the cover of *Le Petit Journal*'s illustrated Sunday supplement 15, no. 704 (April 24, 1904), showing dozens of her blue-clad crew dramatically dying and drowning as their ship blew up under the eyes of nearby Japanese combatants. This is one of seventeen supplement covers in that year about the faraway war.

Published in Paris, *Le Petit Journal* was for a time, before the turn of the century, France's and the world's best selling daily newspaper, thanks to its high-speed rotary press, huge press runs, and price of just five centimes a copy. After nearly fifty years in print, the supplement ceased publication in 1937. Lurid coverage of this sinking and other disasters of this distant war, in foreign papers and periodicals, and intelligence reporting by a host of foreign attachés on site to their home governments enormously enhanced the prestige of the Japanese Navy in Europe.

The decisive sea battle of the war between the rival empires came in late May 1905 in the Tsushima Strait, when the Japanese fleet ambushed and destroyed most of the Russian Baltic Squadron, entering the strait on the way to Vladivostok from Cam Ranh Bay, Vietnam, after a seven-month, 18,000 mile cruise from Europe. Superior Japanese seamanship and gunnery resulted in a debacle for the Russians on a scale that seemingly confirmed Mahan's analysis. Their losses at Tsushima were catastrophic: 34 (of 38) ships sunk, captured, or interned; more than 10,000 sailors killed, captured, or interned.

Japan's low-cost triumphs at sea and the more expensive ones in battles ashore at Port Arthur and Mukden also prompted an explosion of colorful, celebratory woodblock prints in Japan, perhaps the best of which were by young Yasuda Hampō (1889–1947). Sadly, this stylish imagery was soon replaced by more popular postcard lithographs and photographs.

Source: Bibliothèque Nationale, Paris.

That embarrassment was followed by another a month later: the general court-martial of her commanding officer, Captain Edward Qualtrough, USN, on board *Louisiana* at Gibraltar on a charge of drunkenness at a reception hosted by Samuel Gummere, the American minister in Morocco—a soirée that otherwise included a ride on muleback in dress uniform by guests from *Georgia* and *Nebraska* to and from a hotel in Tangiers. Qualtrough, fifty-nine and a veteran of thirty-eight years of navy service, was convicted. Instead of accepting a six-month suspension and the loss of ten numbers of seniority, he promptly retired, leaving *Georgia* to continue across the Atlantic to home under the command of her executive officer.

Not a trifling amount, $1.6 million, about equal to the price of two *Smith*-class destroyers beginning to join the fleet, but little more than 1 percent of the navy's 1910 budget.

Led by the nearly new USS *Connecticut* at the head of the first division, the great ships passed in review in front of Roosevelt almost in reverse order of age. First were four of the five *Connecticut*-class battleships. Then came four *Virginia*-class ships in the second division, followed by USS *Minnesota* leading three *Maine*-class battleships in the third, and finally the fourth division with a pair each representing the midcareer *Illinois* class and *Kearsarge* class. The oldest ships, *Kearsarge* and *Kentucky*, were not yet ten years old; the newest (*Minnesota*) had been in commission just nine months. Four of the US Navy's twenty-two rear admirals were on board, lending their personal flags and—only for a while for two among them—personal heft to the procession. In their headiest fantasies, the members of the Special Advisory Board commissioned by Hunt had never imagined that in twenty-five years the United States would send such a powerful naval force to sea.

With their white hulls showing an occasional colorful flash of red bottom paint, tan topsides, elegant gold trim, and beneath flags flying under dense clouds of black smoke, the big ships were awe-inspiring. The best known image of them under way, among very many, is probably Henry Reuterdahl's oil painting of the fleet in column of divisions two months after leaving home, exiting the Straits of Magellan on February 8, 1908, after a 10 knot transit of the passage between the oceans interrupted by seven days coaling in Punta

Arenas. Behind USS *Connecticut* (herself led by the Chilean Navy's protected cruiser *Chacaubuco*) stretches a three-and-one-half-mile-long line of American battleships snaking their way in a turn to starboard through the historic strait past sharp-edged peaks. It hangs in the collection of the US Naval Academy museum.

The last time this picturesque strait got so much attention in the United States had been ten years earlier, when in the spring of 1898 the *Indiana*-class battleship USS *Oregon* steamed nearly 14,000 miles from San Francisco to join the Atlantic fleet.

Oregon was the only ship of her class to have been built on the West Coast (the other two, *Indiana* and *Massachusetts*, were built by Cramp and Sons as their hull nos. 270 and 271, Cramp's first battleships). After her acceptance trials, on the West Coast, anyway, *Oregon* was popularly believed to be the best the US Navy had. Perhaps not just there: in February 1902 the *Vermonter*, published monthly in St. Albans, in an article boasting about her former commanding officer, native son Captain Charles Clark, USN (1843–1922), called *Oregon* "the greatest fighting vessel in the world." The two apparently deserved each other; the *Vermonter* went on to say greasily that Clark (descended supposedly from one of *Mayflower*'s pilots, John Clark) possessed *Oregon*'s "sterling qualities as nearly as a human being possibly can."[7]

Out of San Francisco on March 19, 1898, *Oregon* sailed into Jupiter Inlet (north of Palm Beach) on May 24, was at Key West two days later, and off Cuba two days after that, ready to fight. *Oregon*'s arrival was welcomed enthusiastically in Florida.

Sailing alone until Punta Arenas, Chile, where she was joined by the gunboat USS *Marietta*; both accompanied for a short while by the American-built, ex-Brazilian auxiliary cruiser *Nictheroy* out of Rio de Janeiro; coaling only four times on the way; and weathering a storm in the straits in mid-April, *Oregon* had averaged around 10 knots during these nine weeks in transit (on her best day making good nearly 16 knots), arriving off Cuba in time to join in the Battle of Santiago Bay. She would have been slightly faster had not *Marietta* held her to 7 knots sometimes during the two weeks the two sailed together.

Her sprint to join the war—in Rio de Janeiro Clark learned of Dewey's triumph at Manila Bay—prompted not only enormous attention from the press but later at least two sappy poems, one an eight-stanza piece by John James Meehan that began:

> Lights out! And a prow turned toward the South,
> And a canvas hiding each cannon's mouth,
> And a ship like a silent ghost released
> Is seeking her sister ships in the East.

And ended mercifully thirty-four lines later with:

> When your boys shall ask what the guns are for,
> Then tell them the tale of the Spanish War,
> And the breathless millions that looked upon
> The matchless race of the Oregon.[8]

Ships moving between the Atlantic and Pacific Oceans continued to use this long route around the tip of South America, past Reuterdahl's handsome peaks, for only seven more years. In August 1914 the Panama Canal opened "the path between the seas" (the phrase is the title of David McCullough's award-winning 1978 canal history). *Oregon*'s "matchless race," reported daily to a rapt American readership and often based entirely on rumor and imagination, had been a powerful stimulus to its construction.

Captain Clark, who'd taken command of *Oregon* barely two days before she sailed from San Francisco, remained in command only until late summer. Sickened by "tropical fever," he was relieved in August for medical reasons, and never again served at sea. After command tours at the navy yard on Philadelphia's League Island (where the Schuylkill and Delaware Rivers meet) and the city's naval home, and an assignment as president of the Examining and Retiring Board, he retired as a rear admiral in 1905. *Oregon* was decommissioned at the end of World War I for the last time, three years before Admiral Clark died in 1922. What was left of his famous command was finally scrapped, perhaps ironically, in Kawasaki, Japan, in 1955.

Under a front-page headline announcing "Fleet Steams Southward As Cannons Fire Salute to Commander-in-Chief," the *Washington Times* of Monday evening, December 16, 1907, posed a question about the Great White Fleet's dramatic departure from Hampton Roads earlier that day. "Why Is It Going?"

the newspaper asked, and then went on to offer readers seven possible reasons. "To demonstrate to the world America's naval prowess? To show Congress the need of a still greater navy, in order to protect equally the Atlantic and Pacific coasts? To show Congress the necessity for more navy yards and better docking facilities on the Pacific Coast? To drill the officers and men in battle formations, and general fleet maneuvers on a large scale? To strengthen the Monroe Doctrine, by showing our South American cousins the power back of it? To restore to the United States the balance of international naval power in the Pacific Ocean? To be ready for possible war with Japan?"

Fourteen of the original sixteen made it all the way around. Only *Maine* and *Alabama* dropped out, detached from the fleet before it departed San Francisco for Honolulu because of their high consumption of coal. (Replaced by *Nebraska* and *Wisconsin*, the original two then continued home through the Suez Canal together.)

The cruise was much harder on its four flag officers than it was on its sixteen major combatant ships, reflecting the fact that the admirals were all over sixty, while none of the ships had yet reached her tenth birthday. In San Francisco on May 9, 1908, after months of incapacity because of painful attacks of gout, Rear Admiral Evans was formally relieved by the commander of the second division, Rear Admiral Charles Thomas, USN. (That Evans served so long in uniform is a marvel. As an ensign in January 1865 he'd been wounded four times leading a Union landing party in the assault on Fort Fisher.) Next, Thomas, like Evans sixty-two years old, retired on schedule six days later, only to have a heart attack and die suddenly in July.[9] Beginning May 15, Rear Admiral Charles Sperry, USN, the youngest of the four by just a year, commanded the fleet until its return home, only to die in 1911. Alone of the four, Rear Admiral William Emory managed to make it almost to seventy.

It fell to Secretary George Meyer, in his report to the president of December 4, 1909, to say frankly: "the senior officers of our navy are old for the responsibilities and arduous duty required in the modern battleship. They are much older than similar officers in the other principal navies of the world. Not only is this the case, but flag officers arrive at the grade of rear admiral so late that even those of longest possible service do not get adequate training as subordinate flag officers before assuming the chief command."

Rear Admiral Evans (1846–1912, USNA '64), the fleet's commander for the first quarter of the cruise, supposedly had said on sailing that his ships were

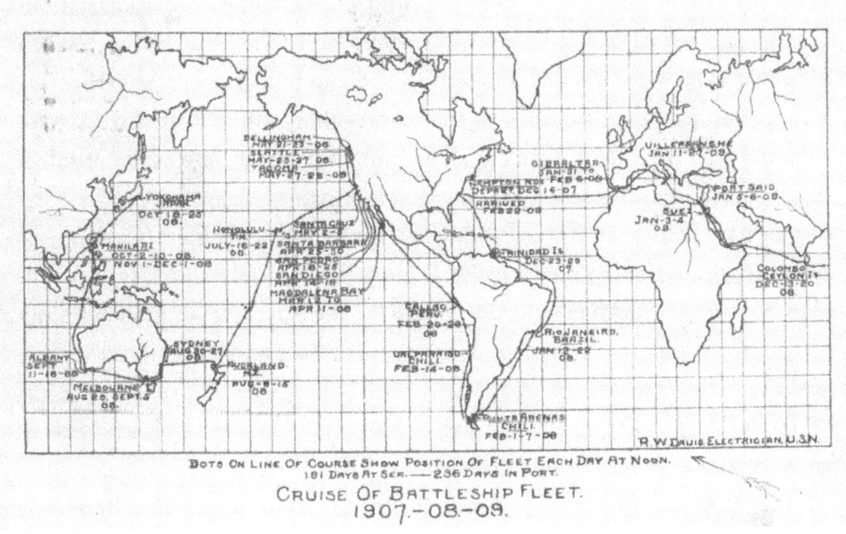

FIGURE 4.3. "Cruise of Battleship Fleet. 1907-08-09," chart by Roy Davis.

The return of the Great White Fleet to Chesapeake Bay on Washington's Birthday, February 22, 1909, after fourteen months deployed was met with an explosion of celebration and ceremony not dampened by the wet, cold weather. A reporter from the *Chicago Tribune* calculated that a grand total of 2,344 gun salutes were fired by the 3 inch saluting batteries on board the ships and atop the walls at nearby Fort Monroe. Some were honoring Roosevelt, present in the presidential yacht *Mayflower*, some honoring President Washington, some seemingly just adding to the festivities of welcome.

By every measure the cruise was an operational triumph. It was, as well, a political success. Significantly, the fleet's welcome in Japan was remarkably warm, "the welcome of a nation," the *Tribune* wrote, "hurt by the reports that they were secretly our enemies. It cannot be denied that the fleet went to Japan with suspicion in its heart. It came away with feelings that at present, at any rate, the Japanese are inspired only by feelings of boundless friendship."

During its fourteen months (434 days) deployed, the fleet spent 243 days in various ports and the balance at sea, cruising sedately (except during bouts of heavy weather approaching Auckland, between Manila and Yokohama, and in the Central Atlantic) and economically at an average speed of 10 knots. The longest overwater leg, seventeen days, had come between Honolulu and Auckland.

This chart of the deployment of battleship *Vermont* with the fleet was hand drawn by an electrician on board, Roy Davis.

Source: Roy W. Davis Collection, Naval History and Heritage Command.

ready "for a feast, a frolic or a fight." Feast or frolic certainly; formation station-keeping and occasional gunnery drills aside, his battleships did nothing in 1908 that a like-sized fleet of contemporary ocean transports (or for that matter, cruise ships today) couldn't do, but had it come to it, that the sixteen were fully prepared for a fight wasn't at all so evident. First, there was the problem of getting to the action; the fleet managed its circumnavigation not by relying on nine navy colliers but by chartering nearly fifty foreign colliers (forty-one of them British). Access to these civilian ships and their essential stocks of coal in wartime would be problematic, one reason for the Royal Navy's globe-girdling naval base system, for which the US Navy had no counterpart. And second were the well-known design and construction deficiencies that would have impaired the fleet's fighting and damage-control performance (such as excessive top hamper weight and mislocated armor belts).

Standing aboard USS *Mayflower* for the last time, a grinning Roosevelt welcomed the fleet home fourteen months later. The Great White Fleet's arrival, battleship *Connecticut* in the van, the much smaller scout cruiser *Salem* in the rear, twenty-three combatant ships between them, all steaming in column at 6 knots, was greeted by another kind of fleet entirely. *Mayflower* was there, with the President and Mrs. Roosevelt and their two sons on board. So was the dispatch boat *Dolphin*, with members of the Senate and House Naval Affairs Committees; the lighthouse tender *Myrtle*, with representatives of the Department of Labor; the steamer *Brandon*, in from New York with a boatload of Navy Leaguers; and, not last, steamer *Washington*, carrying a full load of senators, representatives, and their families.

In less than two weeks Taft would take the oath of office, and the president would become once again merely "Colonel Roosevelt." In time, he'd regret the demotion and campaign to reverse it.

Scientific American's special navy issue of February 20, 1909 (vol. 100, no. 8, published just before the returning fleet appeared in column off Hampton Roads), featured another of C. McKnight Smith's cover illustrations for the popular weekly magazine, this one a view from off the starboard, forward quarter of battleship *Florida* (BB-30) steaming downwind. *Florida*, not yet laid down at the New York Naval Shipyard and still more than a year away from launching, represented the last word in prewar American dreadnought design: coal-fired steam turbine power protected by a foot of armor plate, and a main battery of ten 14 inch guns. In December 1917 she'd be a part of Battleship Division Nine as it sailed into Scapa Flow to join the Royal Navy's Grand Fleet.

That magazine issue included a superb centerfold, also by Smith, anticipating by a few days the triumphant return of the Great White Fleet to Hampton Roads. Its imminent arrival prompted *Scientific American*'s detailed look at the principal navies of the world ten years after the Spanish-American War. Four separate articles in the magazine toasted the modern American navy, the chief one ("Comparative Strength of the Navies of the World") making a persuasive case that by most measures of war-fighting capacity (all but number of hulls alone), the United States boasted in 1909 the second navy in the world, behind only Great Britain and just ahead of France.

Any excuse at all was justification enough for a newspaper or periodical to conduct a census of the combatant fleets of the world after the turn of the century, listing them in rank order on the basis of simple numbers or some complex judgment of comparative fighting strength. Readers seemed to have an insatiable appetite for this information, a reflection as much of interest in naval forces as expressions of the highest technology extant, as of the political tensions that seemingly flexed just below the surface of even polite diplomatic conversations during the early 1900s. The secretary of the navy needed no such excuse. Making judgments about what his navy could do, and what it needed to perform and improve, was part of his charter.

Secretary Meyers's 1909 report to the president (the first of two) concluded with just such a numerical analysis of "sea strength" of the world's eight principal powers, one different from *Scientific American*'s. Counting only the chief types of combatant vessels afloat, the United States with 139, he wrote, stood third in this census, behind England and Germany and ahead of France and Japan. Third also on the basis of vessels under construction or authorized (45, among them 19 destroyers and 20 submarines), but second looking at the cruder measure of gross war-ship tonnage alone (682,785); more than 1 million tons behind the Royal Navy but a scant 73,000 tons temporarily ahead of Germany's Imperial Navy. (German construction under way would soon move Germany's tonnage ahead of the United States.)

Meyer's predecessor, Vernon Metcalf, had in 1908 endorsed the General Board's recommendation of a new construction program encompassing four

FIGURE 4.4. "No Limit."

Puck magazine's cover for September 22, 1909 (vol. 66, no. 1699), showed five nations playing a high-stakes poker game with their combatant fleets. Uncle Sam, German emperor Wilhelm II, French president Émile Loubet (in fact out of office since 1906), King

Edward VII of Great Britain, and the Japanese Meiji emperor are seated clockwise around the card table with their stakes scattered on the floor beneath them. The Meiji emperor, right hand in the air holding a ship, is saying, "I see your cruisers and raise you a dreadnought!" The cover satirized the costly competition, but underscored the extent to which the naval arms race dominated the international politics of the prewar era.

The cover artist was Philadelphia-born Louis Glackens (1866–1933), one of a pair of brothers who were both artists. Glackens worked at *Puck* over the magazine's last two decades, illustrating covers and drawing cartoons. After the magazine was sold to Hearst in 1917 and collapsed the next year, Glackens moved to drawing cartoons for the *New York Tribune* and working on early animated films in Hollywood.

Source: Library of Congress, Prints and Photographs Division.

big-gun battleships (enough to constitute a second division), four scout cruisers, ten destroyers, and four submarines. Apparently based entirely on considerations of affordability, and of course with no hint of what was to come, Meyers recommended, as the century's second decade began, that the US Navy ship construction program should include only two new battleships and a single repair ship. His report for 1910 would recommend only another two, and two submarines.

During the next several years, and under Secretary Metcalf's three successors, the size of the US Navy slowly crept up. Just before the war began in Europe, the Navy, now under Secretary Josephus Daniels's direction, stood at sixty-two principal combatants (battleships and cruisers), fifty destroyers, and thirty-six submarines, only a few of the latter truly ocean-going.

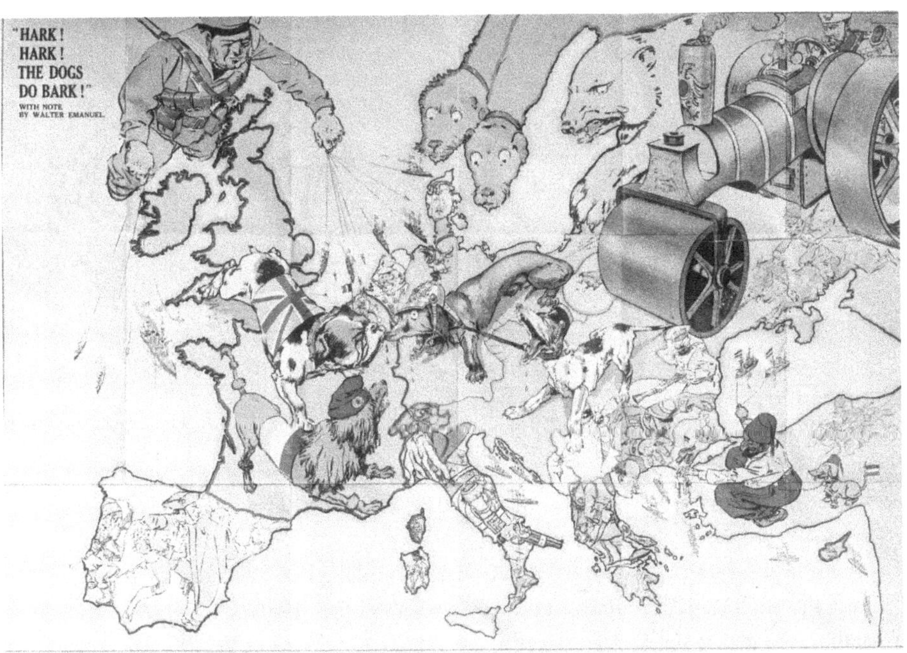

FIGURE 5.1. "Hark! Hark! The Dogs Do Bark!"

Seemingly abandoned in the decades after the Crimean War by her traditional European allies, Great Britain and France, in the 1880s the Ottoman empire pivoted toward Germany for political, military, and financial support. Later, both found good reasons to fear the ambitions and armies of Tsarist Russia, believed to have been remarkably revitalized in the decade since that empire's humiliating defeat by Japan in 1904–5, and Turkish-German ties grew closer still.

Turkey's formal alliance with Germany developed in stages, beginning on August 2, 1914, with a secret treaty in which Turkey promised to join with Germany against Russia should the Russians attack Germany's ally, Austria-Hungary. (The treaty followed a period during which German advisors had reshaped the Ottoman Army to a more modern model, after which German officers commanded certain important formations in the field.) The diplomatic climax came three months later, on November 10, when Turkey, bolstered now by German gold and two Imperial German Navy cruisers flying Turkish colors, declared war on Russia, on her allies France and Great Britain, and for good measure also on Belgium, Serbia, and tiny Montenegro. The Turkish declarations came two days after declarations of war against Turkey, first by Russia, and then by Britain and France.

The apparently crushing weight of Russian arms, initially approaching 1.5 million men and potentially many millions more after general mobilization, was represented in this contemporary British comic map by a steamroller driven by Tsar Nicholas II heading toward East Prussia.

As described by William Wohlforth in the April 1957 issue of *World Politics*, by 1914 friends and foes alike believed that Russia had absorbed the lessons of the Japanese war and had been immeasurably strengthened since that fight by military reform, record harvests, railroad expansion, industrial development, and a years-long "Great Program" of rearmament, most of this funded by French bank loans collateralized by French fears of German ambitions. (Moreover, the threat of revolt in Russia, originally raised in January 1905 almost inadvertently by the monk Father Gapon and that exploded in rioting at the end of that year, had seemingly receded after 1907, following which the durability of the tsar and empire seemed doubtful no longer.)

German and French intelligence shared this view of a restored Russian colossus, one that historian Christopher Clark, writing much later with the clarity of hindsight, described in *The Sleepwalkers* (HarperCollins, 2013) as "an absurd over-estimate of Russian economic progress and military strength."

As depicted on the map, while the Russians are rolling into Germany, a fez-wearing Turk squatting atop Asia Minor is idly playing with ships in the Black Sea with one hand, and pinching shut the Dardanelles (through which 40 percent of Russia's exports and much of its imports passed) with the other. The usual focus of Ottoman anxieties about Russian aims, Istanbul, which the Russians possessively called "Czargrad," is inconspicuous here.

At the time, the image of an unstoppable Russian juggernaut was reinforced by fearsome estimates in the foreign press, such as the oddly precise one that appeared in the *Seattle Star* on August 4, 1914, claiming the Russians could field fully "4,762,300 soldiers." Boldly describing itself as "The Only Paper in Seattle That Dares to Print the News," the *Star* offered other military manpower estimates, too. Without identifying its sources, the newspaper credited Germany, Austria-Hungary, and Italy (the Triple Alliance, so long as Italy remained on side) together with nearly 12.7 million soldiers, and the Triple Entente (Great Britain, France, and Russia) with 9.7 million. In fact, the real number was some three times higher: some 60 million or more troops were mobilized by both sides, one-third of them by the Central Powers, and one-fifth from Russia alone.

(General Vladimir Sukhomlinov, once chief of the Russian general staff and after 1909 the minister of war, had confidently assured the tsar in 1914 that Russia's army was better prepared to fight than it had ever been. Sukhomlinov, distracted by a new and youthful bride, turned out to be wrong, and Christopher Clark right: several years of homicidal fighting later, Russia found herself in the west pressed back against her sixteenth-century border, and Sukhomlinov—since tried, convicted, jailed, and released—in flight from his homeland, destitute, and in disgrace.) On March 2, 1917, with what little was left of the famed guards regiments no longer loyal to him, the tsar abdicated. When Grand Duke

Michael declined to succeed, and the young tsarevitch was rejected by the Duma, after three centuries of the Romanovs the government of Russia was left to whoever could grasp it. Ultimately that was Lenin, and later Stalin. The two would reshape not only Russia but also the world.

Cartoon maps such as this one were unaccountably popular early in the century. According to the Imperial War Museum, this poster was originally printed in Britain in 1914, by Johnson-Riddle and Co., Ltd., and later reprinted in Hamburg, Germany, as an example to Germans of British propaganda.

Source: Imperial War Museum, London.

Chapter Five

"The Guns of August"
and USS *Tennessee*

Europe was a heap of swords piled as delicately as jackstraws; one could not be pulled out without moving the others. Under the terms of the Austro-German alliance, Germany was obliged to support Austria in any conflict with Russia. Under the terms of the alliance between France and Russia, both parties were obliged to move against Germany if either became involved in a "defensive war" with Germany.

—Barbara Tuchman, *The Guns of August* (New York: Macmillan, 1962), 22

And so, like a nightmarish game of chess where all possible moves are bad ones, the world went to war.

—Peter Frankopan, *The Silk Roads: A New History of the World* (London: Bloomsbury, 2015), 306

Barbara Tuchman's Pulitzer Prize-winning *The Guns of August*, about Europe's descent into the Great War, described an almost mindless, mechanical process through which six great empires and a cluster of lesser states suddenly found themselves fighting desperately in late summer 1914, either implementing or responding to a military strategy apparently paced largely by schedules, sending thousands of German troop trains flowing first to the country's western border—carrying 3 million men, nearly ninety thousand horses, and tons of ammunition—and seven weeks after that to its eastern border. By the time the fighting was over, more than four years later, four of the six empires had collapsed, eventually ushering National Socialism, Fascism, and Communism onto the stage, and the surviving two—Great Britain and especially France—were utterly exhausted, and no longer global creditors but debtors.

Also fully spent were the generations who'd fought the war on both sides of no man's land. Robert W. Service, the Canadian poet, balladeer, and sometime ambulance driver, got that terrible cost about right in introducing his collection of poems, *Rhymes of a Red Cross Man* (Barse and Hopkins, 1916):

> ... For through it all like horror runs
> The red resentment of the guns.
> And you yourself would mutter when
> You took these things that once were men,
> And sped them through that zone of hate
> To where the dripping surgeons wait;
> And wonder too if in God's sight
> War ever, ever can be right.

Service was among the remarkable thirty or so volunteer ambulance drivers who went on to fame as poets or authors (Hemingway, MacLeish, cummings, Maugham) or, if not fame, at least to passing admiration (Dos Passos, Bromfield, Masefield) after the war. This shared experience masked great differences, the subject of James McGrath Morris's *The Ambulance Drivers: Hemingway, Dos Passos and a Friendship Made and Lost in War* (Da Capo Press, 2017).

Tuchman's book was published the year after one by German historian and Hamburg University professor Fritz Fischer, entitled in English *Germany's Aims in the First World War* (W. W. Norton, 1961), but more descriptively in the original German, which might be translated as "Germany's Grab for World Power." Fischer's thesis in this work (buttressed by a second book in 1969, *War of Illusions*) was that the infamous "war guilt clause" of the Treaty of Versailles was correct: that Germany's government *was* responsible for the outbreak of World War I, and explosively, that German war aims in World War II flowed directly from those of World War I.

In the half-century since *The Guns of August* was published, and especially during 2014—World War I's first centennial year, a natural book marketing opportunity—many other scholars have reexamined the history of the Great War, and sought anew to identify whose was the guilt and what were the motives and objectives; to describe what happened on its several fronts, and why; to judge the performance under terrific pressure of the chief political and military persons of the age. Among the most notable recent authors are six writing in English: Christopher Clark, Charles Emmerson, Max Hastings, Dominic Lieven, Margaret MacMillan, and Sean McMeekin.[1]

The current answer—much more complex than the assignment of blame exclusively to Germany by Article 231 of the Treaty of Versailles, signed in June 1919—reads like a riff from Agatha Christie's *Murder on the Orient Express*: everybody did it, all six and Serbia were together responsible. Still, some scholars are yet not convinced. Isabel Hull's *A Scrap of Paper* (Cornell University Press, 2015) supports the "Germans as bad guys" conclusion. So does Ian Kershaw early in *To Hell and Back* (Viking, 2015). He blames the notorious "blank check" (a barely 300-word-long telegram wired on July 6, 1914, by Kaiser Wilhelm's chancellor to Emperor Franz Joseph's foreign minister) for unleashing the Austrian ultimatum to Serbia of July 23, and for all that followed.

Everything about World War I was a surprise (which says something about war planning, confirmed since many times): its stunning beginning; its great length; the horrible loss of life in the trenches and in no man's land to blanket artillery barrages and massed machine guns; the inutility of cavalry; the irrelevance of costly capital ships; the use of poison gas; the invention of tanks; the roles of barbed wire, submarines, aircraft, trucks, dirigibles, and especially railroads; the belated participation of the United States; the treaty provisions at the end, and their grim consequences a generation later.

The first surprise for many was that the war happened at all. During the peaceful final few years of the nineteenth century, a Polish industrialist, Jan Gotlib Bloch (1836–1902), asked, *Is War Now Impossible?* (Grant Richards, 1899), the hopeful title of a single-volume, English-language abridgment of his six-volume, 3,000-page treatise in Russian, *The Future of War in Its Technical, Economic, and Political Relations*. He concluded that in Europe it was.

A decade later Norman Angell's best selling second book, *Europe's Optical Illusion* (Simpkin, Marshall, Hamilton, Kent and Co., Ltd., 1909), captivated readers by his more nuanced answer to Bloch's question:

> [it is] not that war is impossible; [this from the book's synopsis] but that it is futile—useless even when completely victorious, as a means of securing those [m]oral or material ends which represent the needs of modern civilized

peoples, and that on a general realization of this truth depends the solution of the problem of armaments and warfare . . . that military power is socially and economically futile, and can have no relationship to the prosperity of the people exercising it . . .

That it is impossible for one nation to seize by force the wealth and trade of another—to enrich itself by subjugating, or imposing its will by force on another; that, in short, war even when victorious, can no longer achieve those ends for which peoples strive. The forces which have brought about the economic futility of military power have also rendered it futile as a means of enforcing a nation's moral ideals or imposing social institutions upon a conquered people.[2]

That said, not everyone believed that a new era of lasting peace was in the offing.

Some of their contemporaries who had studied war and history came to a very different conclusion than did Bloch and Angell. One who did was Colonel Charles Ardent du Picq (1819–70), of France. Nothing in du Picq's own four wars, the last fatal to him, suggested to him that a fifth was impossible. His *Études sur les combats* (Librairie Hachette, 1880) led him to conclude that will, discipline, determination, and solidarity produced "the resolution to advance," decisive in combat of the future. The strategic emphasis on "offensive to excess" that du Picq's theorizing prompted was to serve France very badly in the fighting to come.[3]

Another who disagreed with Angell was Rear Admiral Alfred Mahan, USN, by far the most influential of the several academic strategists in the decades around the turn of the century. ("Academic" because Mahan was a historian; his actual service at sea during the Civil War and later was undistinguished.) The two, Mahan and Angell, wrestled politely in the pages of the March and June 1912 issues of the *North American Review*, as genteel as a fight can be when four pages into his critique the assailant (Mahan) announced, "The fundamental proposition of [Angell's] book is a mistake . . . The entire conception of the work is itself an illusion based upon a profound misreading of human action."[4]

Mahan (1840–1914) was the century's giant among contemporary sea power theorists, which included men such as Sir Julian Corbett of England, Admiral Raoul Castex of France, and Vice Admiral Wolfgang Wegener of Germany; he also put in the shade those who looked to the land beyond salt water, geo-strategist Halford Mackinder among them, who thought in terms of command not of the sea but of the "world island." (Nicholas Spykman's competing "rimland" theory came only in time for the next war, not this one.)

In 1894 Mahan's first two of four books—*The Influence of Sea Power upon History, 1660–1783* and, in two volumes, *The Influence of Sea Power upon the French Revolution and Empire* (both Little, Brown and Co., 1893)—were paired in an over-the-top review by Teddy Roosevelt in the March issue of *Political Science Quarterly*:

"Captain Mahan . . .," Roosevelt wrote, "has even done more than write the best book that has ever been written about naval history . . . he has written a book which . . . may be regarded as founding a new school . . . Until Captain Mahan in these two books revolutionized the study of naval history, no one had attempted to show exactly how naval power made itself felt in the struggles between the different races and nationalities of mankind, nor exactly how far reaching its influence had been and was likely to be upon the destinies of the great master races."[5]

From Mahan's two books Roosevelt took away a Mahanian precept that shaped both his thinking about the worth and mission of navies, and the structure of the fleet that the American navy would have at sea at the beginning of World War I:

mere commerce-destroying is not of decisive weight in the result of a great war. It is a valuable adjunct to other operations, but it is only an adjunct. It may greatly irritate and annoy an enemy, but it can only seriously cripple him if the commerce-destroying is carried on with the help of great fighting fleets. This is a lesson that we in America especially need to learn. We are very apt to think that all we need to do, as far as our fleet is concerned, is to build fast cruisers and harass an enemy's merchantmen; whereas we need to have the lesson taught again and again, and yet again, that we must have a great fighting navy, in order to hold our proper position among the nations of the earth and to do the work to which our destiny points.

Mahan's first book was translated into German and Japanese, and both navies sailed carrying copies of *The Influence of Sea Power upon History* on board for the professional education of their officers. The Royal Navy didn't need the crib sheet that Mahan's book provided to aspiring great sea powers. Its historical experience was, after all, much of the foundation for the Mahanian analysis. Besides, several years before Mahan, the Royal Navy and its supporters in Parliament had settled on a simpler basis for structuring their fleet. Conscious in the decades after Trafalgar of the irreplaceable role a superior Royal Navy had played in Great Britain's security and economy, and, as the end of the century approached, focused initially on France and Russia, Great Britain based its standard not on what its fleet should be able to *do*, but more simply on how big it should *be*. Size, Britons had come to believe, really did matter. The answer was at least twice as large as the navies of both its strongest rivals on the Continent. The Naval Defense Act of 1889 formalized this "two power standard," carried forward for the next fifteen years and not formally renounced until 1921–22.

Otherwise, Mahan's influence was global, even though he was misleading. History describes the past, and it can explain the present, but it cannot tell us much about the future, which is what Mahan and his acolytes were attempting to wrest his research into doing. During the first big war after his books came out, blockade (a form of the "mere commerce destroying" he dismissed so easily), and not the collision of great fleets at sea, turned out to be decisive. Germany's submarine assault on shipping in response to impasse on the ground and starvation at home threatened Great Britain with defeat, a very near thing until the reluctant introduction of convoys. Then Britain's continued throttling of the sea lanes into Germany—and the prospect of American infantry divisions materializing one after the other on the Western Front—forced Germany to acknowledge defeat, even with armies deployed in foreign fields and a fleet at anchor at home. The proud, breathtakingly expensive cruisers and battleships of both sides had relatively little to do with that outcome. A very different naval force—one focused less on the line of battle and much more on husbanding your own trade and attacking the enemy's—would have served each side better.

The best short critique of Mahan is that found early in Edward Miller's *War Plan Orange* (Naval Institute Press, 1991): "lacking modern examples [Mahan] had looked back to warfare in the age of sail. He had no genuine appreciation for certain new weapons of the logistics of steam navies. His fascination with the climactic battle and scorn of direct attacks on trade led him to discount the havoc of attrition that an outgunned nation could wreak with expendable light craft and submarines . . . Mahan was a mediocre strategist of modern war" (37).

Mahan's vision had found its explicit expression in assistant secretary of the navy Roosevelt's sailing orders to Commodore Dewey in 1898 and in President Roosevelt's orders to Rear Admiral Evans in 1907. Not long thereafter, that same vision dangerously misled several of the war's principal combatants, who after the inconclusive Battle of Jutland and during the last two years of the war painfully discovered a mismatch between their costly fleets and reality on the high seas. Those who adopted Mahan learned at the end of May 1916 that his convictions, however persuasive, could not serve as prescriptions.

Mahan aside, those persuaded by Norman Angell's bold antiwar argument—and they were many, the Briton's small book was prefaced by eight pages of quoted extracts from admiring reviews, and went through many printings—were stunned by the onset of hostilities in August 1914 in defiance of his tightly reasoned thesis. For their part the combatants were astonished, too, by the quick failure of their war plans, which had been written and rewritten ceaselessly in the decade before the war.

Everybody but Great Britain—whose standing army, not much more than a glorified colonial police force, was tiny by European standards, and whose intention was to stay out of any fray across the Channel—had at least one war plan. Even the Serbians (usually spelled "Servians" then), who'd started it all with the assassinations near the end of June of the heir to the Austro-Hungarian empire, Archduke Franz Ferdinand, and his wife, had one. Theirs directed five regular and another five freshly mobilized divisions against Austria-Hungary. So did the Romanians. France's general war plan, its seventeenth iteration since the process began, contemplated a major offensive against Germany to the north and south of Metz-Thionville by four armies, focused on the recapture of Alsace and Lorraine, lost in the Franco-Prussian War and mourned ever since. (As executed, Plan 17 left French defenses in Germany's actual attack corridor to the north near fatally under strength.)

For their part, the Austrians also had two plans: one weighted against Russia and Serbia, the other emphasizing Russia; both optimistic in view of the dual monarchy's chronically underfunded army, victim of the monarchy's nearly tribal politics. So, also, did the Russians: Plans 19A ("Austria") and 19G ("Germany"), developed beginning in 1910, the pair reflecting uncertainty about where the initial threat lay. Work had begun on a twentieth Russian mobilization plan in 1914, but it wasn't completed by the time war erupted later in the year. That timing was unfortunate for the Russians, who went to war with a four-year-old plan that didn't fully use the increased railroad capacity just completed, and mistimed the mobilization of Russian railroads and of troop units, coordination deficiencies compounded by the fact that Russia possessed half as many tracks on which to haul troops to the front as did her enemies, eighteen versus thirty-six.[6]

Countless staff man hours had been expended in the iteration and reiteration of these plans, heedless perhaps of the observation by von Moltke the Elder that "no operation extends with any certainty beyond the first encounter with the main body of the enemy." A caution echoed more pungently by the boxer Mike Tyson, who once explained that "everybody has a plan until they get punched in the mouth."

None of the future combatants understood that they would be sending antique armies, generally like those that Napoleon could have mustered, right down to the colorful red trousers of the French infantry, the plumed helmets and breastplates of French cuirassiers, the glittering accoutrements of Austrian Lancers, and the towering karakul sheepskin hats worn by Cossacks, against modern weapons whose industrial-strength lethality neither Napoleon nor his successors during the following century could have imagined. Ignorance difficult to fathom, given the careful observations of countless handsomely uniformed attachés who'd toured the lethal battlefields of the Russo-Japanese War and reported home what they'd seen. Some 8 million to 10 million men in uniform would die instantly or more slowly from their wounds during the course of the Great War. Three times that number survived their wounds.

Germany's plan, as finally envisioned in 1905 by Count Alfred von Schlieffen as a gigantic sweep through Belgium, pivoting on Diedenhofen-Metz and swinging to scoop up Paris while a small force covered East Prussia, was amended beginning the next year by his immediate successor, Helmuth von Moltke the Younger. (Inconveniently, Von Moltke's uncle, chief of the German general staff in 1857–71, had the same first and last names as his nephew, necessitating identifying him as "the Elder," and his nephew as "the Younger.") The younger Von Moltke is usually charged with responsibility for the plan's failure by progressively weakening the armies assigned to the pivot through Belgium and Luxembourg and the final assault on Paris.

That assertion oversimplifies the flaws in the German plan, launched by the invasion of neutral Belgium on August 4, 1914—which plucky nation, astonishingly, didn't yield but resisted—and with an attack on the city of Liège the next day.[7] Albert I, king of the Belgians, is supposed to have explained to the Germans that Belgium "was a nation, not a road." The price for his brave stand was horrible: 1 million of Belgium's 8 million citizens became refugees during the first year of the war.

In late summer 1914 Germany's expectation was that the war on the Western Front was going to last exactly six weeks (some on the German general staff, reported the Bavarian ambassador to his capital, optimistically thought as little as four), ending in mid-September 1914 with triumphant countrymen entering Paris at the climax of a great assault that managed its swift pace by circumventing entirely the powerful line of French fortresses that ran from Belfort, through Epinal and Toul, to Verdun.[8] That accomplished, the new veterans of the Kaiser's army were to turn around and speed by rail east across Germany, to hurl themselves against the Russians, initially fixed at their border by a nine-division-strong German holding force but now presumably finally fully mobilized and threatening Prussia with their millions. Final victory in this bold, two-front war—fought one front at a time—would surely follow.

In fact, it didn't. The failure of Von Moltke's carefully derived, but, as it turned out, wildly unrealistic, timetable (stalled by the Belgian Army and all the reasons that Bloch and Angell had pondered) condemned Germany almost certainly to lose the war, because a delayed victory would eventually turn not on a combatant's immediately available military strength—the product of frantic mobilization everywhere in Europe during late summer and through the fall of 1914—but rather upon the comparative economic strength of the competing alliances during all the war years.

In the key measures of this comparison, the Central Powers (Germany, Austria-Hungary, Turkey, and Bulgaria after the defection of Italy) were deficient as compared to their four adversaries (Great Britain, France, Russia, and later Italy; exchanging in 1917 the United States for postrevolution Russia). And as the war progressed, that economic balance grew ever more unfavorable.

So said Stephen Broadberry and Mark Harrison, both professors of economics at the University of Warwick, some fifteen years ago. "World War I had some distinct features," the two wrote in the introduction to *The Economics of World War I* (Cambridge University Press, 2005):

One is that economics decided the outcome of the first war in a direct and straightforward sense, even more than in the second. The military decision of World War I was expected on the western front, where the richest countries engaged most of their forces. Yet the military decision never came. It is true that there were victories and defeats, and that the front became considerably less stable during 1918. But the fact remains that the military struggle ended in ceasefire, not surrender, with the German army still standing on foreign soil. If Germany's war effort had become unsustainable, it was because of the failure of its economy, not its army.

But perhaps not, although around the end of 1916, the German high command apparently came to the same conclusion as did the two English professors nearly a century later: By the turn of the year, the fight in Europe had long since become economic, not military, and—unlike in the east against Russia—in the west Germany couldn't win the war on the ground. It was that grim realization and growing hunger at home which led to the resumption of unrestricted submarine warfare by the Kaiser Marine, a desperate effort to break the stalemate by forcing the British out of the war with a weapon far from the thinking of Prussian generals (and German admirals, and Admiral Mahan himself) when the shooting began in August 1914: the U-boat.

Until World War I the submarine had existed more as a promise than as a threat, notable when at sea more for drowning its crew than for anything else. Little in its prior, nearly 300-year-long history (counting not from Leonardo da Vinci's hint of an idea, but a century after that from Cornelius van Drebbels's odd, grease-coated submersible in the Thames River) gave reason for real confidence that a submarine could be made to work, until John Holland's SS-1 did in March 1898. A few years later, Germany's first functional submarine sailed from Kiel, and soon after that, in December 1906, the German Navy commissioned its first submarine, the kerosene-fueled U-1.

The chief focus of the German naval construction program that began in 1898 under Rear Admiral Alfred von Tirpitz, however, was capital ships, combatants that could challenge the Royal Navy's cruisers and battleships on equal terms. The hugely expensive and hugely provocative program (provocative at least in the eyes of the British, who saw the German Grand Fleet as a direct challenge to a century of uncontested British supremacy at sea) would turn out, after mid-1916 and the Battle of Jutland, to have been a poor investment. Not so the relatively small amounts spent on the construction of a fleet of torpedo-firing and mine-laying submarines. As early as December 1912 the Kaiser, not exclusively in charge of national security policy in the fractious German system but always outspoken and influential, was urging an increase in U-boat production, explaining that they could be used to torpedo British troop ships on the way to France. Nothing came from that particular meeting, but the future utility of submarines was clearly not a new subject.

Beginning in February 1917 and for months thereafter U-boats (more than one hundred boats a year were entering the German fleet, more than making up for losses) were sinking more than a half-million tons of shipping per month, denying island England the food and fuel needed to continue to fight the war. These were losses that new construction could not replace.

The war's greatest irony is that at the bitter end the possibility of victory for Germany hinged not on its powerful army, the lethal instrument of Schlieffen's carefully constructed plan, and not on its enormously costly High Seas Fleet, but on a neglected bit of the Imperial German Navy, U-boats, and on the fantastic possibility that the British Isles, home to the world's most powerful navy, could be defeated by submarine blockade in defiance of what Mahan taught and his acolytes believed.

An enduring surprise was that the war, once joined, lasted so long. "Modern wars are short and sharp," Army Lieutenant Wirt Robinson, 4th US Artillery, an instructor in military science at Harvard, had sagely reminded readers of *Collier's Weekly* a dozen years earlier.[9] "The average duration of the five great European wars from 1859 to 1870 from the declaration of war to striking the decisive blow was but seven weeks," he wrote (deliberately beginning his count late enough to exclude thirty months of fighting in Crimea). Later, the Spanish-American War proved no exception; it, too, was over weeks after the shooting began. The wars fought in the Balkans after the turn of the century were also short, seemingly validating Robinson.

Astonishingly, not only those who couldn't know better—junior officers who'd never been in a fight or out of the saddle, worrying about having the correct uniform soon to witness their foe's surrender—but also those others whose vantage point and sources were much more elevated, and so perhaps should have known better, expected a short war. (Or none at all: as late as July 27, 1914, Ambassador James Gerard in Germany was telling Washington, "I have reason to believe matter will be arranged without general European war.")

Among the latter was the American ambassador to Great Britain, transplanted North Carolina newspaperman and publisher Walter Page, who served in London from April 1913 until October 1918. It soon fell to Page to deal with frightened Americans (and also to manage the diplomatic and consular business of the Germans and the Austrians in London, whose embassies were turned over to his charge during the first few days of August; and later that of the Turks). Describing those first days in a private letter to President Wilson on August 9, he wrote:

> nervous women . . . who came in and asked absurd questions . . . Crazy men and weeping women were imploring and cursing and demanding—God knows it was bedlam turned loose. I have been called a man with the greatest genius for emergency by some, by others a damned fool . . . Men shook English banknotes in my face and demanded United States money and swore our government and its agents ought all to be shot. Women expected me to hand them steamship tickets home . . . These absurd experiences will give you a hint of the panic . . . English, Germans, Americans—everybody has daughters and wives and invalid grandmothers alone in Germany. In God's name, they ask, what can I do for them?[10]

Later, on November 18, 1914, Ambassador Page passed on to Secretary of State Bryan (the senior pacifist in Wilson's cabinet) what he'd heard directly from the general commanding the British Army in France, General Sir John French, "that he now regards the result of the war as practically determined. His opinion is that the Germans have done their utmost and there will now be a slow victory of the allies, won perhaps next spring." General French comes across as a naïf or worse, but Ambassador Page wasn't. He'd referred to the war as "the Grand Smash" in his reports and letters to Washington.

French's naïve optimism was buttressed by a report from Frederick Palmer (1873–1958), the veteran American war correspondent—covering his sixth conflict since 1897, and described admiringly in the US press as "having seen more war than any other American"—just back from Berlin with the fantastic news that German commanders "know that they will be beaten." Palmer's views clearly carried special weight: during the war years to come, his strategic and military insights were quoted nationwide in some 1,400 newspaper stories. The only possible reason peace would be delayed, French and Palmer seemed to agree, was the allies' insistence that Germany pay an enormous indemnity to Belgium for the latter's full restoration. Later Palmer spent some of the war years as General Pershing's press liaison and as a censor for the American Expeditionary Force. He would come "to hate war bitterly and unrelentingly," as revealed in his well-regarded book *The Folly of Nations* (Dodd, Mead and Co., 1921).

The end of the war in 1915 was foreseen by another authority, the celebrated French "pythoness," Mme. de Thèbes (an aging clairvoyant named Anna Victorine Savigny in real life, "Thèbes" lent her a suitably mysterious ancient Egyptian aura), who, New York City's *Sun* explained on March 28, had successfully predicted the San Francisco earthquake and, in November 1913, the start in 1914 of the Great War. Such visions had special power in the first few decades of the century, when people high and low unabashedly consulted seers and mystics to communicate with the past or perceive the future.

In 1914 Mme. de Thèbes predicted that the war would end the next year, leaving behind it a Germany that was a republic. The famous clairvoyant's obituary in the *New York Times* in December 1916 catalogued her successful predictions before listing her three big misses in 1914: Kaiser Wilhelm's assassination in September, a French invasion of Germany in October, and the end of the war in November.

General French, a cavalry officer tragically in above his head in command of three British Army corps on the line, lost his job in December 1915. By then, at the battles of Mons, the Marne, Aisne, Ypres, and Loos, more than 150,000 Tommies had lost their lives on the Western Front under his inept command. Among the near 60,000 British casualties at Loos in September (including three division commanders) was Lieutenant John Kipling of the 2nd Battalion, Irish Guards, the only son of the 1906 Nobel laureate for literature, Rudyard Kipling, the empire's favorite poet and storyteller. His son's disappearance on that battlefield prompted Kipling—suffering deeply from guilt, he'd pressed his son into national service despite disqualifying vision problems—to launch a desperate search for him, then to write a poignant memorial poem, "My Boy Jack," and later still to pen a series of short "epitaphs" in rhyme which hinted that the famous bard of empire and its army might be rethinking the war he'd so enthusiastically supported.

French wasn't the only failure at the front. One of the explanations for the horrific slaughter was encapsulated then and since in the phrase "donkeys leading lions." That's the explanation Jay Winter of Yale recently espoused, describing "the yawning gap between the ordinary decencies of the men who went to war and the blindness of the men who led them into a kind of battle the world had never seen before, a kind of battle they could not control. Their errors, their blindness, their arrogance—in some cases, their criminal incompetence—sentenced millions to hardship, mutilation, and death."[11] Compared to Scott Anderson's in *Lawrence in Arabia: War, Deceit, Imperial Folly and the Making of the Modern Middle East* (Doubleday, 2013), Winter's savage assessment is relatively mild. "Europe's imperial culture had fostered a culture of decrepit military elites—aristocrats and aging war heroes and palace sycophants—whose sheer incompetence on the battlefield, as well as callousness toward those dying for them, was matched only by that of their rivals." Anderson continued, "Indeed, in looking at the conduct of the war and the almost preternatural idiocy displayed by *all* the competing powers, perhaps the most remarkable feature is that anyone finally won at all."

The *New York Times*'s banner headline for Sunday, August 2, 1914, spanned all eight columns of the paper's front page: "Germany Declares War on Russia, First Shots Are Fired; France Is Mobilizing and May Be Drawn in Tomorrow; Plans to Rescue the 100,000 Americans Now in Europe."

Among the most surprised when the fighting erupted on the Western Front, with the rush of four German armies west into Belgium that began the following Tuesday, were tens of thousands of Americans in Europe—many there without a passport, suddenly essential for cross-border travel—who practically overnight found themselves stranded without money or credit anyone would accept, and no way home.[12] The same day the *Times* announced the start of the war, the *New York Tribune*'s front-page war reporting included news of a cable sent from Dover by a stranded American to the Associated Press. Under the headline "U.S. Transports for Relief of Marooned American Tourists," Howard Carroll (a "New York author and businessman") wrote: "the alarm and excitement among Americans anxious to return home cannot be exaggerated." Carroll went on to say, "Permit me through the Associated Press to suggest that in this crisis the United States government make such representations to the European powers as will insure for passenger steamers sailing for

American ports a truce of six to eight weeks pending the return of Americans to their homes. Otherwise incalculable hardships will be imposed upon an army of innocent people, whose only fault is that they have visited Europe as usual to spend countless sums of money." Very soon, much greater "incalculable hardships" would fall on millions.

The war announcement was one of sixteen stories about the war in the *Times* that day, including one that reported Kaiser Wilhelm had mobilized 4 million men, and another that said the British Foreign Office considered the "situation," meaning the preservation of peace, "absolutely hopeless."

Under a column heading that announced "Transports for Refugees Being Considered by State Department," the same Sunday issue of the *Times* reported that "State Department officials admitted that a most serious problem was confronting them in the plight of Americans abroad. They estimated that at least 100,000, and possibly as many as 300,000, were scattered throughout Europe." In fact, no one knew how many wealthy tourists—or less well-heeled Americans, living on the Continent because their business, education, or heritage was there—were trapped abroad. Estimates ranged from as low as 40,000 to the *Times*'s upper-end guess of more than seven times that many. Their numbers soon threatened to overwhelm the resources of a hastily improvised "Committee for American Residents in London for Assistance of American Travelers," chaired by Herbert Hoover, then a consulting mining engineer living large in the British capital.[13] (Hoover would later parlay his brilliant performance as head of the Commission for Relief in Belgium during the war and his service after that in the cabinets of two presidents into an unsuccessful single-term presidency.)

Assistant Secretary of War Henry Breckinridge, chief of an interagency relief commission quickly assembled in Washington and dispatched to Europe to help these desperate citizens, began his October 14 after-action report to Secretary of War Lindley Garrison by setting the stage for his commission's arrival on the Continent two months earlier. "The natural result of the outbreak of the European conflagration was the stranding of 125,000 American tourists, students and residents sojourning abroad," he began, introducing a new, and too low, count of Americans temporarily trapped in Europe.

> The transatlantic lines were paralyzed, their ships either being taken by their respective Governments for military purposes or kept in port by the

fear of capture by ships of war. The credit system of Europe collapsed. In some countries moratoriums were instituted. In others the practical results were the same. Holders of the best collateral—letters of credit, travelers' cheques, etc.—could not realize thereon. Railroads were given over entirely to military operations. One could not move, could not get money, often was dependent for food and shelter on a landlord extending credit. And finally there seemed no prospect of the early release for commercial purposes of any great fraction of European shipping. And the United States had no ships! Well there was a degree of consternation among our stranded citizens. Natural that their plaint should cross the Atlantic and engage the American public and the American government.[14]

By September 11, with Breckinridge's help, 72,000 Americans were believed by Herbert Hoover's relief committee already to have fled Europe for the United States. On one particularly busy day, September 12, the westbound fleet of seven passenger liners scheduled to depart for the United States (it included RMS *Lusitania*, very briefly commissioned in the Royal Navy as an armed merchant cruiser) reportedly would sail carrying 1,200 passengers in steerage alone.[15] Sadly, little more than one year later *Lusitania*'s name would again be on everyone's lips, the ship having been sunk by a single torpedo from U-20 just south of Queenstown, Ireland, with 1,195 people drowned.[16]

It became USS *Tennessee*'s unique mission to address both problems: to carry $1.5 million of government money and another $3 million in privately owned gold to Europe, the treasure on board to pay off travelers' checks and letters of credit, and then to move some distraught American civilians off the Continent, and across the Channel to ports in England, where they could board chartered vessels back to the United States.[17] The expectation on board her seems to have been that, urgent work done, the cruiser would head west for home around the end of September.

The *Philadelphia Inquirer* wrote that *Tennessee* sailed with between $5 and $8 million, in the same story on August 5 that reported how Germany "served notice on the United States that no Americans will be allowed to leave Germany while the army is being mobilized. This is to make sure that no reservists get away in the exodus of foreigners." Three days later the *Inquirer* confirmed the $8 million amount, and quoted Captain Decker, her commanding officer, as explaining that *Tennessee* would "go up the English Channel lit up like Luna

[Amusement] Park" to ensure she would not be confused for a combatant. (A year later the flow was the other way, when 96,000 pounds of gold coin, the equivalent of $35 million, and millions more in securities arrived for safekeeping in New York from the Bank of England.)

That notion of a return home in early autumn was probably reinforced by the fact that *Tennessee* had sailed with great haste, and when she left New York for Falmouth was only marginally ready for sea. Months later, in February 1915, Rear Admiral Victor Blue, USN, chief of the Bureau of Navigation, looked back and reminded his operations counterpart, Rear Admiral Bradley Fiske, USN, that "the *Tennessee* and *North Carolina* were sent away hurriedly last August with officers and money to supply the needs of American citizens who had become stranded on account of the outbreak of the war in Europe. As the service was urgent and temporary these ships were taken from a reserve status and given scarcely more than Navigation Complements which were sufficient for the purpose of their mission." In plain language, "navigation complement" meant that each cruiser had barely crew enough on board to sail the ship safely, but not a "fighting complement," a crew of sufficient size to man main and secondary batteries, take her into combat, and effect damage control should it come to that. No one in Washington expected that it might.

Admiral Blue's "urgent" recommendation to Fiske—responding to her commanding officer's bleak, month-old assessment of his ship's unreadiness for battle while it later sailed in the eastern Mediterranean—was that *Tennessee* and *North Carolina* be relieved on station by the much smaller, unarmored "peace cruisers" USS *Des Moines* and USS *Chattanooga*. The two had been described dismissively in *Scientific American*'s all-navy issue of December 7, 1907 (vol. 97, no. 23) almost as chum, as designed to perform in time of war "various naval duties which would not call for vessels either of great speed or serious fighting power." Blue reaffirmed his recommendation two months later.

A month after that, on March 11, Rear Admiral William Caperton, commanding the cruiser squadron of the US Atlantic Fleet to which the two ships nominally belonged, endorsed Blue's call for *Tennessee*'s and *North Carolina*'s swift return, noting that "two of our most important and heaviest cruisers are over three thousand miles away from their main body in the midst of a European war, weakened by lack of officers and men, and one in addition by a foul bottom, at a time when our diplomatic situation is somewhat delicate." He suggested—an idea that seems obvious today—that if the secretariat wanted to have ships available for the transportation of refugees and other peacetime operations, then chartered merchant vessels should provide the lift, supported by one of the navy's schooner-rigged gunboats then operating in the Caribbean, either USS *Machias* or USS *Marietta*.[18]

Blue's recommendation and Caperton's suggestion notwithstanding, *Tennessee* was to remain in European waters for nearly a year altogether, brushing up hard in mid-November against Turkish sensitivities in a way that the American ambassador to Constantinople, Henry Morgenthau, and others nervously feared might have accidentally triggered "evil results for Americans," and later brilliantly performing a politically sensitive rescue mission that no one had foreseen when she first sped from New York in late summer for the British Isles.

At 9:34 p.m. on August 6, 1914, one day out of the Brooklyn Navy Yard and hours late, USS *Tennessee* finally steamed from her overnight anchorage at Tompkinsville, Staten Island, for Falmouth, England, with these millions in gold coins stowed in shell rooms D-23 and D-24 in sealed, 300 pound kegs, each one containing $50,000 in US $20 "double eagles."[19] Four days later, on August 10, the *Wall Street Journal* reported that Chubb and Son had provided insurance for the valuable cargo, charging a premium of $1.50 per $1,000 in gold, about double the usual rate. "Had the gold been shipped on an English steamer, liable to capture," the *Journal* concluded, "the rate would of course have been higher, if not prohibitive."

Sailing had been delayed nearly twelve hours by the late arrival of the civilians' gold, held up in Bankers Trust's offices downtown by goosey insurers exposed to all the risk they could afford to assume by the $40 million already at sea, half that total just out of New York City in American Lines's plain and aging SS *St. Louis* and Norddeutscher Lloyd's handsome four-stacker, SS *Kronprinzessin Cecilie*, newest of the line's famous "Four Flyers." (The fabulously elegant *Cecilie* boasted a first-class dining room that rose through three decks, described by Douglass Burgess as "decorated with winged cherubim and pastoral scenes . . . watched over by allegorical figures in Grecian robes . . . Over all, set like a diadem in a crystal crown, was a bust of the princess herself.")[20]

They needn't have worried about the treasure *Kronprinzessen Cecilie* carried. Eight years old when she sailed from New York on July 25, 1914, the luxurious steamer never made it to Bremen with her $11.1 million in gold and silver and 1,200 passengers. Diverted to Bar Harbor, Maine, by Norddeutscher Lloyd management while under way home to Germany, to avoid the risk of capture, her passengers, mail, and millions were offloaded there, and she was soon interned nearby in Boston.

Confiscated in February 1917 just before the United States entered the war, *Kronprinzessen Cecilie* spent the last few years of World War I transformed into an American troop transport named USS *Mount Vernon*, presumably minus the glittering, gilded putti of her decoration. In one of the war's lesser ironies, on September 5, 1918, westbound in a convoy off France, the new USS *Mount Vernon* (the third ship of that name) was hit by a single torpedo fired by U-82, but managed to limp back across the Atlantic to Boston after urgent repairs in the dry dock at Brest. The attack killed thirty-six men and wounded fifteen. U-82 got away.

The first year of the war saw fortunes in gold move across the Atlantic, as the international economy tried to cope with effects of the war, and national treasuries made payments or sought safety for their reserves. In August 1915, the *New York Times* reported: "Seven Carloads of English Gold Reach New York . . . Sent in a Battle Cruiser." According to the *Times*, forty armed men guarded the $52 million in gold (48 tons packed in 800, 120 pound boxes) and securities that then moved by fortified train from Halifax to New York City.

Described simply as "boxes of metal," tens of millions of dollars in bar gold and gold coin of various countries were shipped to Canada and the United States in Royal Navy ships and merchant vessels of the Allan and Donaldson Lines, usually landing in Halifax for further movement by rail to bank vaults in Ottawa, New York, or Washington. When the White Star Lines's SS *Laurentic* was sunk by mines off northern Ireland January 25, 1917, £5 million of this gold in transit was lost, but almost all was recovered later by divers. All the rest of the treasure seems to have been moved safely.

There's nothing in the unpublished, four-volume war history of the Bank of England, 1914–21, or in *Tennessee*'s deck log to substantiate the junior Beach's statement that returning home in 1915, *Tennessee* brought with her "gold bullion of the Bank of England" on the way to transfer to Canadian banks. Nationality aside, her route home made that impossible.

Under a headline that announced "16 Tons in Tennessee's Chest, Sail Ho!" page 4 of the next morning's issue of the *New York Tribune* showed its readers what these kegs full of "gold doubloons" had looked like while temporarily stacked on *Tennessee's* deck under the watchful eye of her new executive officer, Lieutenant Commander Earl Jessop, USN, looking suitably serious in a rumpled dress white uniform, and armed with a holstered pistol on his right hip.

The first $1.5 million of *Tennessee's* small fortune came from an appropriation hastily approved by a joint resolution of Congress for the "relief, protection, and transportation of American citizens in Europe, and for personal services, rent and other expenses." The other $3 million had been amassed by Benjamin Strong Jr., the new president of the Bankers Trust Company, of New York, and nine other titans of American banking. There was to have been $2 million more in gold on board, but at the last minute J. P. Morgan managed to get credit support from the Bank of France. Confusingly, the *Tribune* reported *Tennessee* had sailed with $8 million on board; other papers reported $5.867 million. Some newspaper reports following *Tennessee's* return to New York said, probably correctly, she'd returned with an unexpended $169,000, but the exact amount of the fortune she sailed with the year before isn't completely certain.

New York bankers had been careful to emphasize that this initiative wasn't merely to serve clients of the ten banks that were represented on the committee that had pushed it through, but that "all holders of American travelers' checks and letters of credit issued by responsible concerns will be recognized, irrespective of whether the issuers are contributors to the fund or not. The sole object of this shipment is to provide for all who are in need and to give them the means of securing the funds necessary to maintain them in London and to furnish them with money for their return to the United States at the earliest possible moment."[21]

The $3 million of bankers' gold resting quietly in casks down in ammunition storage spaces below *Tennessee's* armored deck as she steamed east represented a potential bonanza to Captain Benton Decker, USN (1868–1933, USNA '87), her new commanding officer—a fortune he first claimed in writing on October 23, 1915, while *Tennessee* was midway through her port call at Brindisi, Italy. Decker then recalled, or learned before anyone else remembered it, that a curious article in Chapter 14 ("Instructions for Officers in General") of the 1913 edition of *Navy Regulations* gave him what seemed to be an unimpeachable, personal claim to an enormous fee for the service of hauling this gold across the Atlantic in a US Navy ship under his command.

The article, no. 1510 ("Gold, etc. taken as freight"), provided that

> when gold, silver, or jewels shall be placed on board any ship for freight or safe-keeping, as provided by the Articles for the Government of the Navy, the commanding officer shall sign a bill of lading for the amount and be responsible for the same. The usual percentage shall be demanded from the shippers, and its amount shall be divided as follows: One-fourth to the commander-in-chief, one-half to the commanding officer of the ship, one-fourth to the Navy Pension Fund. To entitle the commander in chief to receive any part of the amount, he must have signified to the commanding officer of the ship, in writing, his readiness to unite with him in the responsibility for the care of the treasure or other valuables. When a commander in chief does not participate in division, two-thirds shall inure to the commanding officer of the ship and the remainder to the pension fund.[22]

Decker's share under the article's formula totaled a generous $20,000. (The Navy's Pension Fund was to get the remaining $10,000.) This at a time when the secretary of the navy and his fellow cabinet officers received $12,000 annually; when a senior captain serving at sea was paid just under $5,000 a year; and when an annual income of $1,500 put a family solidly into America's middle class.

Early in October, with *Tennessee* now coaling in Brindisi from USNS *Vulcan* and preparing to sail for Beirut, Decker wrote the bankers in New York asking for his commission. (Earlier, in June, both the Bureau of Navigation and the secretary of the navy had told Decker he was not "required" to collect the percentage.) In December the bankers replied that his request could only be considered if first "sanctioned and approved" by the secretary. Decker's request was duly forwarded to Secretary Daniels, who passed it on for comment to Commander Ridley McLean, USN, the navy's judge advocate general (JAG), its senior counsel.

Commander McLean (1872–1933, USNA '94), in 1902 the author of the original *Bluejacket's Manual,* had no legal education whatever. McLean, whose sea duty had included riding USS *Connecticut* around the world as part of the Great White Fleet in 1907–9, served as the JAG during 1913–16 and then returned to a successful career at sea: taking command in turn of *Columbia, New Hampshire, Nebraska,* and *Arkansas*; eventually rising to vice admiral in 1927; and dying suddenly in that grade while in command of Battleship Division Three.

None of the incumbents between 1880, when the JAG position was established, and 1950 was a lawyer. Remarkably, such was the influence of line officers that not until 1950 did Congress pass a law, PL 586 (64 Stat. 109), that required the Navy's judge advocate general, the service's senior lawyer, actually to be an experienced attorney. The chief business of that law, passed by the 81st Congress, was enacting the Uniform Code of Military Justice, thus "unifying, consolidating, revising and codifying the Articles of War, the Articles for the Government of the Navy, and the disciplinary laws of the Coast Guard" into a single code.

Nested deep within that act, on page 147 of 149, in Article 140, Section 13, lay the operative language: "Hereafter The Judge Advocate General of an Armed Force . . . shall be appointed from among those officers who at the time of such appointment are members of the bar of a Federal court or the highest court of a State or Territory and who have had not less than a total of eight years experience in legal duties as commissioned officers." Passed by Congress on May 5, 1950, the bill was signed into law by President Truman the next day.

McLean's five-page analysis of Decker's claim certainly sounds lawyerly today, down to its reminder that almost two years earlier, his recommended amendment to the operative article in Navy Regulations—that any transportation of treasure during war, insurrection, or "turbulence" be done without charge, without diversion, without responsibility, and without pay—was ignored. Decker's claim, therefore, was obedient to the express provision of the article and the secretary, wrote McLean, could and should do nothing that would attempt to divest Decker of his rights.

A year after he submitted it, Decker's claim against the Bankers' Trust Company was still bouncing around Washington. On October 9, 1916, Secretary Daniels sent him a report on its progress since the previous April 17, when Decker had raised the claim again with the secretary. Daniels told him that "in view of the fact that other departments were concerned . . . and in order that no injustice might be done you," he'd spoken with Secretary of the Treasury William McAdoo, President Wilson's son-in-law. They'd both agreed it was necessary to consult with Wilson before responding. Such a consultation with the president of the United States, Daniels explained, could not happen before November 7, after which time (and after further discussion with Secretary McAdoo) Decker could expect his reply. Sadly, nothing in any available archive tells what happened next to his claim.

Also on board with *Tennessee*'s crew was a mixed bag of fifty-seven official passengers heading for Europe. The group included Ambassador Joseph Willard, returning to begin his second year at the embassy in Madrid after vacationing at home in Virginia; Assistant Secretary Henry Breckinridge with several uniformed aides; Breckinridge's deputy from the State Department, Percival Dodge, and a covey of consuls; John Grier and four other civilian bankers to baby-sit the specie, a condition of the treasure's commercial insurers reluctantly agreed to by the government, and the national director of the American Red Cross, Ernest Bicknell, and a second Red Cross representative. Suitable berthing limitations required that ten others bound for Europe be diverted to USS *North Carolina* (ACR-12), soon to leave Boston and sail for Europe on a parallel relief mission, but minus the gold.

Tennessee had been built as a flagship, with accommodations appropriate for a squadron commander, her commanding and executive officers, 19 wardroom officers, plus 12 junior and 10 warrant officers—a total of 44, with half in cramped, austere surroundings. Reflecting his rank, Ambassador Willard moved into the baronial accommodations of the flag cabin aft. The other senior civilian visitors on board *Tennessee* likely displaced some of the twenty-eight ship's company officers from officers' country and the wardroom, spaces that, even so, probably featured standing room only during this top-heavy crossing. According to the Red Cross's Bicknell, those junior civilians who were crowded out from berthing below decks sat topside in daytime beneath *Tennessee*'s great guns on folding stools, and slept in the same place at night on folding cots. Some of the ship's dispossessed junior officers probably also camped out on deck among the passengers.

FIGURE 5.2. Captain Benton Clark Decker, USN.

This photograph of Decker by photographer George Bain was taken in October 1911, when then-Commander Decker was midway through a tour as the third commanding officer of the scout cruiser USS *Chester*. An "insult to my uniform," on the Santo Domingo waterfront by barracks guards that April, as Decker described it, which soon became the stuff of stiff diplomatic exchanges, seems to have been the highlight of *Chester*'s Caribbean deployment. Decker was promoted to captain in July 1913 and retired in December ten years later, having been since 1918 a temporary rear admiral.

He was the third generation of navy officers in the family, starting with William Augustus Weaver, whose service began in 1811. Decker's son, Benton Weaver Decker (1899–1983, USNA '20), and his grandsons, Benton Weaver Decker Jr. (1922–59, USNA '45) and Edward Albert Decker (1922–2008, USNA '46), followed their father and grandfather into the family business in turn. The fifth in that lineage, then-Lieutenant Commander Benton Weaver Decker, age thirty-seven, died in 1959 near Iwakuni, Japan, when his Douglas-built A3D "Skywarrior" Bureau Number 130362 crashed on May 28, killing the crew. Originally built to deliver nuclear weapons, by 1959 the type no longer had an attack mission, and had been reconfigured to carry electronic warfare (EW) equipment. EW aircrews disliked the big, unstable aircraft as much as had its original heavy attack aircrews, who morbidly joked that its designation stood for "All 3 Dead."

Captain Decker and Ambassador Willard rubbed up against one another abrasively at the American embassy in Madrid, where Decker was the naval attaché until 1918, when Willard had him and the assistant attaché, Lieutenant Commander Carlos Cusachs, USN, abruptly recalled to Washington and fired. Inevitably, in the poisoned atmosphere of the postwar navy secretariat and during the presidential election of 1920, their reliefs for cause were addressed by Congress.

Joseph Willard, a failed Democratic candidate for the governorship of Virginia and probably now remembered only as one of Washington's famed Willard Hotel family, served as the American ambassador to Spain from July 1913 to July 1921. Willard might have felt beleaguered during and after this wartime brouhaha: four of his eight-man staff at the embassy were commissioned officers of the US Army or US Navy.

In June 1914 Willard's daughter, Belle Wyatt, married Kermit Roosevelt, the second son of the former president, in the chapel of the British Embassy in Madrid, where the presence of the groom's father at the ceremony riled some local politicians, who unhappily recalled Teddy Roosevelt's starring role in the Spanish-American War barely fifteen years earlier.

Styled "the father of news photography," George Bain founded the New York City–based News Service, one of the first news picture agencies, in 1898.

Source: Library of Congress, Prints and Photographs Division.

Captain Decker (1867–1933, USNA '87) had taken command of *Tennessee* on August 5, the day after he was detached from the Naval War College where he'd been a student and then one of two captains on its staff, and the day before she sailed. He'd suddenly become the cruiser's twelfth commanding officer, but only the seventh who served in the grade of captain, a promotion he'd received barely a year ago. (The other five were a gaggle of junior officers—one was a mere lieutenant—place-keepers who held command generally while the ship was in overhaul or otherwise tied up in port for an extended period. Once *Tennessee* was wrecked and on the beach in 1916, "command" of the forever immobile hulk briefly devolved on even more junior officers.)

Decker's nine tours of sea duty before 1914 prepared him well for command of an armored cruiser. In March 1889, some nineteen months after he left the Naval Academy, Naval Cadet Benton Decker, then twenty-one, was one of seven cadets on board the squadron flagship, the screw steamer USS *Trenton*. The young Decker survived her sinking in a great tropical cyclone at Apia, Samoa, with a relatively minor injury, and so emerged largely intact from a catastrophe that saw her and three other US and Imperial German Navy ships destroyed, and 115 of their sailors drowned. (An ongoing Samoan civil war had seemingly opened an opportunity for Germans and Americans to advance rival imperial interests in the Western Pacific, hence the presence of the ships. In 1899 the islands were partitioned into American and German Samoa.) Every one of the six merchant ships in port Apia that March sank also.

Only HMS *Calliope*, the sole Royal Navy ship in the port, escaped the harbor for the safety of the open sea in time. Astonishingly, despite *Calliope*'s example of good weather sense and seamanship, the American squadron commander, Rear Admiral Louis Kimberly, USN, and his several ships' commanding officers were exonerated by then-Secretary of the Navy Benjamin Tracey, who piously viewed the lethal storm as an unforeseeable "visitation from Providence in the presence of which human efforts are of little avail." Tracey's conclusion would find its echo in Secretary Daniels's generous treatment of her commanding officer when *Memphis*, née *Tennessee*, went aground in twenty-seven years' time.

Eight years later, after service with ship's company in the cruisers USS *Baltimore* and USS *Newark* (Cramp's nos. 254 and 258) and in the obsolete monitor USS *Miantonomoh*, Lieutenant Junior Grade Decker was in battleship USS

Indiana (Cramp's no. 270) during the battle of Santiago, Cuba. On January 26, 1915, then in the Mediterranean commanding *Tennessee* and dealing with the frustrations of his cruiser's asthmatic engineering plant, Decker recalled unhappily this long-ago first combat tour in *Indiana*.

"It was my lot at the beginning of the Spanish War, to be on the INDIANA," Decker wrote from Alexandria to Rear Admiral Fiske, Secretary Daniels's aide for operations for only another few months. (The personal and professional relationship between the two, Daniels and Fiske, soon edged over into open hostility. Later Fiske would be one of the leaders of the uniformed navy's postwar assault on the secretary.)

> The ship, with others, was sent before the outbreak of the war to Dry Tortugas. It was considered at the time that this was a demonstration to put pressure on Spain. On the passage to Dry Tortugas the boiler tubes were in such bad condition that the ship could not make the speed required, and was taken in tow for a time. A number of boiler tubes were shipped to Key West and the boilers re-tubed in great haste and with great inconvenience by boilermakers of the fleet. The ship's bottom was foul and divers were sent from the north to clean her bottom, which was done in a hasty manner, but as well as practicable under the conditions. Fresh water could not be obtained for her boilers so after re-tubing they were filled with salt water. On the passage from Havana to San Juan the ship could not maintain her speed; the boilers were forced; the crown sheets came down, and the ship was virtually a cripple from that time on.[23]

Although her problems forced *Indiana* to miss entirely the excitement of the chase of the fleeing Spanish squadron, Decker managed to distinguish himself in charge of a shore rescue party sent off *Indiana* to succor survivors of the battered and beached Spanish destroyer, *Pluton*.[24]

A tour in the transport USS *Panther* (ex-SS *Venezuela*, Cramp's no. 263, later reconfigured as a repair ship) in 1899 was followed by Lieutenant Decker's first command, USS *Quiros*, a 400 ton, former Spanish Navy gunboat with a crew of just thirty-seven, then part of the US Navy's tiny Philippine Squadron. After three years in the new battleship USS *Virginia* (1907–9) followed by shore duty, in July 1911 Decker, now a commander, became USS *Chester*'s commanding officer. He took her out of commission nineteen months later, then went to the War College, from where he left abruptly in late summer 1914 to join USS *Tennessee* on her cruise to Europe and the war.

Tennessee sailed for Falmouth, England, with a pickup crew, from her new executive officer, Commander Jessop, until then commanding officer of the destroyer USS *Benham*, DD-49 (Cramp's no. 385), on down, to junior enlisted men. Approximately seven hundred sailors were aboard when *Tennessee* got under way, significantly shorthanded. As a receiving ship tied up in port for the past three months, she'd not had a full complement assigned, and so her departure was made possible only by hasty impressment of officers and enlisted sailors from along much of the Atlantic Coast. The battleship USS *Utah*'s crew and the crews of several torpedo boat destroyers under repair at the Brooklyn Navy Yard were especially hard-hit by the levy, as Jessop's own hasty reassignment proved.

Six months later, at sea in early January 1915, the hard-pressed Jessop considered *Tennessee*'s muster list and concluded that "it is impossible to arrange any system by which this vessel can be prepared for battle in the proper sense of the word . . . there are not sufficient officers." Tellingly, the shortage was concentrated in officers assigned to the gun batteries and to gun fire control. "Instead of having twenty-three officers available for this work," Jessop reported to Decker, "we have Seven, which would demonstrate how impossible it would be to effect an efficient battle organization." That shortage was not corrected before *Tennessee* sailed home.

Lieutenant Harold Bowen, USN (1883–1965, USNA '05), *Tennessee*'s new chief engineer and the junior of her two lieutenants, characterized reporting crew members dismissively as "the ragtag and bobtail of the Atlantic Fleet." Bowen didn't think much of the crew, and he didn't like Captain Decker much, either. He called the skipper a "sundowner," providing readers of his 1954 autobiography, *Ships Machinery and Mossbacks* (Princeton University Press, 1954), with Webster's definition for the term, "a very strict captain," and then with his own, "a[n] S.O.B." The allusion was to commanding officers who insisted liberty parties (including officers) return to the ship in time for the evening meal, sharply cramping their sampling the seductions of nightlife ashore.

Bowen's forty-six-year-long navy career, from which he retired as a vice admiral, revealed him to be prickly and famously hard to please, but in fact *Tennessee*'s under-strength engineering gang seems to have had little experience with coal-fired steam plants (by late 1914 the US Navy's transition to oil-fired boilers was already well under way), and this novelty showed as the cruiser worked her way east, nursed through recurring serious mechanical problems by Bowen's overworked, under-strength engineers. That, and not restricted liberty ashore or disciplinary proceedings on board, could account for the engineer's harsh assessment of his boss, who would later display extraordinary sympathy for the thousands of wretched refugees *Tennessee* would carry out of danger, suggesting character and virtues his carping engineer didn't appreciate.

Captain Decker was on the bridge that August night as the distant lights of New York faded behind him, the start of what became an unusual near-year-long cruise that saw his ship arrive in Europe to deliver the bullion, twice ferry tourists and refugees across the English Channel to Falmouth from Le Havre and Rotterdam (where the Dutch apologized fulsomely that neutrality regulations required them to insist that *Tennessee* anchor outside of the three mile limit); unexpectedly sail to Italy to coal instead of returning home, and then continue to the Eastern Mediterranean to add her presence to the geopolitical ferment in the Aegean, and also to move war refugees of many nationalities from ports in Ottoman Palestine to British-controlled Alexandria, Egypt. Between August 16, 1914, when she sailed from New York, and July 30, 1915, when she returned to that city, USS *Tennessee* steamed 20,603 miles and called forty-seven times in foreign ports, thirty-seven times in the Mediterranean Sea. That tally included ten calls (totaling more than seven weeks pierside) at Alexandria between December and June.

When she sailed for England, *Tennessee* had logged just over 129,000 miles steaming since she'd first gone to sea eight years earlier. She was, in the judgment of her new chief engineer, (whose own orders to *Tennessee* had come to him in New York by hasty phone call from Washington only the day before), "not in materiel or personnel readiness to go to sea." Lieutenant Bowen, who'd earlier served on five ships and had commanded a sixth—the aging destroyer *Hopkins* (DD-6)—for some months, wrestled with *Tennessee's* neglected engineering plant for the entire crossing, dealing first with a failed icemaker that threatened the nearly seven tons of fresh meat on board, and managing to extract turns for only 10 knots from the engines for much of the crossing. *Tennessee* finally limped into Falmouth at 17 knots, with the port engine operating normally and the starboard one breathing hard and making partial power. Only part of her weak performance came from plant problems; some resulted from the poor quality of "Colver" brand coal, from a mine near Ebensberg, Pennsylvania, that had been loaded in New York. It had proved to be inferior even to the second grade of Admiralty coal *Tennessee* loaded in her bunkers soon after arrival in England.

His chief engineer's problems and frustrations aside, Decker thought that the crossing—punctuated by the usual battle, fire, collision, and abandon ship drills; boxing and other deck sports; and (adhering to a near century-old navy tradition) a minstrel show with players in blackface—was "comparatively comfortable."

Tennessee entered Falmouth ten days after leaving New York City, just before 8:00 p.m. Sunday, August 16, hours behind *North Carolina*, Captain Joseph Oman, USN, commanding. *North Carolina* had left Boston for Europe on the same refugee extraction mission, but minus the kegs of gold, on August 7, passing the wheezing *Tennessee* on the way east. Moving on, *North Carolina* remained in the Mediterranean to the end of the following May performing the same presence and evacuation missions as *Tennessee*, and finally arrived for fumigation, bottom cleaning, and overhaul at home in Boston June 18, 1915. (Had the catastrophic, amphibious landings at Gallipoli gone very differently than they did in the spring of 1915, *North Carolina* might have followed the invading Franco-British fleet up the Dardanelles toward Constantinople, suggested the American ambassador, making her crew available to protect resident Americans and other neutral civilians during the European allies' seizure of the Turkish capital.)

By the end of the month, the effort to succor Americans on the Continent was going so well that the *New York Tribune* was able on August 30 to print a summary of the work of Breckinridge's relief board that began: "the situation is so greatly relieved at the present time that Americans anywhere upon the Continent can, by applying to the nearest embassy or legation, get in touch with people in this country, and get money if they need any, and can get transportation and passage home if they want it." (The following February Breckinridge and his boss, Secretary of War Lindsay Garrison, both resigned, frustrated by President Wilson's failure to act to heighten US military preparedness, and in particular by Wilson's refusal to stand up an army of reservists.)

Finished with her two shuttles across the English Channel, *Tennessee* steamed

FIGURE 5.3. USS *Tennessee* in the Carrick Roads at
Falmouth, England, August 17, 1914.

The arrival of the cruisers *Tennessee* and *North Carolina* suddenly more than doubled the US Navy's presence afloat on European waters during late summer 1914. The only other American ships already there were the antiquated gunboat USS *Scorpion* (a converted yacht), deployed to the Mediterranean since 1908 and in 1914 the station ship at Constantinople, and the Cramp's-built battleship USS *Maine* (BB-10, the second *Maine*, Cramp's no. 302) on a port visit to Villefranche, France, during a training cruise for Naval Academy midshipmen.

The former crew of USS *Idaho* (built ten years earlier by Cramp's as its hull no. 328) was idling about Villefranche, too. Their battleship, renamed *Lemnos*, had been delivered two weeks earlier to the Royal Hellenic (Greek) Navy, part of a sale that also included her sister ship, USS *Mississippi*, Cramp's no. 327, renamed *Kilkis* and become the flagship of the Hellenic Fleet. Both were soon seized by the French and disarmed for the duration of the war.

Source: Courtesy of Captain David Barnicoat, Falmouth, England.

from Rotterdam to Brindisi, Italy, via Falmouth (arriving on October 12), a move first noted by the *New York Times* on September 30—the same day *Tennessee* got her sailing orders from Washington by cable—under a headline that explained, "Second American Cruiser Sent to Keep an Eye on Turkey." Thinking strategically, the *Times* observed that the port city, on Italy's southern Adriatic coast, lay "directly across the Strait of Otranto from Turkey [Albania today], and is within fifty miles of the Ottoman Empire." The item continued, "The cruiser *North Carolina* already is in the Mediterranean at the request of Secretary [of State William Jennings] Bryan following reports from Ambassador Morgenthau at Constantinople concerning the alarm felt by the Americans and other foreigners there. The presence of the *Tennessee*, in addition to that of the *North Carolina*, is expected to have a salutary effect."

The *Times* didn't comment on (didn't know, likely) how the balance of naval forces afloat in the Mediterranean was undergoing a historic change. The Royal Navy's big ships were moving west, to Gibraltar, where they had easy access to the Atlantic, to where British planners thought the war's greater danger and challenges lay. That shift, leaving in the Central and Eastern Mediterranean cruisers and smaller combatants and tacitly trusting to the French Navy to take up the slack, implemented an understanding that saw Britain assume an obligation for the security of French Atlantic ports in exchange for French help in securing the lifeline from Gibraltar to Suez against the Austro-Hungarian Navy.

"Salutary," as used in the *Times* article, was understatement. Since August 5, even before *North Carolina* and *Tennessee* sailed from the East Coast, Morgenthau had been pressing the Department of State to get a US Navy presence off the Syrian coast, beginning with moving USS *Scorpion* from Constantinople to Beirut (permission to do that denied), then other ships to Smyrna and elsewhere, to quell the clamor of citizens ashore and "prevent anarchy." By mid-December, however, the ambassador would become much less certain about the utility of American warships in or near Turkish waters.

Henry Morgenthau Sr. (1856–1946), the German-born American ambassador in Constantinople while *Tennessee* was in the Mediterranean, was the third in a near continuous run of four American ministers/ambassadors to Turkey who were not diplomats but lawyers or businessmen and also Jews, a concentration that perhaps reflected an odd, turn-of-the-century notion that American Jews were somehow uniquely able to communicate with Ottoman Turks. This was because of the open-handed welcome their co-religionists had received from Sultan Bayezit II, the eighth Ottoman sultan (of thirty-seven), when they were expelled from Spain and Portugal in 1492. Or perhaps this was because Jews represented a natural neutral party, straddling the centuries-long divide between Muslims and Christians in the Levant, and representing the Abrahamic roots of the other two faiths.

That diplomatic roster included Oscar Straus, posted to Constantinople first in 1887–89 by President Harrison, again in 1898–1900, and for a third time in 1909–10 (and after 1906 Theodore Roosevelt's secretary of commerce and labor); Solomon Hirsch, there between 1889 and 1892, also representing Harrison; Henry Morgenthau Sr. in 1913–16 for twenty-six months; and finally, Morgenthau's replacement after a nine-month gap, another Jewish lawyer from New York, Abram Elkus, who remained at the Turkish capital for barely six months in 1916–17. (This tour was terminated by a decade-long break in relations while Turkey morphed from an empire to a republic.) The last two represented President Wilson.

Morgenthau had been the chief of Wilson's 1912 campaign finance committee, raising more than $1.1 million for the campaign ($30,000 of that his personal contribution) from some 90,000 donors, this at a time when a million dollars was real money and the entire electorate numbered fewer than 15 million. Wilson's victory that November over the sharply divided Republicans, with Taft running as the incumbent and Roosevelt campaigning as a Bull Moose progressive, and against a socialist, Eugene Debs, saw Morgenthau rewarded with Turkey, Walter Page with London, and James Gerard, another campaign loyalist, with the senior post in Berlin. Daniels, Wilson's chief publicist, got a plum cabinet post, the navy secretariat.

Constantinople was a consolation prize for Morgenthau, who had hoped for a cabinet post, too. Morgenthau's ties to Wilson were close. Long since back from Constantinople and then tooling up to raise money for Wilson's reelection campaign, at the end of September 1916 Morgenthau described his view of the president to George Creel of the *New York Times* in passionate, almost reverent, terms. "At the time of my decision [to enter government]," Morgenthau said,

I felt the call of religion, the religion of the new democracy of America, which if it means anything . . . means justice, not charity; it means equality of opportunity instead of special privilege. All my life I have believed these things, but I had never fought for them. What I did was to decide to fight.

At the time of my decision I was not entirely clear as to how and where I should make response to my desire for service to real democracy. Woodrow Wilson . . . came as an answer to my uncertainty . . . I read his books. I talked to him. I grew to feel that Woodrow Wilson, more than any other man since Lincoln, had democracy in his heart and in his soul.

As to why he left Constantinople: "I felt that not only this country but the nations of the world had a vital interest in Woodrow Wilson's re-election, for failing to endorse and vindicate him would be a blow to democracy."

After Morgenthau left Constantinople—by train for Berlin and eventually reaching home in late February 1916, repelled from his post by the bloody Turkish "campaign of race extermination" against Armenians that he'd described to Washington, and drawn by the reelection campaign then under way—he took on a brief, secret peace mission. This fruitless diplomatic exercise sent him to Gibraltar the following summer, to attempt to cobble together an agreement with the Turks guaranteeing Turkish territorial integrity in exchange for leaving the war. The initiative quickly failed.

Today Morgenthau is best remembered for his central role during the spring and summer of 1915 publicizing the Ottoman empire's continuing horrific dislocation and slaughter of Armenians, some of whom had taken up arms for Russia but most others persecuted solely because of their nationality and faith. "Unless something can be done," Morgenthau reported to Secretary Bryan on August 11 (in his telegram no. 924, following up several earlier reports), "to arrest this atrocious campaign, these people will be forced from their homes and herded like cattle into the arid and hostile wastes of the interior, where the greater number, possibly excepting those who in desperation embrace Mohammedanism, will doubtless perish by murder or slow starvation . . . I earnestly beg the Department to give this matter urgent and exhaustive consideration with a view to reaching a conclusion which may possibly have the effect of checking this Government and certainly provide opportunity for efficient relief which is not now permitted." One of his suggestions was the mass resettlement of Armenian refugees via a boatlift through the Panama Canal to California, Oregon,

FIGURE 5.4. Henry Morgenthau Sr. (1856–1946), c. 1910.

Morgenthau's family, mother (Babette), father (Lazarus), and ten siblings, immigrated to the United States from Baden when he was ten. Educated at the City College of New York and the Columbia University Law School, by his forties Morgenthau was already a wealthy New York City real estate investor. He met Woodrow Wilson in 1910 and soon became a committed supporter.

Today, Morgenthau is best remembered as the man who exposed and announced the Armenian genocide to the world, who believed (and wrote in his 1919 book, *Ambassador Morgenthau's Story*) that "the whole history of the human race contains no such horrible episode as [the Armenian genocide] . . . earlier massacres . . . have one feature that we can almost describe as an excuse: they were the product of religious fanaticism and most of the men and women who instigated them sincerely believed that they were devoutly serving their Maker . . . the men who really conceived [this] crime had no such motive. Practically all of them were atheists . . . with them the one motive was cold-blooded, calculating state policy."

The Library of Congress holds an extensive collection of Morgenthau's papers, including his correspondence, diaries, speeches, and family papers.

Source: Library of Congress, Prints and Photographs Division.

and Washington. None was implemented, and the Armenian genocide remains a fact of history disputed today only by Turkey.

By the time *North Carolina* and later *Tennessee* steamed into the Mediterranean, the initial naval excitement there was long since over. Early during the second week of August the only German combatant ships in that sea—the powerful German battle cruiser SMS *Goeben* and her escort, the light cruiser SMS *Breslau*—won their race from Pola, the Austro-Hungarian navy base at the top of the Adriatic Sea where *Goeben* had undergone urgent voyage repairs, via the Algerian coast to the safety of the Dardanelles against desultory opposition from the British Mediterranean Fleet. Robert Massie, in his excellent *Castles of Steel* (Random House [2003], 32), described the Royal Navy's effort in August to interdict the two German cruisers as a "debacle." That the two German ships made it safely to Constantinople on August 11 can be attributed to confusing instructions to its fleet from London, and to a very un-British timidity on the part of Admirals Milne (the fleet's commander in chief) and Troubridge (his deputy). Their shared failure was the first hint—the shattering defeat of the British West Indies Squadron off Coronel, Chile, marked by the loss of HMS *Good Hope* and HMS *Monmouth* with all hands, in November would be the second—that the coming war at sea was not necessarily going to go as the Royal Navy confidently expected it would. Troubridge was court-martialed for negligence, for his failure to pursue *Goeben* with his four cruisers. His subsequent acquittal acknowledged that his thin-skinned armored cruisers were in fact not a match for the big-gunned, heavily armored *Goeben*, but he never again was given a sea-going command.

On August 16, in a bit of sleight of hand that included the raising of the red Ottoman crescent flag on both German ships, now renamed *Yavuz Sultan Selim* and *Midilli*, and the outfitting of their Imperial German Navy crews with Turkey's distinctive red hat, the inverted flowerpot fez, *Goeben* and *Breslau* became part of the Turkish fleet.[25] The transformation was a clever riposte to the British seizure weeks earlier of two Turkish battleships just completed at shipyards in the United Kingdom, *Osman I* (originally ordered by Brazil as *Rio de Janeiro*) and *Reşadiye*. The pair's abrupt diversion to the Royal Navy (where they would soon be commissioned as HMS *Agincourt* and HMS *Erin*,

respectively) was ordered by the First Lord of the Admiralty, Winston Churchill, who was loath to export the powerful dreadnoughts as war loomed over
Europe. No compensation was paid to the Turks.

On September 23 Rear Admiral Wilhelm Souchon, the German com-
mander, passed through the same metamorphosis as had his ships *Goeben* and
Breslau, emerging from it as the new commander in chief of the Ottoman Navy.
He assumed a magnificent new title of office, Befelshaber der Schwimmenden
Turkischen Streitkräfte, or Commander of Floating Turkish Armed Forces.

Some ten weeks after Souchon took command, on October 29, with *Tennessee* now in the Aegean after having left Brindisi on October 19, his seven
ships in the Black Sea opened fire on Russian ports. It must have been over-
heard reports of this attack, broadcast by a civilian radio station in the Eastern Mediterranean, that prompted Decker to report to Washington that while
under way to Mytilene, he'd heard "that war had broken out between Russia
and Turkey and that France and England would probably join Russia." His
news was not wrong but premature. Several days later British and French ships
replied to Souchon's attack in the Black Sea, shelling Turkish forts at the bottom end of the Dardanelles. And a day after that, Wednesday, November 4,
Russia declared war on the Ottoman empire, as did Great Britain and France
one day later.

The anxieties of Americans stranded in Europe that urgently pulled *Tennessee*
and *North Carolina* across the Atlantic were nothing as compared to the near
panic in early August of Americans living in the Levant, in those Turkish cities and towns where the horrors of holy war were expected to erupt at any moment against members of the local American expatriate "colony." Beginning
August 5, these fears began to stream into Ambassador Henry Morgenthau's
embassy via overlapping reports from his consuls in Beirut (the shaky W. Stanley Hollis), Smyrna (George Horton and Leland Morris), Jerusalem (Otis
Hazebrook), Jaffa (Jacob Hardegg), and Alexandretta (agent H. E. Bishop, a
Standard Oil employee), and several times from these outposts directly to the
secretary of state—each consul pleading for the presence of American "battleships" to "prevent anarchy" or much worse. The hysteria peaked in early
autumn, after the October 1 Turkish abrogation of the "capitulations," which

for many decades had given Americans and other Western nationals extraterri-torial insulation from Turkish officials and Ottoman law, took away this special protection from privileged foreigners, and after the Turkish declaration of holy war. Hollis was especially nervous, reminding his superiors that the direct descendants of the notorious old tribe of "Assassins" lived in his area, and that they would like nothing better than an opportunity to attack, loot, and massacre non-Muslims.

Leland Morris's August 10 letter to the secretary of state on the situation in Smyrna, copying one sent August 8 to the embassy in Constantinople, and received in Washington on September 4, was typical of these alarms. "The immediate effect of the declaration of war by Germany was the stoppage of almost all exportation and the cessation of cash payments by the banks. Many people were caught unawares and today people of wealth are unable to obtain enough money for daily living expenses . . . From a business viewpoint the outbreak of war at this time means heavy loss to Smyrna. The fruit exportation was just about to commence. This fruit exportation is the principal source of wealth to Smyrna, and its loss will have disastrous consequences." But business aside,

> the [Turkish] order for a general call to arms has had a most deplorable effect . . . the moral effect on the population has been of the worst. This effect is particularly pronounced amongst the foreigners and especially the large English colony. No one will believe for an instant that this mobilization is not intended to end in an open declaration in favor of Germany and Austria . . . The entire English colony is in a state of anxiety and fear, which has a more or less sympathetic reaction upon the members of the American colony.
>
> If Turkey enters the conflict on the side of Germany, the situation will suddenly contain elements of the gravest danger to the entire Christian population. Therefore, I respectfully reiterate my opinion . . . concerning the advisability of having a warship here . . . Practically every member of the American colony has asked that a warship be sent.[26]

Five days later Stanley Hollis, in Beirut, echoed Morris. "The only thing which can save the situation and preserve order and prevent anarchy is the prompt arrival of some American men-of-war," he wrote to Bryan. "A feeling of insecurity combined with nervous expectancy prevails, and not only would some definite news regarding the movement of American men-of-war be gratefully received by practically all classes of the population here, but the mere receipt of such authoritative information concerning the approximate arrival here of some American men-of-war would have a wonderfully tranquilizing effect here."[27]

After two weeks of such increasingly shrill alarms, on August 19, with *Tennessee* in port in England only two days, Secretary of State William Bryan told Morgenthau that the "United States Government is considering sending warships to Turkish waters, but before doing so deems it advisable to sound European powers as to such action." (The Russians soon told the American ambassador in Moscow, "the more the better." His Majesty's Government, for its part, also "would welcome the presence of American warships on the coast of Asia Minor." France agreed. Finally, on September 14, Ambassador Gerard reported that Germany, too, thought "it would be a good thing if [a] neutral warship should be sent to protect foreigners [on the] Turkish coast.") Before he had further news from Washington, Morgenthau told Secretary Bryan, "Unrest is constantly increasing due to fears of war with Russia and expected internal trouble," while reassuring the secretary that he was "personally not in the least alarmed and feel that I can protect the colony."

On August 28 Bryan wired Morgenthau that *North Carolina* would sail the next day from Falmouth to Turkish waters. *Tennessee* followed some five weeks later. The expectation that, their mission in and around the English Channel done, the two cruisers would soon come home had swiftly been proved naïve. The next questions to be raised came from the navy: what would *North Carolina* and *Tennessee* actually be doing in the Levant, and for how long could and would they do that?

A first formal attempt by the navy to get an answer from the State Department to the question of "how long?" came at the end of November, two weeks after *Tennessee*'s notorious incident at Smyrna (about which, see below). Noting the limitations imposed by the Turks on the freedom of navigation of the American cruisers, the navy asked for Morgenthau's opinion as to whether one of the two might not be returned to the United States, explaining that both cruisers had been sent to Europe hastily and needed docking and repair. Three days later, December 3, Morgenthau told Bryan in response that "we are now entering most critical period"; citing a "grave danger" of local authorities misusing power in dealing with American educational and charitable institutions, he recommended leaving both ships in the Eastern Mediterranean.

That said, the ambassador would prove to be of two minds about having these ships with their assertive captains and big guns steaming around offshore of his turf. On December 12, in a wide-ranging telegram (his no. 148; it took nearly three days to be delivered), Morgenthau told the secretary of state that "this government is fast drifting into anarchy . . . Time has arrived for Americans to consider their departure." He went on to reveal some anxiety about the state of mind of his consuls, especially Hollis, and recommended that they not be "entrusted with any power over the cruiser, and as I shall not assume the responsibility of sending a cruiser to any port but Beirut you might recall one of them after the *Tennessee* has been to Alexandria . . . *In my opinion the chances of injuries that may result from misuse of cruisers are far greater than protection they might render* [my emphasis]. I strongly favor retain one cruiser at Beirut but should like the captain instructed he must not permit himself to be involved in any incident . . . and that cruiser is there for refuge and moral influence."

To be available for "refuge," of course, is what had sent *Maine* to the harbor of Havana sixteen years earlier. How, exactly, evacuating frightened Americans from Beirut to a cruiser off the coast would be done wasn't described, but that same idea is what had sent *Tennessee* off Smyrna to Vourla nearly a month before, with consequences that Morgenthau regretted.

Bryan's response said nothing about the ships, but he did say President Wilson agreed that "Americans should be advised to leave Turkey whenever [Morgenthau thought] it would be unsafe for them to remain." The matter should be handled "very guardedly and confidentially" to "avoid frightening friends and . . . attracting public attention."

While Decker eavesdropped on what he thought was news of the outbreak of war, he was racing from Beirut to Lesbos's capital city, Mytilene, in response to a request from Morgenthau that "one of the ships [meaning *Tennessee* or *North Carolina*] proceed direct to Mytilene and to remain there to protect Americans who may desire to leave Smyrna in case of any trouble." Mytilene, on the east side of its island and roughly north of the mouth of the Gulf of Izmir, was one place for *Tennessee* to wait while whatever might be going on in the city, 85 nautical miles away at the far end of the L-shaped gulf, percolated. A better one would be actually inside the Gulf, and that's where Morgenthau, permission from the Turks received, would send *Tennessee* next.

Ground transportation to Smyrna for the captain had been offered by the Turks, but Decker had rejected it, choosing instead to move from Vourla to the port in *Tennessee*'s biggest steam launch. He left *Tennessee* at 8:37 a.m. Just under an hour later, with *Tennessee* now more than seven miles astern, the launch came under fire from the shore. After three shells splashed around the launch—described by Bowen as "well-placed misses," and by Jessop as leaving "no room for doubt that an attempt to destroy was being made"—*Tennessee* prepared to get under way and manned her guns. Had she fired on Smyrna, which she soon threatened to do, the shelling likely would have thrust the United States into war against the Turks.

As Lieutenant Commander Jessop, the senior officer on board in Decker's absence, described it, at around 9:30 loud gunfire was heard on board *Tennessee*. The officer of the deck then reported heavy projectiles hitting the water close to Decker's steamer, close enough to indicate the battery was trying to sink the launch. Next, with Decker's boat now out of sight behind Clazomenae Island, the clatter of machine gun fire was heard on the ship. At this point Jessop responded appropriately, albeit very inconveniently for Morgenthau: he had prepared fires lit in four boilers, manned the main battery (*Tennessee*'s big 10 inch guns), and started preparations to sweep for mines ahead of the ship when she began to move toward the channel. At the same time he radioed a message to Consul Horton, translated from Jessop's diplomatic French,

> The American Consul General in Smyrna,
> The commanding officer left this morning to visit officials in Smyrna, and their fortress fired on him. Inform the governor general that a repeat of this will cause Tennessee to advance into a position to bombard the forts.

At 10:45 the ship radioed the launch to "please report safe arrival by cable. Have steam up." Decker responded a minute later, "Everything O.K." At 11:50, after several unavailing conversations with sentries at an outpost on the southern shore, the launch left to return to the ship, arriving there at 12:50 p.m.

The morning's dangerous incident prompted an urgent telegram the same day from Ambassador Morgenthau to Decker via Horton. (Horton would go on to serve a total of nine years during two postings in the city, but the focus of his career and his sympathies was Greece, not Turkey.) "It has come to my knowledge," Morgenthau wrote remarkably mildly, "that a visit to Smyrna has been undertaken by a naval officer and that he has threatened to bombard the fortifications. Kindly send me details of this incident immediately. The Embassy was officially informed that the port is closed some short time ago." Actually six days earlier.

Horton soon replied from on board the cruiser.

Commander Decker desires to give you following details. Commander was coming to Smyrna on his steam launch to make the usual official visits. He knew that the port was closed to battleships and to merchant vessels but had no information that there was any objection to the launch of the Tennessee going to Smyrna. En route three solid shots were fired on the launch from the shore, one of them just missing the launch. Upon this, the officer left in command of the Tennessee telegraphed me to inform the Governor General that a repetition of this line of conduct would cause the Tennessee to advance to a place from which it could bombard the fortifications. After cessation of fire the Commander communicated with the authorities on shore. They informed him that it was forbidden to continue to Smyrna and the Commander thereupon returned to the Tennessee.

Early the next morning, as instructed by Morgenthau, *Tennessee* steamed for Scio, on the island of Khios ("Chios" and Greek today), some six and a half hours away across the Khios (now "Cesme") Strait and away from any possible trouble. On January 23, 1915, the *New York Times* explained *Tennessee*'s presence offshore of the city and described the incident mildly under headlines that read: "Clears Up Smyrna Incident, Capt. Decker's Mail Report Shows Turks Were Blameless." Daniels's amplifying statement quoted by the *Times* seemed to accept the Turks' explanation, that the shots were meant as a warning to the launch that she was steaming into mined waters, "fired to prevent her from proceeding into danger."

The following week, on January 31, the *Times* explained to its readers that the US Navy, then ranked third among the world's naval powers, was expected

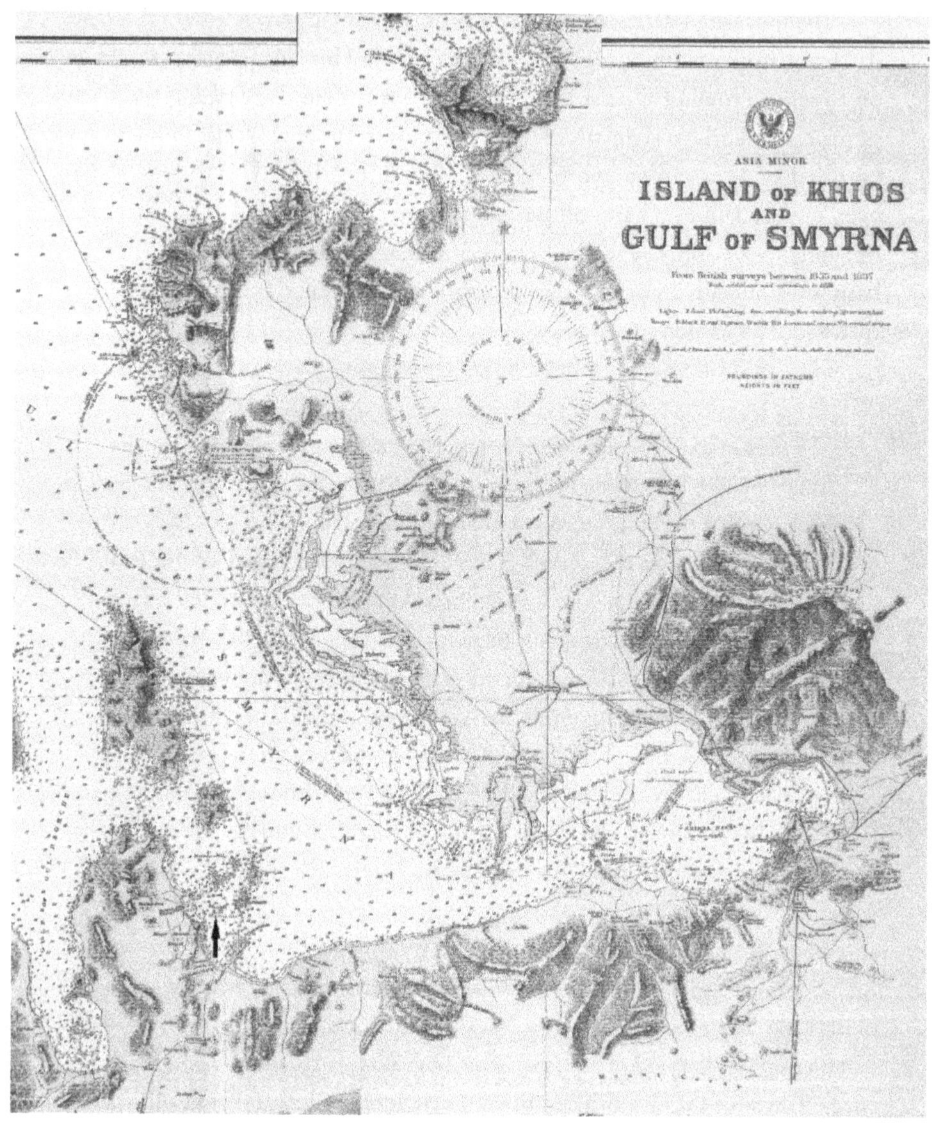

CHART 5.1. Detail from HO Chart No. 5978, "Island of Khios and Gulf of Smyrna from British Surveys between 1835 and 1837, with additions and corrections to 1898" (Washington, DC: Hydrographic Office, March 1915).

Soon after her arrival in the Eastern Mediterranean in early November 1914, *Tennessee* received instructions from Ambassador Morgenthau to anchor to the west of Smyrna, in Vourla Roads, some twenty nautical miles from the closed city, and not far from the coastal railroad line that connected Vourla to Smyrna. There the cruiser could conveniently board fleeing Americans should evacuation of Smyrna be required.

Vourla Roads lies on this chart slightly south of due west from Smyrna amid the Marathussae Islands cluster, at the far end of the melon and vegetable fields and fig tree orchards that lined both sides of the water approaches to the port (see arrow). Smyrna, beyond the mined narrows of the Gulf of Smyrna, here hugs the south shore of the harbor between Mount Pagus and Daragaz Point. A companion chart, HO 3922 ("Archipelago, Northern Sheet," February 1915), showed plans of Smyrna and Vourla anchorages, and eleven other places.

Tennessee's only real excitement during her deployment to Europe came in the roads on the morning of November 16, 1914, when a Turkish shore battery fired several times on her 50-foot launch as Captain Decker, in dress uniform, headed from the ship into the narrows for the city—entirely in Turkish domestic waters, toward a city he knew to be closed to shipping of every type—to pay the usual but apparently now unwelcome courtesy calls on the Turkish governor, Rahmi Bey, and other local officials. Later Becker was careful to establish that, excepting his officer's dress sword, the launch was unarmed.

Becker's boat officer, Lieutenant (junior grade) Norton, was navigating the launch between ship and city, not on this chart but on the essentially identical British Admiralty Chart No. 1645 of January 1893.

Source: Library of Congress Geography and Maps Division.

soon to fall to fourth place behind the French, with the Japanese "coming along strong behind." Great Britain and Germany stood first (with 2.7 million tons) and second (1.3 million tons), respectively. "Within a period of less than six years," the paper continued soberly, "the United States will have dropped from second to fourth place among naval powers."

FIGURE 6.1. "Departure of Jaffa Refugees."

Finished with her gold delivery and English Channel shuttle, in mid-autumn 1914 *Tennessee* steamed from Rotterdam to Brindisi, Italy, and then on to Beirut, a move prompted in part by the anxieties of the Western expatriate community in Ottoman Palestine, but also by agitated diplomatic reporting from the American ambassador in Constantinople, Henry Morgenthau, warning of Turkish persecution of Armenian Christians, and potentially of now-stateless Jews, suspected by the Turks of favoring the allies over the Central Powers. More than simply showing the flag offshore, the cruiser soon took on an unexpected mission: moving fearful and usually impoverished refugees from Palestine to sanctuary in Egypt, which had been under British military control and martial law since November 2, 1914, and with the khedive then in self-imposed exile in Constantinople, officially a British protectorate after December 17.

Soon after the start of the war, commercial steamship service began to collapse in the Mediterranean, reflecting both the growing risk of operations and the effectiveness of the Anglo-French naval blockades at the Mediterranean's exits, and also across the narrow Strait of Otranto. For a while, through autumn 1914 and into the winter of 1914–15, tramp steamer traffic continued sporadically in the Eastern Mediterranean, while vessels of the Greek-owned, American-flagged Archipelago American Steamship Company (all named after American states) also sailed more or less regularly along the Levantine coast. With the termination of scheduled Italian service in the Eastern Mediterranean the following spring, expatriates and other residents in Ottoman Palestine fully realized their isolation and vulnerability, but anxieties about their safety had been building since soon after the war began.

This photograph by Wesley F. Moore shows the departure on February 14, 1915, from Jaffa of one such emergency evacuation. *Tennessee* would arrive in Alexandria three days later (after shuttling between Jaffa and Haifa), her eighth time in that Egyptian port since mid-December!

The *New York Times* estimated that already by mid-January 1915 some 6,000 such refugees had been relocated to relative safety. According to typed passenger manifests attached to her deck log, between December 1914 and June 1915 *Tennessee* alone transported seven shiploads of stricken refugees, 5,400 of them, citizens of all ages and from some dozen different nations. Most refugees appear on these rosters under a last name and nationality only, and many apparently traveled without identity papers of any kind.

Other refugees were carried by USS *North Carolina*, USS *Des Moines*, and the collier USS *Caesar*. A more complete count by Stanford Shaw in 1991 suggested that the total number of refugees delivered to Alexandria by the improvised American task force (also supported by the collier *Vulcan*) might have been more than 11,000, moved in sixteen separate cruises. The Israel Genealogical Society puts that number at a precise 11,277 and is the source for the identification of *Fiorino* as the first ship to move refugees to Alexandria, arriving there on December 18. *Tennessee* and her consorts moved these thousands—expelled from their homes in Palestine—"gratuitously," meaning for free.

Source: Naval History and Heritage Command.

Chapter Six

"Its Memory Be Blessed
for All Eternity"

The outbreak of the war found about 100,000 Jews in Palestine, most of whom had been dependent upon relatives and the pious Jews of Europe for their subsistence. This aid was abruptly cut off . . .

When Turkey entered the war, she gave the choice to the Jews in Palestine who were nationals of the enemy countries to become Ottoman subjects or leave; about 600 Jews were expelled, and an additional 7,000 voluntarily departed.

The plight of the Jewish population was further aggravated by the Government requisition of grain, petroleum, vehicles and beasts of burden, and by the visitation of a plague of locusts.

—*Ninth Annual Report of the American Jewish Committee,*
November 1916, 22–23

When in 1928 the third great locust swarm of the twentieth century arrived in Palestine and neighboring Syria, people were evidently better prepared to control the voracious migrating grasshoppers than they'd been when similar swarms arrived in 1915 or in 1900, or for that matter in all the years during and since biblical times. In the Old Testament's Book of Joel, swarming locusts ("a mighty army without number") were described as leaving behind them only destroyed wheat and barley, dried-up grapevines, and withered trees: "That which was left by the creeping locust hath the swarming locust eaten, and that which was left by the swarming locust hath the grass locust eaten; and that which was left by the grass locust hath the corn locust eaten." According to the prophet Joel, it was left to mankind only to weep and howl.

The September 1928 issue of *Popular Science Monthly* reported that the "invading host of locusts was driven back by flame guns and poison sprays. Since ancient times these insects have periodically ravaged the Palestine crops, bringing famine. This year scientists and military men rushed mobile field units to meet the enemy. First, powerful portable lamps were used to attract the insects into traps. Then the flame guns and poison sprays were brought into action, slaying the insects and their unhatched eggs." *Popular Science* said nothing about how effective these new weapons actually were, and, after several paragraphs about locusts, it moved on to items reporting on a meeting of the League of Nations Health Organization, and on Guglielmo Marconi's improved methods of radio beam transmission.

Efficacy aside, neither flame guns nor poison sprays (for use against insects, anyway) had been available during 1915; nor, apparently, were storks, locusts' usual predator, about in sufficient numbers to provide any natural control over the swarm that darkened the skies and coated the ground between Jerusalem and Damascus that second year of the Great War.[1] Photographer Lewis Larsson of the American Colony in Jerusalem took many photos of the 1915 swarm—among them pictures of the Garden of Gethsemane, lush before and devastated after the locusts passed—that could have been illustrations in the prophet Joel's book. In 1915, despite hasty establishment of a locust control commission by the Turkish Fourth Army's dictatorial commander, General Mehmet Djemal, and its requirement that every male between the ages of fifteen and sixty living in Jerusalem, Beirut, or Damascus collect 20 kilograms (nearly 45 pounds!) of the insects and their eggs or pay a fine, control was again ineffective. Although the winter grain crops were largely harvested when the swarm materialized and so escaped destruction, vineyards, olive groves, orange and apricot orchards, and vegetable gardens suffered terribly, and so did the people dependent on these foodstuffs for nourishment and their livelihood.

But in 1915, a year into the Great War, those living in Ottoman Palestine were suffering from more than the current plague of locusts. Among the resident expatriates, Jews from the Balkans and Russia, who'd fled persecution in their homelands during the prior three decades, arguably suffered the most.

Most of the fighting and dying during World War I happened in a very small part of the globe, a space barely forty degrees of latitude and longitude square . . . a patch on the surface of Eurasia often fought over, but hardly big enough to rank this as a global conflict in other than European eyes. What made this a "world war" was less where it was fought than the distant origins of many men brought into the fight from the colonies of the principal combatants (more than a million from India alone, for example). Putting aside the war at sea, the war's ground combat theaters included the principal European fronts, Turkey and the Levant, and, on a much smaller scale, East Africa.

Were it not for the colorful and near-mythic figure of "Lawrence of Arabia," personified by actor Peter O'Toole, supported by a brilliant cast, in a very long film directed by David Lean—a film released more than fifty years ago and restored and rereleased every decade since—it's possible that many people today would know nothing about World War I in the Middle East. That despite T. E. Lawrence's autobiographical *Seven Pillars of Wisdom* (published in some half-dozen notably different first editions during the 1920s), which tells something very loosely like the same story as the screenplay, and remains in print today. A more reliable history of the war and a more readable biography of the man can be found in war correspondent Scott Anderson's *Lawrence in Arabia: War, Deceit, Imperial Folly and the Making of the Modern Middle East* (Doubleday, 2013).

World War I in the Levant had several focal points. One, in Arabia, involved the Ottomans and the Arabs, the latter seeking their independence from the debilitated Turkish empire—Lawrence's war. Another focused on the defense of the Suez Canal, British since 1875, and the artery of the best route to India, against a Turkish assault. (That attack, when it came in February 1915, was repulsed with almost laughable ease.)[2] A third was in the Dardanelles, where Germans and Turks cooperated successfully to keep closed the back door to Anglo-French resupply of their Russian ally through the Black Sea. A fourth involved France and England, each maneuvering for postwar position on the ground and for access to influence and oil. Yet another was a campaign by Zionists to carve a homeland for Jews out of lands sacred to all three Abrahamic religions, successful eventually only after the near-destruction of European Jewry during World War II. And finally, there was one in Ottoman Palestine, where the Turks took the opportunity the war presented to renounce international agreements regarding the status of foreigners and aggressively to purge nonbelievers from coastal *sanjaks* (districts), with the goal being to "Turkify" the country (Morgenthau's word), to strengthen political control, suppress minorities, and restore Muslim orthodoxy. Many thousands of these resident infidels were Jews, the earliest of whom had come to the Holy Land in the 1880s from central and southeastern Europe; they were followed by a second wave of refugees a generation later from Russia, fleeing pogroms and repression.

On September 8, 1914, the Ottoman government in Constantinople announced the end of its "capitulations" to foreign governments. These were centuries-old agreements that until then gave to these governments legal control over their citizens living as expatriates in the empire, and the authority to defend these controls and their citizens' status by force. (One such agreement had been reached with the United States in 1830, coupled to a trade accord and to US technical assistance in the reconstruction of the Ottoman Navy, destroyed at Navarino four years earlier.) Suddenly, those holding Austro-Hungarian or Russian passports, soon open to classification as "belligerent nationals," became subject to deportation, internment, or (a day later when general mobilization was announced) to forcible conscription. Deportations back to Russia began in October but apparently were halted the next month following a protest by Ambassador Morgenthau.

It's likely that the first of an estimated 11,300 Jews with foreign citizenship who were to succeed in escaping were the 698 on board an Italian steamer, *Fiorino*, from Jaffa to Port Said in mid-December 1914. The rest followed during the next nine months. *Tennessee*'s first movement of refugees came the day after that Christmas; the cruiser's passengers from Jaffa to Alexandria included 21 French nuns fleeing Jerusalem among 475 other refugees. All 496 were landed ashore in Egypt on December 29.

"The subject of the Jews and their treatment in Palestine has been an interesting one to me," Decker later explained to a lecture audience. "The Zionist movement was not approved by all the leading Jews, but the work done by the Zionists in Palestine enriched the world. They made the desert to blossom, and people that will do this are entitled to their reward." Decker's speech echoed what he'd written to the secretary of the navy on February 15, 1915, in a "Report on the Conditions in Palestine with Reference to Zionism," where he identified Zionism to be "undoubtedly one of the great movements of the world." It was a remarkable sentiment in an era when polite antisemitism was generally fashionable in the upper levels of American society, government, and business. In 1913 that prejudice had managed to derail Louis Brandeis's appointment to Wilson's cabinet as attorney general.

At the end of February, after six refugee deliveries to Alexandria (there would be another two), Captain Decker and his crew were honored by the grand rabbi of the Comité d'Assistance aux Réfugiés de Syrie et de Palestine, Rafaello Della Pergola, with a small silver plaque, and words of generous praise and gratitude. A few days later Secretary Daniels and Secretary of State Lansing separately relayed to Decker appreciative notes from the French ambassador and also from Brandeis, then an attorney in private practice but confirmed the next year (after a nasty four-month battle in Congress) to a seat on the Supreme Court, where he remained until his death in 1941.

Her months-long humanitarian mission nearly finished in early summer 1915, *Tennessee* left Beirut for Jaffa (128 miles away, now Tel Aviv-Yafo, Israel) on June 26 with the ship's band playing "Home, Sweet Home," with a slender, 610 foot-long pennant flying to mark her homecoming. The *New York Times* described it as "the longest that ever trailed astern a modern man of war." Just before departure, reportedly, the crew sang their own version of the popular song "It's a Long Way to Tipperary." The first and last verses of the parody,

> Back to New York City where I was bred and born,
> Back to New York City, where they taught me right from wrong.
> Of all the countries I have seen, have nothing on Broadway.
> I long to drink my crème de menthe in a New York cabaret.
>
> Since we've performed our duties in these Oriental lands,
> I hope to see us sailing soon for dear old Yankee land,
> For there my friends are waiting to greet me by the hand,
> And I'll surely appreciate New York town when I get there again.

On June 30 her classmate, the cruiser USS *Washington*, arrived at Alexandria to relieve *Tennessee* in the Mediterranean. In turn, three days later and still flying her mammoth pennant, *Tennessee* left Alexandria for Barcelona, six days to the west, after disembarking her tenth and last load of refugees and taking on a thousand tons of coal. A second leg toward home.

Her passage through the Mediterranean and across the Atlantic was slow at

11.5 knots. "The ordinary cruising speed of this ship is assumed to be 12.5 to 15 knots," Decker's engineer, Bowen, had reported to Decker six months ago. Because of the drag of *Tennessee*'s foul bottom, he'd explained, she had to develop an extra 1,087 shaft horsepower to make 12.5 knots, and 2,658 extra to make 15. The cost of that additional horsepower was paid in "extra consumption of coal, larger steaming watches, more wear and tear on boilers and machinery, more labor expended in cleaning and overhauling boilers, and conversely less labor available to keep the plant in condition."

Out of Barcelona on July 15 after six days in port, and through Fayal, westernmost of the central Azores Islands, in two days not long thereafter, *Tennessee* finally entered the port of New York on the last day of July 1915. Several days short of one year after suddenly leaving New York, *Tennessee* was finally back at home. Next, Decker thought, would come extended liberty for the crew, fumigation for vermin and rats, hull cleaning, and major engineering maintenance before his ship deployed back to sea.

Three weeks after *Tennessee* reached home, on August 25, the Department of State received Morgenthau's telegram no. 374 (inexplicably nearly a month after its transmission). In it Morgenthau, who'd had issues with Decker throughout, was effusive in his praise of *Tennessee*'s services to Jews and other refugees. "I also wish to speak," he wrote to Lansing,

> in the highest terms of the services rendered earlier in the year by the *Tennessee* to the Jewish and other refugees it transported from Jaffa to Alexandria. Many expressions of grateful appreciation of what was done for these people have since reached me, and I cannot speak too highly of the kindly assistance given them by Captain Benton C. Decker and his officers and men. The use of our cruisers for this purpose has meant much extra work and inconvenience for their officers and crews. But they have satisfied an urgent need, and . . . their ready and gracious help to those in anxiety and distress will long be remembered by their grateful beneficiaries.[3]

Months before that, in early May in Alexandria, passed assistant surgeon Renier Straeton, USN, *Tennessee*'s medical officer, had reported to Decker formally in writing—and probably unnecessarily—that their ship was "infested with cock-roaches and bed bugs. The bed-bugs are especially obnoxious, being generally distributed throughout the living quarters of the officers and chief petty-officers quarters. Efforts to exterminate them have not been effective." Worse, Straeton wrote, "rats are overrunning the ship and they have been a constant source of worry to the Medical Officer, on account of the prevalent rat-infection of plague ashore in this port." The presence of such wildlife afloat was usually credited to hitchhikers in the ship's stores brought on board, and to lying alongside wharves in port with lines ashore.

The original plan was to fumigate *Tennessee* by burning sulfur in her living spaces as prescribed in chapter 7 ("Disinfection on the Ship") of Dr. James Gatewood's monograph, *Naval Hygiene* (P. Blakiston's Son and Co., 1909). Medical inspector Gatewood's enormous book, 779 pages long and generously illustrated, was more than a handbook. The publication of *Naval Hygiene* was simultaneously proof of the new navy's increasingly serious scientific interest in maintaining crew health—Gatewood was an instructor in the navy's medical school—and of the rise in professional status of ship's surgeons, who through the nineteenth century had been seen as little more than tradesmen afloat with medical instrument toolkits. The index to that single chapter listed fifty-seven topics, everything from "The vital causes of disease" to "The health of the port."

In fact, not until September 7, after *Tennessee* had first lifted marines to Haiti twice (first an infantry regiment from Philadelphia that left August 10 for Port au Prince and Cap Haitien, and second, on August 26, an artillery battalion with its guns from Annapolis and Philadelphia) did the navy finally find time to rid *Tennessee* of her many four- and six-legged stowaways. At the government quarantine station at Reedy Island, public health officers redirected *Tennessee* to the navy yard, explaining that sulfur fumigation would damage the ship's electrical systems, something Gatewood had said nothing about.

And so, after *Tennessee* tied up at the wharf in the navy yard's back basin the next afternoon, the complex fumigation process began, not according to Gatewood but instead using hydrogen cyanide gas. This procedure had been developed by Dr. Norman Roberts, one of five medical doctors working in the busy Division of Fumigation and Disinfection of the Port of New York. He'd developed the technique for using the deadly gas in arriving immigrant transports, a procedure performed many times a year at the nation's busiest port of entry.

The driver behind the search for the most effective, economical, and safe ship fumigation procedure was not the fairly limited needs of the US Navy but rather the flood of immigrant ships into ports on the East Coast, carrying with them presumably unwashed and unhealthy hordes looking to start new lives in the cities, towns, and rural places of America. (The danger inherent in their movement probably peaked during 1910–11, when cholera attacked Naples, the principal port from which emigrants left southern Europe for the United States. The Neapolitan city government and the national government in Rome deliberately concealed news of the epidemic, fearing that American authorities would obstruct the profitable business.) The flow into the United States continued until restrictive laws of the 1920s slowed immigration to a trickle.

By late 1915 the US Public Health Service had identified and evaluated the effectiveness and economics of three familiar fumigants: sulfur dioxide (Gatewood's choice, also the choice of the Treasury Department's quarantine regulations), carbon monoxide ("funnel gas"), and hydrocyanic acid gas, Roberts's agent. The easy winner was the last: deadly to insects and rodents, relatively cheap, and easy to use carefully.

Tennessee had been tied up since midafternoon on September 8, 1915, at the wharf in Philadelphia Navy Yard's back basin with all her doors and hatches shut, for fumigation. To look at her from ashore it would seem like nothing was happening on board at all. She appeared, through September 9 and 10 at Philadelphia, almost perfectly inert. *Tennessee's* fires were out and cold; her generators shut down. (Electrical power for lighting came through cables snaking aboard the ship from the shore.) Even the air inside the hull, especially the air, wasn't moving: *Tennessee's* ventilators and fire room uptakes were closed; fans and forced air blowers stilled; stacks capped; gun doors dogged shut. Some two hundred members of her crew were on leave; hundreds more were on liberty. Even *Tennessee's* brig prisoners were elsewhere, held temporarily on board the transport USS *Hancock*. (The two ships, *Tennessee* and *Hancock*, would be in port together again late next summer under less happy circumstances.)

Only five men were inside the hull during fumigation: Dr. Roberts, the Public Health Service's fumigation expert; Drs. Robertson and Beddoe from *Tennessee's* medical department; and two unnamed first-class petty officers, presumably volunteers selected on the basis of unknown criteria, speed on foot surely being one. Each had a preplanned route through the sealed ship to the main deck, passing on the way his share of the 10 quart cedar buckets—400 in all, every waxed bucket holding a measured dose of water and sulfuric acid—and dropping into each a bagged single ounce of sodium cyanide, as he jogged past heading for open air. In an hour over midnight on September 10 all five were done and on deck. Behind them hydrogen cyanide gas fumes spread through the ship, killing everything alive. When it was all over, Decker reported "excellent results" to the navy secretariat.

Bottom cleaning and an overhaul remained before *Tennessee* would be ready for sea. Her hull below the waterline was so foul, Decker had reported to the Navy Department on January 26, that its drag cost the ship nearly 1.5 knots of speed at cruise. Making turns for 15 knots, *Tennessee* on the way home from the Mediterranean actually made good just over 13.

Captain Decker's tour in command of *Tennessee* in the Mediterranean had been a triumph, prompting a shower of letters of appreciation, among them a letter from Aristide Briand, the French prime minister, expressing gratitude for the cruiser's good work in the Eastern Mediterranean, a performance naturally attributed to his leadership. Another came from a local source:

November 14, 1915

Dear Captain,

On behalf of the Committee of Refugees in the name of the Jewish Community of Alexandria, and in the name of entire Jewery, I have the honor to present you with this small souvenir as a token of our profound gratitude for the work of love and pity accomplished by you in favour of our unhappy brethren expelled from Palestine.

May God bless you, the officers and the crew of this glorious ship. May He pour out his benedictions on the Great Nation on whose behalf you have accomplished this admirable and humane act, which has poured out glory and triumph for the cause of Justice.

This glory has already been acquired by your flag—the shadow of which has protected exiled women, children and the aged. Your deeds shall eternally be engraved on the hearts of our people. Your devoted care and noble thoughts shall form the object of our songs and legend will praise them in the History of Israel.[4]

FIGURE 7.1. USS *Memphis* on shore at Santo Domingo, August 29, 1916.

Memphis's deck log described the swift destruction of the ship that Tuesday afternoon. At 4:10 "gigantic swells" began breaking across her decks while at anchor in the open roadstead some 460 yards from the nearest land, in 7.25 fathoms with 70 fathoms of anchor chain out. Ten minutes later, pressed by great waves, she began to drag her anchor west-northwest toward the shore. "Each great roller," wrote the officer of the deck, "picked the ship up and threw her hundreds of feet."

At 4:33 the big ship touched bottom for the first time. *Memphis*'s attempt to get under way three minutes later, full speed astern on the starboard engine and ahead on the port engine, failed due to low steam pressure, and minutes later the engine room log recorded that "heavy seas were coming into the engine rooms."

Memphis ended up just before 5:00 p.m., high and hard aground, displaced about 1,250 yards from her anchorage into only 19 feet of water forward and 12 feet aft. At the time, before her bottom was crushed, she'd been drawing some 27.5 feet. There the cruiser lay, listing 5 degrees to port, her bow just 40 feet from shore. An engineering survey soon concluded the ship couldn't be salvaged.

The news of this catastrophe in the Caribbean Sea reached Washington just before midnight; coincidentally, earlier that same day President Wilson had signed into law the munificent Naval Act of 1916, promising the navy an astonishing 143 new combatant ships: 10 battleships, 16 cruisers, 50 destroyers, and 67 submarines! The act's generosity went far toward satisfying the president's somewhat ambiguous call the previous February 3 before an assembly of the Businessmen's League in St. Louis, Missouri. New York City's *Tribune* and *Evening Post* reporters both quoted Wilson as asking for "incomparably the greatest navy in the world." Skeptics present thought they'd heard him ask instead for something much less sweeping, a meaningless request for "incomparably the *most adequate . . .*," and that's how the published, official transcript of his speech to the first session of the 64th Congress records what he said. Weeks later Senator Benjamin "Pitchfork" Tillman, then chairman of the Senate's Naval Affairs Committee, was quoted in the *Tribune* as saying Wilson must have been "drunk on applause" to have gone so far. Tillman, from South Carolina, supported a navy *third* to none, and second only to Great Britain's. The photograph was probably taken by Carl M. J. von Zielinski, who is known to have taken others very like it. In August 1916 he was ten months away from retirement as the US vice consul in charge at Santo Domingo.

Source: Naval History and Heritage Command.

Chapter Seven

USS *Memphis* (CA-10)

Welcome to you Memphis and Good-bye Old Tennessee.
Good-bye to you Old Tennessee, Good-bye from those who love you
And in the list of naval ships there's no name shines above you . . .
So three cheers for you Tennessee from out of a thousand hearts
Just remember, though you're leaving, our friendship never parts.
Welcome to you Memphis, a good name yours shall be
Just keep up in the future the past of the Tennessee.
You've come to a grand old cruiser who has never known a shame
Although she's sorry to lose her own, she is proud to bear your name.
So welcome to you, Memphis and good-bye old Tennessee
And a thousand cheers to both of you the Memphis = Tennessee.

—Poem by boatswain's mate W. E. Gerhart, USN,
Decker Papers, Hoover Institution Archive

Captain Benton Decker remained in command of *Tennessee* for nineteen months, until January 29, 1916, moving to USS *Washington*—soon to be renamed *Seattle*—the same day, when he and Captain Edward Beach, the latter eighteen numbers on the lineal list Decker's junior, exchanged ships and commands in Port au Prince. Orders for the swap had been issued in Washington, DC, just before Christmas.

The unusual, almost causal, exchange was a personal convenience to both men, and supported by the flag officer riding in *Washington*, Rear Admiral William Caperton, USN, commanding the Atlantic Fleet's cruiser squadron for another six months or so. As described by Ensign Justin Miller in *Tennessee*'s deck log, the change of command, a ritual usually heavy with pomp and ceremony, seems to have been almost perfunctory. At 8:00 a.m. in the harbor of Port au Prince Captain Beach of USS *Washington* came on board *Tennessee* for forty-five minutes, for what could have only been a walkaround, a stroll. Approaching 9:30, Decker left *Tennessee* to glance in turn at USS *Washington*; by 10:15, barely forty-five minutes later, he was back aboard. At 2:00 p.m., "an inspection of the ship was made by the Captain accompanied by Captain E. L. Beach, U.S. Navy. At 2:25 all hands were called aft and Captain Benton C. Decker, U.S. Navy was officially detached, and Captain E. L. Beach, U.S. Navy, took command."

In early June, after little more than four months in command of *Washington* and less than two years at sea since the start of the war in Europe, Decker asked for duty ashore. He learned on June 16 from Assistant Secretary Roosevelt that he was to be sent to the Naval War College, and left the ship ten days later for shore duty in Newport, Rhode Island, where he would remain until ordered to Spain the following May. USS *Washington*, for the next ten months under the command of Decker's successor, Captain DeWitt Blamer, USN, was renamed *Seattle* that November. (Like Decker, Captain Blamer knew something about shipwrecks. He'd been an ensign on board the nearly new protected cruiser USS *Charleston* when, during her first cruise, she went aground on the Guinapak Rocks off Luzon in the Philippines on November 2, 1899, and had to be abandoned. Remarkably, no lives were lost.)[1]

Beach's short letter to the secretary of the navy reporting his assumption of command of *Tennessee* reflected the informality of it all. He was, he wrote, "satisfied with conditions" on board his new ship, although the usual drills "were not carried out on account of the [unexplained] exigencies of the service," and no inspection of the ship below the main deck had been made. Beach accepted command "subject to future inspection."

Tennessee quickly became Captain Beach's favorite of the fifteen ships he rode in during his long navy career. "I loved that magnificent ship," he wrote in his autobiography, "even if later her name was changed, and she became a desolate wreck."[2]

The highlight of Beach's short tour in command of *Tennessee* was a three-month cruise that began in the early spring of 1916, transporting a senior US government delegation to ports in South America to follow up on the agenda of the First Pan American Financial Conference, held in Washington the year before. That conference's broad purpose had been to reorder trade and investment relations in the hemisphere in the face of capital and shipping shortages and of other market distortions, all fallout from the war in Europe. Secretary of the Treasury William McAdoo, leading the delegation, and the bankers and captains of American industry he took with him on board all saw business opportunities for the United States in these disturbances. In fact, the expected opportunities didn't materialize, and the delegation came home empty-handed.

On March 8, five weeks after the Decker-Beach exchange of command, with Beach on the bridge, *Tennessee* sailed from Norfolk with McAdoo and his new wife, President Wilson's youngest daughter, Eleanor. She was half his age and, unknowingly, was to be the second of three Mrs. McAdoos. (The last one, Doris Cross, was one-third his age when they wed in 1935, about a year after he and Eleanor were divorced.) McAdoo was young in spirit, anyway; Beach remembered in his autobiography that McAdoo had won every game of hopscotch played out on deck, that athleticism in addition to having "a complete, beautiful command of nonblasphemous profanity." The sailors, Beach reported, "loved" the secretary, thinking that he was like them.

On board with the senior couple were eight other "commissioners," two of their wives, and a dozen staffers. The large official party heading for Brazil, Uruguay, Argentina, Chile, and Peru (Peru then, again, suffering from bubonic plague) must have forced the relocation of all of the ship's senior officers from their staterooms for much of the cruise. Weeks later the commission returned via the Panama Canal, the prospects of its meetings overwhelmed by the reality of the distant war's impact on the world economy.

Beach's special affection for his new command was prompted by *Tennessee*'s uninterrupted, high-speed, single-day passage that April through the Strait of Magellan, entering the Pacific and beginning the leg for home. The day's climax was a thrilling six-hour transit of the Strait's dangerous Crooked Reach, the towering, rocky sides swept by the cruiser's eight searchlights while *Tennessee* ran the Reach westbound in the dark "on a twisting, snake-like course, through boiling currents and between wicked rocks, seen and unseen," her engines turning at maximum revolutions per minute (rpm). By comparison, the transit of the recently opened Panama Canal that followed—with *Tennessee* towed much of the way through by the ten-year-old-Canal Commission steam tug *Mariner*—was memorable, too, but much less exciting. Photographs of *Tennessee* under tow through the Canal's great cut make her look reluctant and disabled. Heading across the Gulf of Mexico via Havana and then up the coast, *Tennessee* returned to Hampton Roads on May 8, where McAdoo's party disembarked. Another thirty years passed before navy ships began to be supplanted by aircraft as the vehicles of choice for official US government travel.

Soon after her return, approaching midsummer 1916, Admiral William Banks Caperton, USN (1855–1941, USNA '75), who until then had passed as the navy's expert in the international politics of the Caribbean, left the squadron and his flagship, and moved west to become the commander in chief of the Pacific Fleet. His relief in the Caribbean was Rear Admiral Charles Pond (1856–1929, USNA '76), six numbers junior to Caperton, who broke his flag in what was now *Memphis* on July 19.

In 1909–11 Pond, then a captain, had been the third commanding officer of the armored cruiser USS *Pennsylvania* (ACR-4), operating in the Pacific. (He'd been in command during Eugene Ely's historic first landing on and take-off from a ship by an aircraft, granted while *Pennsylvania* was tied up in port San Francisco on January 18, 1911.) *Pennsylvania* (Cramp's no. 317), after the 1912 USS *Pittsburgh*, was almost an early draft of *Tennessee*, and so Pond likely quickly felt at home in his handsome quarters aft on the gun deck of his new flagship.

Although Pond had served on six ships and commanded five (USS *Iroquois*, the station ship in Hawaii; USS *Supply*, the station ship in Guam; the ex-army transport USS *Lawton*; the auxiliary cruiser USS *Buffalo*; and also *Pennsylvania*), all in the Pacific, he was a hydrographer and surveyor, not at heart an operator. Pond's professional reputation in the navy was based largely on the quality of his technical contributions—which included an epic magnetic survey of the sea floor from El Salvador to Alaska in 1883, and work laying the trans-Pacific cable around Midway Island in 1903. His obituaries usually mentioned that it was Pond who in 1901 selected the site for the naval station at Pearl Harbor, Hawaii.

Had he been a better seaman, or had any experience at all in the Caribbean and with its annual hurricane season, *Memphis*'s history and his biography might have played out very differently than they did.

On the late August afternoon when *Memphis* died, Admiral Pond was ashore in Santo Domingo attending a lecture on "Dominican Antiquities" in the capital's cathedral arranged by the US vice consul, Carl von Zielinski. He had invited Beach to join him, Pond explained to the Court of Inquiry, but the captain had declined. So, too, had Chaplain Charles Ellis, and Pond's flag secretary, Lieutenant Cleon Maudlin. Hence Admiral Pond observed *Castine*'s remarkable escape and *Memphis*'s terminal distress, "heavy seas . . . sweeping over her nearly to the tops of her stacks," standing alone on the shore. "I believe that Captain Beach and all the officers on the MEMPHIS did everything in their power," he continued in his statement to Secretary Daniels dated September 8, "to save the ship and that the disaster was caused by an Act of God which none could foresee or fight against with success."

"There were no indications that I recognized of approaching bad weather," Captain Beach wrote the day after the wreck, from the US consulate in the city, in his report to Secretary of the Navy Josephus Daniels about the catastrophic loss of *Memphis*. "Throughout this day there were only light breezes and a normal barometer." Out of smooth seas on this beautiful, tropical afternoon, he explained to the secretary, suddenly came a long, easy swell, breaking as heavy surf on the waterfront, followed by lines of breakers, growing enormous as they ran toward the shore. By 4:20 p.m., while *Memphis* tried unsuccessfully to get steam up and under way, "the sea came, and without breaking, flowed across the decks . . . These seas, getting higher and higher, simply pushed across the decks . . . across the forecastle and quarterdeck . . . across the boat decks, the lower and upper bridges, and the tops of the ventilators." "Finally," he reported, "these mountains of water were as high as the smoke stacks."

A since-lost photograph by Clarence Baxter, a newspaper editor from New Jersey then serving in the Dominican Republic as general receiver of customs, reportedly showed *Memphis* aground that afternoon with "only the ends of two masts projecting a few feet above the water," meaning that her four smokestacks—more than 70 feet above the waterline—had been overtopped, and seawater had been piped down them directly into the fire rooms below.

Later, Captain Beach would testify that "it is my belief that never in the knowledge or experience of man has there been such a sudden, tremendous, almost inconceivable upheaval of the seas as that which occurred at Santo Domingo on August 29, 1916. It was utterly beyond experience, conception or imagination."

After half an hour of this battering, *Memphis* was hard aground some three-quarters of a mile northwest of her anchorage, her bottom stove in and her engines torn from their foundations. "The ship brought up in her present position about 4:55 p.m.," Beach stated.

Lines were immediately sent ashore, boatswain's chairs rigged, etc. The first person reached the shore at 5:05 p.m. Soon five lines were rigged and were in operation. I ordered that first the injured from the fire and engine rooms be sent ashore, and next, the sick.

The men were formed in lines or groups, and each, in turn, was directed to go ashore in the boatswain's chair. Officers were in charge of the different lines. There was not, in one single instance, the case of a man volunteering to go ahead of his turn. At no time . . . was there the slightest disorder in the personnel of the MEMPHIS' ship's company. They did, each man, what he was told to do, and when that was finished either found some other work to do, or else quietly waited for orders.

Beach's contemporary descriptions of the disaster are generally trustworthy, and his son's in *The Wreck of the Memphis*, written fifty years after the fact, are both thrilling and imaginative. That book, published more than a decade after the great success of the junior Beach's first novel, *Run Silent, Run Deep*, mixes to superb effect technical descriptions of the stricken cruiser and her sudden destruction with what can only be a novelist's invented dialogue to personalize the drama. (In the 1970s Beach returned twice to writing fiction, sequels of a sort to his first novel.)

Astonishingly, given the chaotic conditions above and below decks, good order and discipline were preserved while the crisis swiftly played out under azure skies—*Memphis* rolling repeatedly through as much as 90 degrees of arc; salt water cascading through ventilating trunks and hatches, and even down her stacks; her keel battering the sea floor; and everywhere deep in the hull machinery being wrenched from its foundations, engine fires going out, and steam escaping through ruptured pipes—and the ship was abandoned. The epicenter of the disaster was below in *Memphis*'s two main engine rooms, where conditions were especially lethal. It was there in the port engine room that chief machinist mate George Rudd and machinist mate Charles Willey earned the Medal of Honor, Rudd posthumously, for their heroic performance of duty that afternoon. A third Medal of Honor was similarly awarded to the engineer officer, Lieutenant Claude Jones. Inexplicably, the medals were awarded fully sixteen years after *Memphis* was wrecked. Then Commander Jones (on his way to rear admiral) got his formally from President Hoover.

All three men were cited for "extraordinary heroism in the line of his

profession while serving on board USS Memphis at a time when that vessel
was suffering total destruction from a hurricane while anchored off Santo Domingo City 29 August 1916." The citations contain the only official, unambig-
uous reference to a hurricane as being the source of the great waves that caused
the ship's loss.

Rear Admiral Pond, then age sixty, remained in command of the squadron only until November 22 when he was relieved, apparently for reasons that
friendly reports attributed to his being "deeply affected . . . when the armored
cruiser Memphis was driven ashore . . . His nerves suffered from the shock and
he has been in poor health ever since." (By then the much smaller scout cruiser
USS *Salem* had been ordered to replace *Memphis* as the squadron's interim flagship.) The bout of infirmity in 1916 that prompted Pond's exit from squadron
command after only several months wasn't terminal, however; Pond lived another thirteen years, eleven of them in retirement, dying August 1929 at age
seventy-three in Oakland, California.

By 1916 American ambitions in the Dominican Republic already had a decades-
long history, one that began in 1854 with the first of three attempted annexa-
tions of the former Spanish and later—briefly—French colony, and now independent state. Two more annexation attempts came in the 1860s, soon after the
end of the Civil War. The second, begun in 1868, failed in the Senate despite
the strong personal support of President Grant, who adopted the commercial
and strategic arguments being made by proponents of annexation, and claimed
personally to believe that this "rich territory" with its population of 120,000
was "capable of supporting 10,000,000 people in luxury." Grant lost to strong
opposition led by Senator Charles Sumner, chairman of the Senate's Foreign
Relations Committee.

Two years later the hard-to-kill idea had its final try for approval when
the Senate voted on an annexation proffered this time by the republic's occasional president, Buenaventura Báez—then shopping his impoverished country around and hoping to make a lot of money in the transaction—and finally
killed it. After that, with annexation evidently truly dead, during the next century interest in the United States turned to seeking its alleged benefits through
periodic armed intervention.

So it happened that the *Machias*-class gunboat, USS *Castine* (PG-6), then more than twenty years old and in commission for the third time, spent most of August 1916 running errands along the south coast of the island of Hispaniola, a very junior member of the US forces at sea and ashore implementing and enforcing the writ of the three-month-old American military government, the second American intervention to force aside Dominican political leadership in little more than a decade.

That military government remained in place until 1924, although Americans continued to control Dominican customs receipts and, accordingly, the country's revenues until 1941, and to exert other controls for a further six years after that. (A third and perhaps final military intervention came in 1965.)

Finishing one such mission, very early on Monday morning, August 28, *Castine* returned to Santo Domingo, and anchored in darkness in 5.5 fathoms on the shallow water ledge directly below the old city. In the 1910s the capital was home to the most important port by a significant margin of all those in the Dominican Republic. As reported by American consul Clement Edwards, during a representative year of that decade Santo Domingo alone handled more than one-third of all the steam and sailing vessels moving in the country's foreign commerce, leaving the remainder to be divided up among the small country's eight lesser ports.

Castine's deck log for the midnight to 4:00 a.m. watch on August 28, 1916, has her dropping anchor at 3:20 a.m. due south of the Santo Domingo light with Torrecilla Point, the rocky bluff marking the eastern entrance to Santo Domingo harbor, lying slightly south of east (at 097° true) some seven-tenths of a mile distant.

Lieutenant Commander Thomas Withers began his *Proceedings* article, published in July 1918, nearly two years after the loss of *Memphis*, by reporting that the cruiser was wrecked by "enormous seas which were *unaccompanied by any wind whatsoever*." Withers then explained *Memphis*'s exposed position to the magazine's professional readership, an explanation relevant to *Castine*'s choice of anchorage, too. "It had been found advantageous to anchor as far to the eastward as practicable," he wrote, "in order to get what lee [shelter] we could from the point on the Duarte [western] side of the Ozama River . . . The prevailing wind and sea were from the southeast and the anchorage was almost always rough." "The anchorage at Santo Domingo City is very restricted, and there is no protection from east to west through south. The westerly current caused the ship to ride heading east. The anchorage is on a narrow shelf or

FIGURE 7.2. USS *Castine* (PG-6).

Authorized in March 1889, built at Maine's Bath Iron Works, and first commissioned in October 1894, USS *Castine* was in service during twenty of the next twenty-five years, sailing in the North Atlantic, South Atlantic, and Indian Oceans, and the East China and Mediterranean Seas. She and her sister ship, the class's namesake, USS *Machias* (PG-5), were well armed but thin-skinned, nothing to send into serious combat.

After her escape in late summer 1916 from the big waves off Hispaniola and following another year in the Caribbean, *Castine* became part of the patrol force off Gibraltar during World War I, remaining there until the end of 1918. She was struck from the Navy Register and sold in August 1921, to sink under tow off Louisiana in December three years later. Her wreck has since been found.

This photograph is autographed by Fleet Admiral Chester Nimitz, USN, who rode *Castine* as a lieutenant in command of the Atlantic Fleet's Submarine Flotilla in 1912–13.

Source: United States Navy Photo Archive (NH 58098).

ledge. This ledge is so narrow that the 10-fathom curve is but a few yards inside of the 100-fathom curve. The danger of such an anchorage had been fully realized and everything was habitually kept in readiness to get underway upon short notice."[3]

As recorded in *Castine*'s log by Ensign Morris Lenney and Lieutenant (junior grade) Roscoe Schuirmann, the officers of the deck during those days, August 28 and most of August 29 were quiet on board, with typically beautiful Caribbean summer weather: temperatures in the high 70s and low 80s, and winds generally from the north at a few knots. The barometer, centered on 30 inches of mercury and moving lazily only a few tenths around that pressure, hinted at balmy conditions to come.

Both days the ship's routine was punctuated by prescribed magazine inspections and the usual gun battery drills, and by the equally routine disciplinary hearings on deck by *Castine*'s commanding officer, Commander Kenneth Bennett, USN, addressing at morning's captain's mast the lapses in discipline to which bored sailors ashore or afloat in the tropics were always susceptible.

At 10:30 a.m. on Tuesday, August 29, *Castine*'s deck watch saw a British schooner, *Canada*, stand out to sea, followed not too much later by a Dominican steamer, SS *Santo Domingo*. Next, a navy tender, USS *Potomac*, a chunky, twenty-year-old former New York City tugboat armed with two 3 pound guns, came out of the Ozama River, soon to turn west and head for open water. All routine movements. Then, near midafternoon, Lieutenant Roscoe Schuirmann, twenty-five (who went on to a decorated navy career, service in World War II, and flag rank), recorded a change in sea conditions that would soon shatter the tranquility of what had been another lazy day swinging at anchor.

"At about 3:15," Schuirmann wrote in the deck log, "ground swells began to increase in size." Twenty minutes later Captain Bennett came back on board—he'd been visiting *Memphis*'s dentist—and immediately ordered preparations to get *Castine* under way. "Sea making rapidly," Schuirmann recorded now, "and breaking in 5 fathoms of water." Pushed up onto the shallows, the waves that were swelling apparently spontaneously from quiet water grew while Schuirmann watched them turn into rollers high enough by 3:40 to prohibit *Castine* from safely taking her sailing launch onboard. The small boat with three in her crew was directed seaward, to wait behind the long, rolling seas for better conditions. The three unfortunates would soon drown, the only lives lost from *Castine*'s crew. At 4:00 *Castine*'s deck watch saw *Memphis*'s motor sailer capsize as

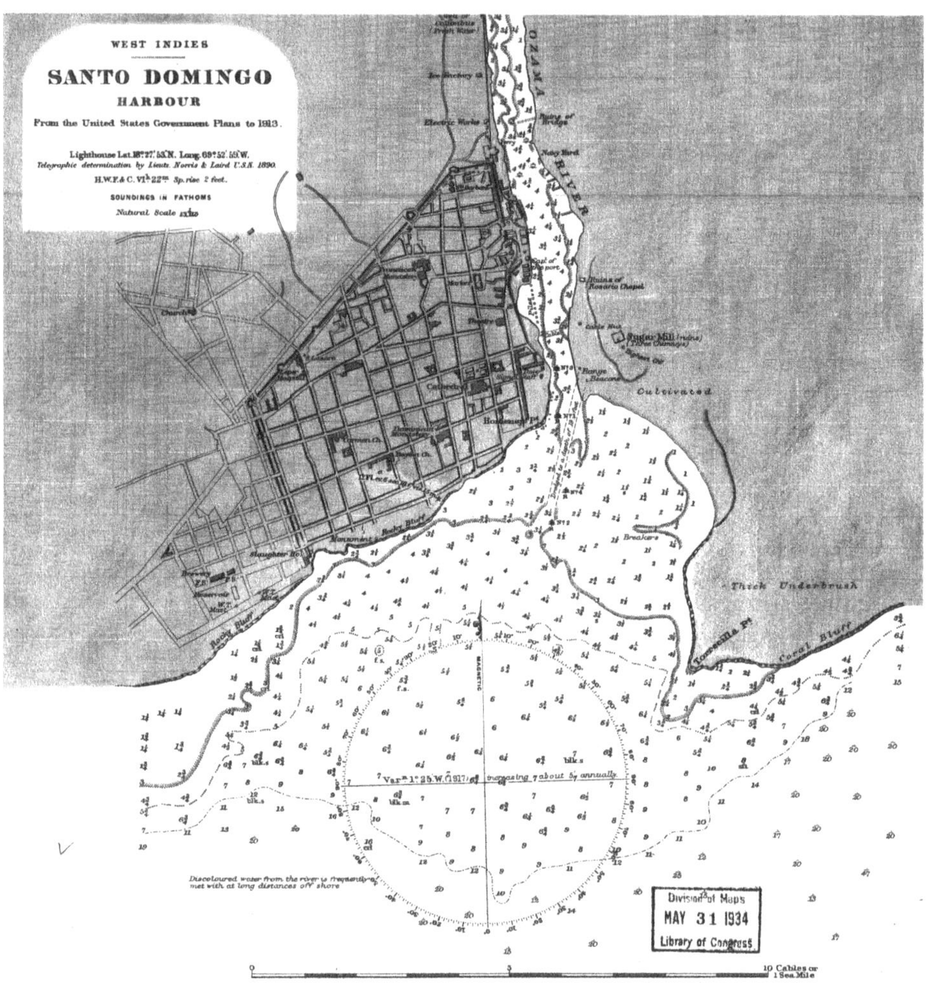

CHART 7.1. Detail from Admiralty Chart No. 472 ("Harbours and Anchorages on the Coast of Haiti and S[an]to. Domingo," September 15, 1896), "Santo Domingo Harbour from United States Government Plans to 1913." Scale 1:13,110.

The night of August 28 *Memphis*, flying the flag of the new commander of the Atlantic Fleet's cruiser squadron, Rear Admiral Charles Pond, USN, and *Castine* were both anchored in about 6 fathoms of water on the shallow-water ledge directly below the old city, south of the lighthouse near 18°28′N and 69°53′W and west of Torricelli Point.

The 1913 edition of *The West Indies Pilot*, published by the US Hydrographic Office, sounded cautious about Santo Domingo Harbor's shallow roadstead, shown in this chart, which it advised "offers a very indifferent anchorage." "In threatening weather," *The Pilot* continued, "it would be advisable to put to sea. A very heavy sea is likely to cause a vessel to drag [her anchor], especially when anchored westward of the lighthouse."

All US Navy ships in these waters were very familiar with the harbor and its landmarks: the large brewery that marked the extreme western limits of the city, and away to the east, across the Ozama River, the three chimneys of a derelict sugar mill standing almost in line with the narrow dredged channel that admitted ships past the bar and up the river to the capital's piers, customs buildings, and office of the captain of the port. August 29 at Santo Domingo was a typical summer day in the Caribbean: temperatures peaked at midday in the low 90s, winds blew out of the north-northeast at under 10 miles per hour, and barometer readings through the day remained right around 30″, but in mid-afternoon, a series of threatening swells rose dramatically on the seaward horizon.

Source: Library of Congress Geography and Map Division.

she came out of the Ozama River. (That boat would be found adrift by USS *Castine* almost a day later. All but six of the thirty-eight on board her drowned, too.)

Castine was spared *Memphis*'s fate because at 4:04 p.m.—just half an hour after Bennett had ordered her to sea—the gunboat managed to get under way with steam from her no. 1 boiler driving both her triple-expansion steam engines. Probably because the engine room watch spent the next few hours dealing with the emergency, the gunboat's second boiler wasn't even lit until 7:15 p.m. It didn't come on the line until 10:20 that night.

Lieutenant Schuirmann's log entry describes *Castine*'s frantic hours between 4:00 and 8:00 p.m. "Seas breaking on all sides of the ship. All boats except motor whaleboat washed away and ship filling through poop hatches. Wire on quadrant of steering gear carried away. Stood toward Torrecilla Point and as impossible to turn backed. When light stood about 30° by estimation ship passed first line of breakers and turned with engines, during lull stood out to southeast. Turned all hands to clearing wreckage and water from after compartments. Relieving tackles on steering gear rigged out emergency tiller on rudder head would not stay on." "About 5:30," Schuirmann continued, "passed breaking seas." *Castine*, steaming southeast at one-third speed, was now finally through the ranks of powerful waves that had for the past hour flushed out the anchorage and run on to batter the shore. Futile attempts to "cat" (stow) the anchor had resulted in nothing but holes punched into the bow, so now, clear of Torrecilla Point, she "slipped" (dropped) that anchor, one of her two, over the side with 5 fathoms of chain still attached. A quick muster revealed that seven crew members had been injured.

From 8:00 until midnight *Castine* continued southeast through high seas, sometimes, according to the new officer of the deck, Ensign George Greene Jr., USN, through heavy rain squalls and in the face of storm- and hurricane-force winds. At 5:05 the next evening, August 30, *Castine* anchored again off Santo Domingo, this time in twelve more feet of water, slightly south of her previous anchorage. Since escaping the waves, she'd spent her time under way apparently searching for drifting boats, at rest at anchor only for an hour off Port Palenque, a single-ship anchorage twenty-one miles southwest of Santo Domingo that served nearby sugar plantations.

That tiny, and duckling-ugly, USS *Castine*, less than half *Memphis*'s length, beam, and draft and displacing one-tenth of the cruiser's tonnage, survived with the loss of only three lives the same seas that killed *Memphis* and dozens of her crew is remarkable. When it was all over, Rear Admiral Pond praised Captain Bennett in what was by navy standards incandescent prose: "The saving of the *Castine* from what, to everyone watching from shore, seemed to be sure destruction, was due entirely to the consummate skill and cool, persistent courage of her commanding officer, Commander Kenneth M. Bennett, and the able assistance rendered him by every officer and man, particularly those of the engineering force. I doubt if in the whole history of the U.S. Navy there is a record of more skillful seamanship than was exhibited by Commander Bennett upon this occasion." That praise was echoed three months later, on November 11, unofficially but to no less effect, in the authoritative weekly *Army Navy Register* explicitly comparing *Castine*'s escape to safety in the open sea with that of HMS *Calliope* during the great Apia cyclone of March 16, 1889. "The achievement of Commander Bennett should not pass unnoticed," the journal noted. "Daring, resourceful and hanging on with bulldog tenacity, Bennett saved a ship that seemed to be doomed, demonstrating that a high order of seamanship still prevails in the United States Navy to grapple with an emergency." "The Calliope had less seaway, for the small harbor of Apia was filled with warships breaking from their anchorage and going on the reefs, but the Calliope's rudder and steering gear stood the strain. Comparison of the size and force of the seas cannot be made; but, granting that the Samoan elemental chaos had greater power of destruction, the sea upheaval at Santo Domingo City apparently had the Castine at its mercy and only Bennett's skillful use of his engines saved her."[4] Later, during World War I, Bennett (1874–1935, USNA 1895) commanded the cruiser USS *New Orleans* (CL-22) and the battleship USS *Wyoming* (BB-32). His obituary in a Hoboken, New Jersey, newspaper (his home town) imaginatively credited Bennett with saving his ship from "a tornado in Haiti . . . while a much larger vessel stationed at Haiti was completely wrecked" nineteen years earlier.

As the month-long Court of Inquiry examining the destruction of *Memphis*, convened first off Santo Domingo in the old transport USS *Prairie* (ex-SS *El Sol*, Cramp's no. 267) and then completed at the Norfolk Navy Yard, revealed in its 482-page report in autumn 1916, during his first few weeks in command of the squadron Admiral Pond had taken a very light strain on the line, providing Beach with almost no instruction or guidance. None other than what might have set the stage for the catastrophe to come: Pond had insisted that for reasons of coal consumption economy, *Tennessee* have only two boilers on the line while at anchor, providing only enough steam to power her "dynamos" (electrical generators) and auxiliary machinery. It took the steam from at least four or better six boilers to move the ship, and so for insurance Beach separately required that four other boilers be primed with coal and ready to light when his ship was at anchor. On August 29 fires were laid under boilers 13, 14, 15, and 16, but without quick lighting material. This meant that each required three "shovels of fire" from the two boilers on the line and then took as much as forty-five minutes to build up enough heat and steam pressure to power both main engines.

Under the battering of the seas, either there wasn't enough time for *Memphis* to raise sufficient steam to get under way even on one engine, or there would have been time enough for that but for the failure of an auxiliary steam pipe in the port engine room that crippled the ship's propulsion plant at the critical moment during *Memphis*'s effort to escape grounding. The pipe's failure and its role in the wreck was a subject of Admiral Pond's second cable to Washington that night. Reflecting his reports to Washington, the next day's *New York Times* headline stated, "Cruiser Was Clawing Her Way to Safety When Main Pipe Burst," over a story that explained how "the bursting of a steam pipe accounted for many of the casualties on the Memphis and perhaps in part for the destruction of the vessel. 'Steam was gotten up and the engines were working,' Admiral Pond cabled, "when the main steam pipe burst.'" In *Memphis*'s engine room log for August 29 that pipe failure isn't granted such central importance. Much more important was the constant wetting of the boiler room fires and flexing of the hull that quickly tore the plant out of alignment.

The formal inquiry was followed three months later by Captain Beach's general court-martial, held in USS *Connecticut*, in port Philadelphia.

Over three days just before Christmas, Beach's court-martial (no. 33198) heard charges alleging that he had improperly hazarded his ship, "in consequence of which she was cast upon the shore"; had "through inattention and negligence" suffered a vessel of the navy to be stranded; and had been "culpably inefficient in the performance of his duty." Found guilty of two of the three charges, Beach was sentenced to be placed at the foot of the captains' seniority list until he'd lost twenty numbers. In a decision that seems incomprehensible today, Secretary of the Navy Josephus Daniels, on review the following February, reduced that loss to just five numbers.

Daniels's view, and the general belief then, was that *Memphis* had been victim of an unpredictable "act of God," a tsunami suddenly coughed up by a submarine earthquake nearby.

Such extraordinary groundings had happened before. Just weeks after the "St. Narciso Hurricane" of late October 1867 sank dozens of ships and killed hundreds of people in the Virgin Islands, Porto Rico, and Hispaniola, a November tsunami lifted the screw sloop of war USS *Monongahela* high atop Frederickstadt, St. Croix. Awkwardly at rest, though generally intact, on the sands, she was finally refloated and restored to duty in 1868. The sidewheel steamer USS *Susquehanna*, then in port St. Thomas, managed to ride out the waves that had grounded *Monongahela*, and so narrowly missed a similar or worse fate.

The next summer, in mid-August 1868, the storeship USS *Fredonia* and the sidewheel gunboat USS *Wateree* were destroyed by another such "tidal wave," this one off Arica, Peru (now in Chile), following an earthquake at the boundary of the Nazca and South American plates now estimated at 8.5–9.0 on the Richter Scale. The wave sank *Fredonia*, drowning all but five members of her crew. *Wateree*, much stouter, survived after a fashion with the loss of only a single man: "a tremendous rising of the sea," explained her captain, had ripped the gunboat from her anchorage and thrust her onto the beach more than a quarter-mile past and a dozen feet above the high water mark. The Peruvian steam corvette *America* was among the several other vessels lifted and dropped onshore by the same wave. (The beached American gunboat remained planted ashore and was used as a building until another tsunami nine years later destroyed what the first wave had left.)

Considered, but discounted, by Captain Beach's supporters then and by his son much later was an explanation that the killer waves had come instead from a category one hurricane, which between August 27 and September 3 rose in the Lesser Antilles, tracked south of Hispaniola roughly along 15°N, and ultimately hit Belize.

Pond's personal and direct responsibility for *Memphis*'s immobility wasn't addressed in any of the legal proceedings that followed the shipwreck. He didn't testify before the court, as much later the junior Beach clearly believed Pond should have volunteered to do. "It is significant that nowhere in the record of proceedings is there testimony by the Cruiser Force Commander," Beach Jr. wrote, "as to why *Memphis* had steam on only two boilers."

Nowhere was it brought out that her commander had protested this order, or that previous policy had been to keep four steaming. So far as the evidence placed before the court shows, this was purely the Commanding Officer's decision.

The reason for this seeming lack must be partly surmised. [Beach Sr.] never alluded to it, but [civilian counsel] was less reticent. The defense had asked Admiral Pond to testify, and was very disappointed when [Pond] asked to be excused. [Beach Sr.] would not countenance [counsel's] proposal to invoke the statutory right of calling [Pond], and refused to permit the evidence to be presented otherwise.[5]

Captain Edward Beach Jr.'s account of the loss of his father's ship, *The Wreck of the Memphis*, was published by Holt, Rinehart and Winston in 1966, the fiftieth anniversary of the ship's loss, and then reprinted in 1998 by the Naval Institute Press as part of its "Classics of Naval Literature" series. Beach Jr.'s introduction noted that the reprint marked the eighty-first anniversary of the loss of USS *Memphis*.

The idea that a tsunami killed *Memphis* was congenial to young Beach; it made his father the victim of an unforeseeable act of God, rather than a captain guilty of presiding over a fatal lapse in readiness for sea that cost him and the navy his ship. Hispaniola lies atop one fault and very near the intersection of two tectonic plates, in a high-risk earthquake and tsunami area; however, there's no other evidence of a Caribbean earthquake that day, and the source of the surge remains controversial.

The unidentified author of the *Richmond* [Virginia] *Times-Dispatch*'s full-page story of December 31, 1916, headlined, "What Happened on the Seabottom That Wrecked the *Memphis*," believed the cruiser was the victim of just such a wave. Confusing volcanic activity that didn't happen with a submarine earthquake that might have, the piece was subtitled: "How a Volcano Bursting through the Ocean Floor Raised a Series of Titanic Waves That Picked the Warship Up Like Giant Hands and Threw Her on a Shallow Shore Two Miles Away." The text was helpfully illustrated by two "simplified diagrammatic representations," the first showing a "sealed submarine volcano" at rest, and the second, such a volcano erupting. A third line drawing depicted "How the Memphis,

Drawing Twenty-seven Feet of Water, Was Lifted Up from Her Moorings in Forty Feet of Water and Was Hurled across the Intervening Two Miles. Striking the Ocean Bed As Each Wave Passed Her, Until She Was Landed and Wrecked in Two Feet of Water on the Shore of San Domingo Harbor."

Confirmation of all this seemed to come from a reliable eyewitness on shore, one "Captain" Theodoor de Booy, a midcareer Dutch American archaeologist then on Santo Domingo for the third time, doing fieldwork for the Heye Museum of the American Indian in New York City. De Booy, whose local authority derived from five years of fieldwork in the Caribbean—it's unclear where the honorific "Captain" came from—was quoted in the *Bridgeport* [Connecticut] *Evening Farmer* and other newspapers as explaining that an undersea disturbance off Dominica in the British West Indies the day before must have been the source of the great waves that pushed *Memphis* aground.[6]

Other contemporary accounts of *Memphis*'s shipwreck accepted the tidal wave theory without question, and also without the benefit of an understanding of plate tectonics, which could have helped to explain the source of a submarine upheaval that might have caused a tsunami to wash up on the southern shore of Santo Domingo. The root source of that theory, however, had been published in Germany only a year before the wreck, in a seminal book by Alfred Wegener (1880–1930), *Die Entstehung der Kontinent und Ozeane*, translated into English and republished nine years later as *The Origin of Continents and Oceans* (Methuen and Co., 1924). But another forty years or so had to pass before Wegener's brilliant insights became a part of settled geoscience. So, an unsettled submarine volcano somewhere to the east-southeast of Santo Domingo it was.

The navy, in the person of its secretary, shared the *Times-Dispatch*'s analysis. Secretary Daniels's June 27, 1919, letter, effectively exonerating Captain Beach, explained that "the storm which occasioned the loss of Captain Beach's vessel was volcanic in origin and of such unusual severity that that it may properly be considered an act of God which it was humanly impracticable to foresee and to make adequate preparation to meet." This despite *Castine*'s escape, which seemed to prove the opposite.

The story of the late August disaster must have fascinated Americans. Before the end of the year *Memphis*'s shipwreck was reported in more than three hundred newspaper articles, many in papers that served a readership in seaports, where naval matters would have been naturally interesting (such as the *Philadelphia Public Ledger* and the *Honolulu Star Bulletin*), but also in others high and dry in the heartland (such as the *Chickasha Daily Express* and *Tulsa Daily World*, both published in the Indian Territory of Oklahoma), where ships and the sea were unfamiliar and sailors unknown.[7]

Edward Beach Sr. (1867–1943) graduated with the Naval Academy class of 1888 and then embarked on nearly thirty-two years of commissioned service that saw him serve aboard more than a dozen ships (he commanded three others, in addition to *Memphis*: the repair ship USS *Vestal*, the armored cruiser *Washington*, and briefly battleship *New York*, as well as two shore facilities). During the Spanish-American War Beach was the junior engineer in *Baltimore*, next in line behind Dewey's flagship, *Olympia*, as the American squadron steamed into Manila Bay to pick a fight. For the few months in late 1918 that spanned the November armistice and included the surrender of the German High Seas Fleet at Scapa Flow, Beach commanded *New York*, the American squadron's flagship, his second wartime tour afloat and his last command at sea.

Beach Sr. devoted himself to the navy and, the catastrophic loss of *Memphis* aside, he served it with evident dedication and extraordinary professionalism, first as an engineer and then, when the two officer branches were integrated in 1900, as a line officer during thirty-one years of commissioned service. His failure to be promoted to flag rank was the price Beach paid for his failure to get *Memphis* under way from Santo Domingo to escape sudden destruction.

Five years later Beach retired from the navy and left his last command, the shipyard at Mare Island, to join the faculty of Stanford University as a lecturer in naval history, the university's first faculty member in that role. At Stanford Beach taught two courses, a survey of American naval history ("emphasizing the influence and effect our naval policy has had on the development of the United States," on Tuesday and Thursday mornings and open to all but freshmen) and a senior seminar on "the American Navy in the Spanish-American War." The *Daily Palo Alto*, since 1892 Stanford's student-run newspaper, later gloated contentedly in its December 6, 1921, issue that in this addition to the curriculum Stanford "stole a march on the oldest college in America," Harvard, supposed then to be standing up its own naval history course taught by Captain Dudley Knox.

The senior Beach died in the naval hospital in Oakland, California, in 1943.

Like his father, the junior Beach retired as a captain, despite a superb navy career that included submarine service during World War II (he was awarded the Navy Cross and two Silver Stars), command of USS *Triton* on her historic 36,000 mile submerged circumnavigation of the world in 1960, and four years as naval aide to the president, usually a sure stepping-stone to flag rank. The junior Beach (1918–2002, USNA '39 and second in his class), is probably best known today as the author of the award-winning *Run Silent, Run Deep*, written while he was President Eisenhower's aide and published in 1955. In 1958 the novel, with its faint hints of Captain Ahab's pursuit of the great white whale, was made very loosely into a movie starring Clark Gable and Burt Lancaster, then Hollywood's A-list male stars. Beach didn't like the film.

Beach wrote twelve other books. His and his father's names identify the hall on the Naval Academy's Hospital Hill that holds the offices of the US Naval Institute.

On December 4, 1917, nearly eight months after the United States entered the war, Secretary Daniels published General Order 350, listing the newly selected names of nineteen destroyers soon to start construction. The first of them, DD-99, was a *Wickes*-class destroyer contracted to Fore River in Quincy, Massachusetts, as its hull no. 305. She was to be named in honor of Rear Admiral Stephen Luce, whose name otherwise was synonymous with the War College he'd founded in Newport. DD-102 (Fore River no. 308) was to be christened "Mahan," after the admiral whose death precisely three years earlier at seventy-four had removed the century's most influential strategist, but not his ideas, from the world scene. Fittingly, perhaps, with USS *Mahan* Fore River set a construction record for its seventy-one destroyers built in wartime; no. 308 was delivered to the navy a little more than five months after her keel was laid down. (Astonishingly, five months was nowhere near the record construction pace for a World War I destroyer. That record is held by the Mare Island Naval Shipyard, where another *Wickes*-class destroyer, USS *Ward* (DD-139), sped from keel laying on May 15 to commissioning on June 24, 1918.)

This swift progress came at a time of enormous expansion of the thirty-two-year-old Fore River yard. Orders for submarines and destroyers in 1916 prompted Fore River's owner, Bethlehem Steel, to open a second yard nearby, at

Squantum. The two yards would soon employ 15,000 men, all furiously busy.[8] The swift expansion hinted at the coming explosive growth of American industrial capacity, which, beginning with World War I, would come to dominate world manufacturing markets nearly to the end of the century.

Some general orders signaled increases to the American fleet, others marked declines. Two weeks after General Order 350, Daniels issued his General Order 354. It listed five ships to be stricken from the register of US naval vessels, the official inventory of navy ships and craft. The five included the destroyers *Jacob Jones* and *Chauncey*, the converted yacht *Alcedo*, the patrol vessel *Rehoboth* (a former fishing boat, sunk intentionally by friendly fire after she developed an uncontrollable leak and had to be abandoned off the French coast just three weeks into her deployment), and the armored cruiser USS *Memphis*.

Five years after *Memphis* came off the register officially, on January 22, 1922, Assistant Secretary of the Navy Theodore Roosevelt Jr., acting for Josephus Daniels's Republican successor, the corruptible secretary Edwin Denby, approved the sale of what remained of the carcass of *Memphis* to the A. H. Radetsky Mine and Metal Company of Denver for $3,000, after earlier contract awards of $15,000 and $6,500 to others had fallen through. At the same time, eight other navy ships, among them battleships *Maine*, *Missouri*, and *Wisconsin*, and the cruiser *Columbia*, were sold for scrap to a Philadelphia company, encouraging *Iron Age* magazine to speculate hopefully that perhaps fallout from the Washington Disarmament Conference would launch a major ship salvage industry in the United States.

Radetsky got the bill of sale and took legal delivery of *Memphis* that March . . . and then nothing happened. Five years later Radetsky conceded it was unable to remove the wreck, and offered to yield its title in exchange for a refund of its purchase price plus interest. Writing in September 1938 in the Naval Institute's *Proceedings*, Robert McClintock, then and for another year American vice consul in Santo Domingo, explained that after "a bewildering series of contracts and subcontracts," in 1937 the salvage contract for the cruiser had been awarded to an unnamed, American-owned molasses company in Cuba that finally managed during the next year or so to get most of what remained of the wreck cut up and hauled away from the island.

FIGURE 8.1. *Arrival of the American Fleet at Scapa Flow, December 7, 1917,* by Bernard F. Gribble.

Friday, December 7, 1917, eight months after the United States joined the war in Europe, Battleship Division Nine, with USS *New York* (BB-34) in the van flying the flag of Rear Admiral Hugh Rodman, USN, steamed into the Royal Navy's anchorage at Scapa Flow in the Orkney Islands, concluding an extraordinarily rough, late autumn crossing of the Atlantic. Coincidentally, that same day the United States went to war against Germany's chief ally, the Imperial and Royal Austro-Hungarian government. (The United States never declared war against the Ottoman empire, in the unrequited hope that the Turks eventually could be induced to abandon their German allies, but diplomatic relations were broken by the Turks in April 1917, when the United States declared war on Germany, and not reestablished until February 1927.)

Battleship *New York* is credited with sinking UB-113, the only German navy ship lost to any ship of the division, in mid-October 1918 by inadvertently steaming into the submerged, nearly new submarine (then on her second war patrol) in the always chaotic waters of the Pentland Firth, just south of Scapa Flow. (Years later Rodman nonsensically described this accidental coup by his flagship as *New York*'s "narrow escape" from an attempted ramming by a submarine—the only successful suicide attempt by any German U-boat during the war, had it been true. "There is every reason to believe," the admiral continued more persuasively, "that the blows of the propeller split the submarine open and sank her," instantly drowning Oberleutnant zur See Ulrich Pilzecker and all thirty-eight of his crew.) Not an inconsiderable achievement, but still only one of 20 U-boats sunk that month and of 202 German submarines sunk during the war. *New York*, for her part, required time in dry dock to patch the hull and replace the starboard propeller.

Admiral Rodman (1859–1940, USNA '80 and the 61st in his graduating class of 62) described his wartime experience, and his forty-year career at sea more generally, in his memoir, *Yarns of a Kentucky Admiral* (Bobbs-Merrill, 1928). Unlike some of his contemporaries, Rodman judged the US Navy to have been very well prepared in 1917 for wartime operations, "even though this opinion be at variance with that of one flag officer at least [a coy reference to Rear Admiral William Sims, USN] who saw no service afloat but has lost no opportunity to criticize adversely the navy in general and in particular, in print and otherwise" (263). Rodman wasn't entirely alone in his defense of his service and its secretary; Admirals Henry Wilson and Ridley McLean were among a few other old salts who publicly supported Secretary of the Navy Daniels against Sims's more broadly based campaign of disparagement.

Rodman's coal-fired battleships entered the huge, sheltered Scottish anchorage fully seven months after the first half-dozen American destroyers, making up Destroyer Division Eight, had arrived at Queenstown, Ireland. The long delay in deploying any heavy combatants to European waters reflected Mahan's precept to concentrate the battle fleet, but also reflected the reluctance of Anglophobic senior American navy officers to commit their capital ships to the distant fight, determined as they were to conserve the fleet's battleships and cruisers for a possible fearsome future in which the Triple Entente had been defeated and the United States alone faced a triumphant Germany across the Atlantic and an emboldened Japan in the Pacific.

Rodman's division was soon redesignated as the 6th Battle Squadron of the British Grand Fleet. On arrival, their British counterparts were pleased by the zeal exhibited by American crews, but surprised by the poor quality of their gunnery. The Americans' gun-laying ability, or the lack of it, turned out to make little difference going forward in the war. The new 6th Battle Squadron's participation in sustaining the blockade between Scotland and Norway across the top of the North Sea had nothing to do with the big ship shootouts that everyone had imagined before the war were going to characterize and decide war at sea in the future.

The American squadron served ably, but without particular distinction, with the Grand Fleet for a few days short of a year before sailing for home on December 1, 1918, several weeks after the armistice that finally ended the fighting that took some 53,000 American lives. (Another 63,000 Americans in uniform died during the war from noncombat causes, most of them slain by the autumn 1918 influenza epidemic that killed millions of others worldwide.) Its contribution to this war effort aside, Battleship Division Nine deployed was a superb training ground for American naval officers in the complex business of operating squadrons of large combatants together, essential knowledge for the war to come.

On departure for home from wartime deployment, *New York*'s commanding officer was Captain Edward Beach, who'd reported on board the flagship just three months earlier from his last assignment ashore, in command of the naval torpedo station on Goat Island in Newport, Rhode Island. His orders to relieve Captain Charles Hughes, USN, and take command of a battleship deployed to the war zone anticipated by nine months Beach's explicit and complete exoneration by Secretary Daniels the following June for his loss of USS *Memphis*. (Later, Hughes got the promotion to flag rank that forever eluded Beach, and went on to become the fourth chief of naval operations before retiring in 1930.)

A year after that, on December 17, 1919, Vice Admiral William Sims, who'd commanded American navy forces in Europe during the war from his headquarters in London and was then back in Newport, again as president of the Naval War College, criticized Secretary Daniels's proposal to recognize with medals some among several thousand naval officers for their service during the war, sharp criticism he repeated early the next year in testimony before a Senate subcommittee.

Sims's and Daniels's relationship had been fraught practically from its beginning. The ambitious admiral's critique quickly exploded into a highly divisive, months-long public controversy—one avidly followed by the American and British press—that segued from arguments about who merited which decoration for wartime service to fundamental questions about the navy's command structure and senior leadership, the Atlantic Fleet's readiness to sail and to fight, and its operations during the war just past. Even the *Harvard Crimson* (Republican to its marrow) jumped into the fray, with a column on "Navy Awards" in its November 9, 1920, issue that dismissed Daniels's term in office as navy secretary as "eight years of willful stubbornness and blind inefficiency." The article suggested darkly that the long delay in announcing the awards had something to do with advancing the Democratic Party's interests in the presidential election, won by the Republicans just the week before. The medals were presented to recipients two days later, on the second anniversary of the armistice.

In this oil painting, Bernard F. Gribble (1872–1962) shows the arriving Americans steaming past the cheering crew of the fast battleship HMS *Queen Elizabeth*, flagship of the commander in chief, Grand Fleet, off to port. ("Big Lizzie" had been in the dockyard at Rosyth a year ago in May, and so had been absent from the huge fight off Jutland.) Visible behind *New York* are five ships, including the battleships USS *Wyoming* (BB-32, Cramp's no. 365), USS *Florida* (BB-30), and USS *Delaware* (BB-28), and an escorting British *Caroline*-class light cruiser, HMS *Caroline*, the last veteran of the Battle of Jutland and a museum ship today in Belfast, Ireland.

The artist seems to have imagined a fifth ship, perhaps USS *Texas* (BB-35), which in mid-February 1918 completed her crossing in heavy weather finally to join her deployed squadron mates more than two months late. She'd been delayed on departure by shipyard repairs required following several days hard aground on Clay Head, Block Island, late the previous September, a blunder made while trying to enter the Atlantic from the Sound. (Her commanding officer, Captain Victor Blue, USN, lost ten numbers of seniority for that professional lapse, but Blue's navigator took most of the blame.)

Among his other works, Gribble, a member of the Royal Academy and official painter to the Worshipful Company of Shipwrights, a London livery company, painted the May 4 arrival of Destroyer Division Eight at Queenstown (*The Return of the Mayflower*); the surrender of the German High Seas Fleet, November 21, 1918; and that fleet's surprise scuttling June 21, 1919, in defiance of surrender, which reportedly Gribble himself witnessed.

Source: United States Navy Art Collection, Washington, DC.

Chapter Eight

The American Navy at War

I have called the Congress into extraordinary session because there are serious, very serious, choices of policy to be made, and made immediately, which it was neither right nor constitutionally permissible that I should assume the responsibility of making.

I advise that the Congress declare the recent course of the Imperial German government to be in fact nothing less than war against the Government and people of the United States; that it formally accept the status of belligerent which has been thrust upon it, and that it take immediate steps not only to put the country in a more thorough state of defense but also to exert all its power and employ all its resources to bring the Government of the German Empire to terms and end the war.

—Woodrow Wilson, April 2, 1917, War Messages, 65th
Cong., 1st Sess., Senate Doc. 5, Serial No. 7265

Wilson moved very far between December 1914 and April 1917. In his second state of the union message to the Congress, delivered December 8, 1914, he'd described the war in Europe as one "with which we have nothing to do, whose causes cannot touch us," and wrote that Americans should be "ashamed of any thought of hostility or fearful preparation for trouble."

The president's antiwar stance soon found its echo in lyricist Alfred Bryan's 1915 Tin Pan Alley hit, "I Didn't Raise My Boy to Be a Soldier," music by "Ragtime Al" Piantadosi. Bryan's chorus had a mother "murmuring through her tears,"

> I didn't raise my boy to be a soldier,
> I brought him up to be my pride and joy.

Who dares to place a musket on his shoulder,
To shoot some other mother's darling boy?
Let nations arbitrate their future troubles,
It's time to lay the sword and gun away.
There'd be no war today,
If mothers all would say,
"I didn't raise my boy to be a soldier."

The cover of the song's sheet music (in an era when you made your own entertainment at home, some 650,000 copies were sold during the first three months after "I Didn't Raise My Boy to Be a Soldier" was released) featured a sappy illustration of a mother in a rocker in front of a fireplace, cradling her kneeling "darling boy" in her arms, while the European war in the trenches raged on in a vaporous cloud above the duo.

While that catchy song played in the background, through 1915, 1916, and into 1917 Americans had watched warily from over the horizon, most of the time lending money and shipping food, matériel, and munitions to the powers of the Triple Entente during the first thirty-two months of horrific ground combat, while the great battles of the Frontiers, Tanneberg, the Marne, Verdun, and the Somme, were fought to bloody indecision on both European fronts, often along lines of trenches dug from the English Channel to the Swiss border.

There was no such indecision at Gallipoli in Turkey, First Lord of the Admiralty Winston Churchill's ill-conceived effort to use the Royal Navy to pry open a front, through forcing the Dardanelles or seizing the Gallipoli Peninsula, where mobility would be possible. At the end of 1915 Great Britain, Australia, and New Zealand finally withdrew what remained of their battered troops from the peninsula after eight wretched and costly months, crippled by their many failures and repelled by an unexpectedly stout Ottoman defense. It was a failure prompted in the first instance by British contempt for the Turks, judged by an anonymous staff officer as "an enemy who has never shown himself as good a fighter as the white man" (quoted by Robert Rhodes James in his 1965 book, *Gallipoli*).

The defeat suggested anew that the British Army's high command had mislearned the lessons of Crimea and the colonial wars of the nineteenth century. But Churchill's resignation as First Lord of the Admiralty while events on the peninsula were still spooling out, his departure from the government, and his acceptance in January 1916 of a commission with the 6th Battalion Royal Scots Fusiliers at the front confirm that he accepted personal responsibility for the debacle.

One war later, in late January 1944, Churchill prompted something very like Gallipoli again: he was the impetus behind the Allied amphibious landings in two-division strength at Anzio, on the west coast of Italy roughly thirty miles south of Rome, dubbed "Operation Shingle." And in December 2020, in the *London Review of Books*, Jonathan Raban, whose father had fought there, reminded his readers that the Allied campaign in Italy ("the most irrelevant and most impotently wasteful of human lives in the Second World War") "was Churchill's brainchild, insisted on by the great man in the face of deep skepticism from both FDR and General Eisenhower."[1]

Casualties from August 1914 to the spring of 1917 soon threatened to deplete an entire generation of men, losses in combat on a scale never seen before, thanks to the industrialization of warfare. In the five-month-long Battle of the Somme alone, casualties—the killed, wounded, or gone missing—on both sides totaled more than 1 million men. There, from July through November 1916, Germany suffered more than 650,000 casualties, Britain some 420,000, and France 204,000.

At sea during the early months, combatant ships of the opposing fleets occasionally met, first in squadron strength at Heligoland Bight, next off Coronel, in central Chile, and the Falkland Islands, then at the Dogger Bank, and finally in enormous force (and inconclusively, despite the destruction of fourteen British and eleven German ships, and the deaths of some 9,800 sailors from both sides) over May 31–June 1, 1916, near Jutland in the North Sea.

The Portsmouth, England, Historic Royal Dockyard is home to the Jutland Museum, which describes Jutland as "The Battle That Won The War." Surrounded by brilliant attractions nearby, among them Henry VIII's *Mary Rose* and Nelson's HMS *Victory*, this small museum needs to reach for attention, but the description is marketing, not history. Jutland's most recent historian, author Nicholas Jellicoe (Admiral John Jellicoe's grandson), concludes in his encyclopedic *Jutland, the Unfinished Battle* (Seaforth, 2017) that the battle's significance lay in the strategic lesson that Germany soon drew from it: that Great Britain's enervating North Sea blockade could not be defeated by surface action. Jutland was followed weeks later, in mid-August, by a German attempt to lure the Grand Fleet into a trap, and after two other desultory tries to engage, both sides determined to stay apart. After that, momentum for a German resort to submarine warfare grew irresistibly.

Not long after newspaper stories about Jutland—what had and had not happened, why the "British had let slip a supreme chance to destroy the German fleet," and what that failure meant for the future—disappeared from front pages, books examining the same subjects at great length appeared. By the end of 1916 more than seventy of them had been published in English, German, Danish, and French in the seven months since the battle.

A standout among these volumes was Rudyard Kipling's oddly organized and hard to classify work, *Sea Warfare* (Macmillan, 1916). His essay collection's obviously patched-together structure is explained by the fact that its contents had appeared earlier in the year as thirteen separate articles in two London newspapers. Kipling's mournful poem "My Boy Jack," mentioned earlier, led off the third and last part of his book, "The Destroyers at Jutland," which text was thriftily recycled from four articles in October's *Daily Telegraph*. (Today's library of books on that battle is substantial, some 574 in all, according to the WorldCat catalogue.)

Four years after that first publishing explosion of Jutland books came the suggestively subtitled *The Battle of Jutland: The Sowing and Reaping of the British Navy* (George H. Doran Co., 1920) by Commander Carlyon Bellairs, RN. His "Sowing and Reaping" phrase might have been borrowed from a private critique of Jutland written a few weeks after the battle by Vice Admiral Doveton Sturdee, RN, victor against von Spee in the Falklands, and in command of a battleship division at Jutland. Sturdee, in a critique of Jellicoe's leadership that Bellairs would adopt (and Andrew Gordon would quote much later), then wrote to Beatty, "It is almost inevitable now that we must reap what we have sown."

Going to sea first at age thirteen, Bellairs (1871–1955) spent eighteen years in the Royal Navy and then went on to a career that included journalism and terms as a member of Parliament before, during, and after the war until 1931. He apparently cut quite a figure as an MP, described by a contemporary paper admiringly as "one of the most striking personalities. Tall, with iron grey hair, beautifully brushed, he wears a monocle with distinction, and what is more, apparently with comfort, and he talks with an attractive voice."

As a prewar MP Bellairs had been a frequent critic of Royal Navy readiness to fight. His *The Battle of Jutland* compiled these criticisms into a single, retrospective text. In it Bellairs roasted Admiral Jellicoe, commander of the Grand

Fleet, describing him, as the *Spectator* wrote in a book review at the end of February 1920, "as a typical example of the officer who knew more about departmental routine ashore than command of a battle-fleet . . . wedded to a fatal defensive theory of war."

The *Weekly Review* several months later, on June 30, 1920, was no more generous: it concluded that Bellairs's case against Jellicoe "looks like a true bill—like a case not for a viscounty, but for a court martial." And the piece continued wistfully to pile up might-have-beens: "if [Rear Admiral Franz] Hipper and [Vice Admiral Reinhard] Von Scheer had been sunk, the clearance of the Baltic offered merely technical difficulties, Russia might have been stiffened, the submarine menace, which within a year was threatening starvation for England, could have been eradicated in a few months."

Bellairs's book attracted Benton Decker's attention, too. Decker, then and for a while longer a temporary rear admiral with his career in decline, was serving as the commandant of the Seventh Naval District with headquarters on Key West. The two, British author and American rear admiral, apparently had met earlier in London, which might account for the fact that it was this particular book on the battle that drew Decker's attention.

In late July 1920, Decker forwarded a copy to Secretary Daniels, using Bellairs's critique to flog his own arguments for US Navy reform in a cover letter: that Jellicoe and Beatty had failed because as administrators they lacked the understanding of war fighting principles which Nelson and Tōgō had grasped instinctively; that teaching such principles to US Navy flag officers was the explicit purpose of war gaming at Newport; and that to ensure preparation for war in the future, the US Navy needed a general staff rather than a clique "controlling the affairs and personnel of the navy in their own interests." Daniels seems not to have replied directly. The clique that was being abused was Daniels's own inner office, and he saw the proposed general staff as a dangerous move away from civilian control and toward despised "Prussianism."

In Decker's view, the issue wasn't which one of them—Jellicoe, the commander in chief of the Grand Fleet and commanding directly its three battleship squadrons homeported at Scapa Flow, or his subordinate Beatty, commanding the Battle Cruiser Fleet based to the south at Rosyth—had failed the other at Jutland (the usual focus of Battle of Jutland analyses then and since), but rather that *neither* Jellicoe nor Beatty was up to his enormous operational responsibilities. Decker found the explanation in inadequate training in peace for operations in war.

Decker's conclusion is very loosely akin to Professor Andrew Gordon's in his *The Rules of the Game: Jutland and British Naval Command* (John Murray, 1996, and Naval Institute Press, 2000). Gordon found the source of Jellicoe's and Beatty's shared failure to lie less in personal lapses than in the history and sociology of the Victorian and later Edwardian Royal Navy, in which Nelson's triumphantly improvisational fleet was converted during the century after 1805 into something very like the Rockettes of New York's Radio City Music Hall: a beautiful, brilliantly turned-out precision dance team, flawlessly executing practiced, scripted maneuvers in close formation, unopposed . . . but at sea. The highlight of that achievement might have been the lock-step precision formation steaming on exhibit during the Combined Fleet exercises of 1903.

An attempt to preserve (more accurately to reintroduce) the possibility of aggressive spontaneity in fleet maneuvers in the presence of the enemy and under fire, and to break away from rigid control by signal from the flagship failed in the aftermath of a deadly collision on June 22, 1893, in the Mediterranean that in minutes sank HMS *Victoria* (drowning 358 men) and dangerously holed HMS *Camperdown*. Among the many dead was Vice Admiral Sir George Tryon, RN, the fleet commander riding *Victoria* and the architect of the signaling and maneuver scheme under which the fleet's two divisions were operating as they approached the anchorage at Tripoli just before the catastrophe. The wreck, the subsequent legal proceedings, and the next edition of the signal book ensured a return to "choreographical certainties of maneuvering," and a fleet led by administrators rather than war-fighters (despite Beatty's later effort to pull in a different direction).

What Jutland demonstrated was that naval officers, no less than their army counterparts, had misunderstood the impact of technology upon the conduct of modern warfare, thinking that the new war could be fought in the old way, but with lines of battle drawn up to face each other farther apart.

By the dreadful standards of World War I on land, the total of lives lost on the water—even adding to the navy statistics those from merchant ships and passenger transports sunk, among them RMS *Lusitania*'s 1,200—was modest, around 65,000, split almost equally, for the Royal Navy and the Kaiserliche Marine; some hundreds more counting lost fishermen and other mariners from elsewhere. The small number reflects accurately the negligible role surface fleet engagements played in the war—not that greater numbers of dead at sea would necessarily convert to greater strategic significance—much more than posturing but less than anything else, to the intense frustration not only of the brave sailors embarked, but also of chastened ministers in the governments of both sides. They, dazzled by Captain Mahan's theorizing—and not yet persuaded by Professor Halford Mackinder's rival concepts—and seduced by the irresistible glamour of big ships and big guns, had misspent fortunes to build the fleets now idling at anchor in home waters.

Mackinder (1861–1947), author of *Britain and the British Seas* (William Heinemann, 1902), concluded in his 1904 essay "The Geographical Pivot of History" that with the development of railroads, the control of the Eastern European "heartland" that had escaped Napoleon now had become not simply possible but more important than control of the seas. This bold idea, contradicting Mahan and the sacred texts of the Royal Navy, would prove itself in the century's remaining hot and cold wars, even as Mahan and his theorizing receded into history.

Still, if you looked hard for it, in January 1917 there was some reason for satisfaction in London with the progress of the war, even as the stalemate on the Western Front continued to gnaw hungrily, and apparently insatiably, through the young troops of the late Lord Kitchener's army.[2]

Granted, Belgium had been swiftly overrun and was still occupied by the Germans, but France hadn't fallen on the German schedule—hadn't fallen at all; the French army mutinies that suggested it still might fall wouldn't begin for another few months, not until after the bloody failure in mid-April of General Robert Nivelle's offensive at Chemin des Dames. Russia, too, was still in the fight; the revolution that would eject the tsar was a month off, and the one fomented by Lenin that would take Russia out of the war altogether and eventually reshape Eurasia was still an unknowable ten months away. Moreover, while the Battle of Jutland the previous spring had fallen far short of the Trafalgar-like victory Britons had trained themselves to expect of the Royal Navy, their Grand Fleet safely ensconced in the great circular anchorage of Scapa Flow was still by every measure the world's most powerful naval force. And the German High Seas Fleet that had seemed so threatening a few years ago was now bottled up impotently in its home ports with its morale collapsing, apparently unwilling to challenge the Grand Fleet in force again, and otherwise incapable of breaching the blockade that was choking Germany.

The engine behind the optimism was just that—the apparent continued success of the British naval blockade of Germany. In January the war cabinet was presented with a confidential memorandum assessing "the Present Progress of the Blockade" that began: "all the evidence available tends to show that, with some minor exceptions, practically no goods coming from overseas are getting through to Germany."[3] Where there was leakage of strategic materials, such as iron ore, wood pulp (for nitrocellulose), and copper, into Germany, the flow was overland through Germany's neutral neighbors, subject to complex metering regimes that depended on British negotiating leverage with each neighbor, not on blockade.

The blockade of Germany had begun with the long-ago outbreak of war in August 1914, a distant blockade almost from the outset because of the danger to enforcers closer to shore posed by mines and submarines. Those dangers displayed themselves quickly and dramatically that September 22, when Cruiser Force C, off the Dutch coast, was savaged by SM (Seiner Majestät) U-9. In an hour the old U-boat sank the antiquated cruisers HMS *Aboukir*, *Hogue*, and *Cressy* in order, trading all six torpedoes on board (five hits) for the three ships and 1,459 of their crew.

The following November Great Britain had announced that the entire North Sea was a military area, and that traffic through it proceeded at its peril. The definition of contraband, cargo subject to seizure, was at the same time expanded generally to include foodstuffs. The German response came roughly three months later, in two parts. The first declared in reprisal "the waters surrounding Great Britain and Ireland including the whole English Channel" to be a military zone, where after mid-February merchant ships, including those of neutrals, found in the zone would be subject to attack by submarines. The second expanded German Navy zeppelin bombing raids to raids across the Channel in January 1915 and, beginning in late May, raids against defenseless London itself. (The huge dirigibles had flown during the first year of the war against Liège and Antwerp.) The terror they engendered on the ground in the British capital was palpable, but the destruction was not decisive, even when supplemented by twin- and four-engine bomber raids two years later—nothing remotely like what German V-missiles were to inflict on the British capital in the next war.

Like Britain, in 1917 Germany was incapable of feeding herself, and the blockade—long since fully in place and supported by fine-grained British economic intelligence to the level of cargoes on individual merchant ships—was inflicting real suffering on the German home front. The suffering has been described as progressing from tolerable dietary reductions in 1915, through severe rationing and pressures on wartime production the next year, toward the edge of a revolutionary crisis prompted by grinding austerity during the two years that followed.[4] More apparent now than it was then, with the blockade entering its third year when the United States entered the war in early 1917, Germany's ability to feed, arm, and even clothe itself had been near fatally impaired.

Echoing very generally what German chancellor Theobald von Bethmann-Hollweg had told the German Reichstag earlier in the day in Berlin, in the mid-afternoon of Wednesday, January 31, 1917, Wilson's Secretary of State, Robert Lansing, learned from Germany's ambassador, Count Johann Heinrich von Bernstorff, that beginning the next morning his country would return for a third time to waging unrestricted submarine warfare, a tactic that had been abandoned the previous May and reconsidered and rejected by the Germans several times since.[5] Now it was rejected no longer.

Before he got to that, von Bernstorff—eight years in Washington, fluent in English, married to an American, and loyally expounding a decision he didn't support—explained in a letter left behind with the secretary that "the freedom of the seas . . . has always formed part of the leading principles of Germany's political program. All the more the Imperial Government regrets that the attitude of her enemies, who are so entirely opposed to peace, makes it impossible for the world at present to bring about the realization of these lofty ideals."

> Since two years and a half England is using her naval power for a criminal attempt to force Germany into submission by starvation. In brutal contempt of international law, the group of powers led by England not only curtail the legitimate trade of their opponents, but they also, by ruthless pressure, compel neutral countries either to altogether forego every trade not agreeable to the entente Powers, or to limit it according to their arbitrary decrees.
>
> The English government . . . insists upon continuing its war of starvation,

which does not at all affect the military power of its opponents, but compels women and children, the sick and the aged, to suffer for their country pains and privations which endanger the vitality of the nation.

The Imperial Government . . . is now compelled to continue the fight for existence, again forced upon it, with the full employment of all the weapons which are at its disposal.[6]

A memorandum attached to the ambassador's letter announced that after midnight in Europe "all sea traffic will be stopped with every available weapon and without further notice . . . around Great Britain, France, Italy and to the Eastern Mediterranean." The "available weapons" he spoke of were, of course, submarines.

The sole exception to this regime was to be a single, specially marked American passenger liner sailing weekly on a fixed schedule and along a prescribed route from the United States to and from Falmouth, England.[7]

Chancellor von Bethmann-Hollweg had said nothing to the Reichstag about hunger at home (his emphasis had been on how the Kaiserliche Marine's enlarged submarine fleet opened a path to victory, and also on global wheat, coal, and shipping shortages), but Von Bernstorff's reference to "starvation" was certainly correct. By the end of the winter of 1916–17, the painful German "turnip winter" just past, the Royal Navy's blockade and its controls over marine freight, policed by the Dover and Northern Squadrons, was so effective that in an economy already dependent on foreign trade before the war, and being badly mismanaged during it, citizens at home were subsisting on short rations of adulterated bread, ersatz sausage, potatoes, turnips, and occasionally "boiled crow." Martin Gilbert, one of Churchill's biographers, has calculated that some three-quarters of a million Germans died of starvation during the war; other estimates go as high as one million.

The resumption announcement, reversing a decision to cease such operations made in May the year before, stunned Washington. Von Bernstorff's message immediately provoked a crisis in German-American relations, beginning with the initial response, a break in diplomatic relations, discussed and unanimously agreed by Wilson's cabinet on February 2 and effected the next day.

Weeks later, in Berlin on February 27, with American-flagged merchant ship losses at sea steadily mounting since unrestricted operations were resumed, the German chancellor explained his government's submarine warfare policy to the Reichstag and to the world in what amounted to an indirect response to the American decision to break diplomatic relations. The next morning's *New York Times* encapsulated Von Bethmann-Holweg's case in a cascade of subheads atop a long, five-column story: "Germany Is "Going Ahead"; Chancellor Regrets Break over U-boats, But Can't Alter His Policy; Our Neutrality One-sided; Evidence by "Submission" to British Restrictions, While We Refuse to Accept Germany's; Denied Breaking Pledges; Tells Reichstag Assurances to Us Were Conditional on England's Adherence to Law; Wilson's Note Required No Answer; U-boats "Surpass Expectations"; Premature to Speak of Peace."

Fully nine weeks passed between the break in relations and Wilson's request to Congress for a declaration of war, during the first seven of which the president and key members of his cabinet (among them the secretaries of war and navy, and the postmaster general) continued to maneuver to avoid joining the war while reluctantly taking half-measures to respond to the crisis, such as arming merchant ships with navy gun crews, and otherwise very slowly edging toward the now inevitable decision.

Forcing that process were the ten American ships sunk one after the other in the Atlantic and the Mediterranean by German submarines in February and March. The first, a twenty-six-year-old freighter, SS *Housatonic*, out of Newport News, Virginia, for London with a load of wheat, sank on February 3, gunned down by U-53, the day after Wilson's speech to businessmen in St. Louis, a city characterized by the *Chicago Tribune* as "the focal point of American Germanism."

U-53's courtly commanding officer, Kapitänleutnant Hans Rose, had made a name for himself the previous October 7, when, seventeen days out of Wilhelmshaven, he'd spent three hours that Saturday in then neutral Newport, Rhode Island, appearing unexpectedly, ostensibly to mail a letter to the German ambassador in Washington. While ashore in dress uniform Rose conducted the usual courtesy calls on his surprised hosts: the naval district commander, Rear Admiral Austin Knight, USN, and the commander of the Atlantic Fleet's destroyer force, Rear Admiral Albert Gleave, USN, the latter on board the *Chester*-class cruiser USS *Birmingham*.

While Rose ricocheted around Newport, his submarine lay tied up in port—both deck guns and eight stowed torpedoes visible—silently illustrating the Kaiserliche Marine's transatlantic reach, and delivering an unspoken message of menace that would a day later be made explicit when U-53 left Newport to start her first war patrol. That Sunday, October 8, once at sea off lightship *Nantucket* (LV-85) and again in international waters, U-53 quickly sank the foreign-flagged steamers *Strathdene, West Point, Stephano, Kingston, Bloomersdijk,* and *Christian Knudsen,* for a total of 22,000 tons of shipping. This while her surprise visit to Newport the day before was front-page news in dozens of American Sunday newspapers. ("German U-53 In and Out in Nimble Time. Plunger Stays But Three Hours in Newport Harbor," on the front page of the Sioux City, Iowa, *Journal* was a typical headline.)

Other ships soon followed *Housatonic* to the bottom, including the schooner *Lyman M. Law* and the steamers *Laconia, Algonquin, Vigilancia, City of Memphis,* and *Illinois.* On March 13, the day after *Algonquin* (out of New York for London with $1.7 million in food on board) was sunk off the Isles of Scilly, Secretary Daniels published "Regulations Governing the Conduct of American Merchant Vessels on Which Armed Guards Have Been Placed." These rules of engagement, laid out in twenty-eight paragraphs, permitted the navy guard detail (an officer, two gun crews, and signalmen) on board to fire on any submarine spotted within two miles of the ship's route, and once engaged required the guard "not to submit to the gun fire of a submarine so long as the armed guard can continue to fire."[8]

The next three, beginning with *Vigilancia,* went down on the same weekend, March 16–17. At the cabinet meeting on March 20, the loss of the trio apparently prompted the still reluctant decision to call Congress into special session to seek a declaration of war. The subsequent losses of the tanker *Healdton,* the freighter *Aztec,* and the schooner *Marguerite* just added to the momentum. An eleventh in the string, freighter *Missourian,* sank on April 4 of still uncertain causes, but in any case too late to affect the decision to go to war.[9]

The crisis in German-American relations was heightened even before February ended by the explosive public disclosure of the "Zimmermann telegram," a leading candidate in the rich field of contenders vying for diplomatic history's dumbest dispatch prize. Arthur Zimmermann, formerly the deputy, had been promoted to German foreign minister the previous November, after his predecessor, Gottlieb von Jagow—a chain-smoking "small, slight man of nervous disposition" in American diplomat Henry Morgenthau's description—was eased out of office. Von Jagow, at the ministry for the past three years, left exhausted by his unsuccessful fight against the resumption of unrestricted submarine warfare. Zimmermann, his successor, knew little about the United States.

His personal knowledge of the country whose great weight would soon fall on the scales in Europe was largely limited to what he'd gleaned looking out the window during a single transcontinental train trip fourteen years earlier, one that began with a few days in San Francisco and ended with a few in New York. Immodestly, he didn't let Count von Bernstorff's well-informed views about America sway him.

Sent in code to Heinrich von Eckhardt, the German ambassador in Mexico, on January 19, 1917, ten days after resumption of unrestricted submarine warfare had been agreed by the Kaiser, Zimmermann's telegram (drafted by a staffer and apparently only hastily considered by the otherwise preoccupied Zimmermann) foresaw that the United States might join the other side once the Kaiserliche Marine's submarines were unleashed on February 1, renouncing Germany's nine-month-old "Sussex Pledge."[10]

In that event, Von Eckhardt was instructed to propose a German alliance with Mexico, offering "generous financial support," holding out as an incentive the heady possibility of reconquest of "lost territory in Texas, New Mexico and Arizona," and encouraging the Mexicans to invite Japan to join in the pact, boldly offering California as the lure. The motive was not justice for Mexico, but to keep the United States preoccupied with events on its borders and in the Pacific, and away from those in Europe.[11]

On February 5 Berlin further instructed Von Eckhardt to open that discussion with Mexico without waiting for a US declaration of war. By then cryptanalysts in the Royal Navy's "Room 40" in the Old Admiralty Building had broken the intercepted text—transmitted helpfully over American diplomatic cable channels (because the German ones had been sabotaged) that had a node in the United Kingdom—into plain language.

The decrypted telegram was finally delivered to Wilson on February 24. On March 1 many US newspapers published the sensational story, the *New York Times* doing so in yet another triple headline bridging all eight columns of front-page text: "Germany Seeks an Alliance against US; Asks Japan and Mexico to Join Her; Full Text of Proposal Made Public." The usual popular source for this history is Barbara Tuchman's admired and outdated *The Zimmermann Telegram* (Viking, 1958). Thomas Boghardt's *The Zimmermann Telegram: Intelligence, Diplomacy, and America's Entry into World War I* (Naval Institute Press, 2012) tells the same story but, drawing more on German sources and on formerly classified cryptologic material unavailable to Tuchman sixty years ago, is more insightful.

A rarity in the highest levels of the German Foreign Office, not a Prussian aristocrat but rather a commoner risen to ministerial rank from the low-status consular service, at first Zimmermann had made a good impression on the American ambassador in Berlin, James Gerard (1867–1951), who was initially attracted by Zimmermann's "plain and hearty manners and democratic airs." Their relationship began to sour soon after *Lusitania* was sunk, when Zimmermann reportedly told Gerard, "The United States does not dare do anything against Germany because we have five hundred thousand German reservists in America who will rise in arms against your government if your government should dare to take any action against Germany."

Gerard served in the German capital from October 1913 until his expulsion when relations were severed in February 1917. "As he said this," Gerard wrote in his popular memoir *My Four Years in Germany* (George H. Doran Company, 1917), "he worked himself up to a passion and repeatedly struck the table with his fist. I told him we had five hundred thousand and one lamp posts in America, and that was where the German reservists would find themselves if they tried any uprising." The expectation that German Americans would rise in insurrection were the United States to go to war against their homeland wasn't unique to Zimmermann. Von Jagow had drawn some comfort from that idea, too. In February 1916, while still the foreign minister, he'd asked Henry Morgenthau, on the way home via Berlin from Constantinople in frustration, about it. "Dismiss any such idea from your mind," the German-born Morgenthau wrote he'd replied, "the first one who attempts it will be punished so promptly and drastically that such a movement will not go far. And I think that the loyal German-Americans will be the first to administer such punishment."[12]

On April 2, 1917, Wilson asked many of the members of Congress, who at the end of 1914 had read his second annual state of the union message denying an American interest in the European war, for a declaration to join in the fighting. That's when Wilson—who'd campaigned for reelection months ago on the proud boast "He Kept Us Out of War" and went on to beat the Republican, Justice Charles Evans Hughes, by only a handful of votes in three states—finally overcame his great fears about how American belligerency would inevitably derail his agenda for the country, and asked Congress for a declaration of war. Earlier the day before, the Oriental Navigation Co.'s armed steamer SS *Aztec* en route from New York City to Le Havre had been torpedoed off Brest by U-46, the ninth American ship to be sunk since February 1, and coincidentally, the first to go down with a navy gun crew on board.

Wilson was halfway through his 3,400-word war message before he turned his focus from submarine warfare to the two lesser reasons for belligerency: German "criminal intrigues" and espionage in the United States, and Germany's attempt "to stir up enemies against us at our very door," referencing the Zimmermann telegram.[13] In passing, Wilson paused to mention the "wonderful and heartening things that have been happening within the last few weeks in Russia," and went on to fantasize, ignoring three centuries of history in a paragraph of pure fiction that, had he read it decades later, would have stunned Mikhail Gorbachev or Vladimir Putin:

> Russia was known by those who knew it best to have been always in fact democratic at heart, in all the vital habits of her thought, in all the intimate relationships of her people that spoke their natural instinct, their habitual attitude toward life. The autocracy that crowned the summit of her political structure, long as it had stood and terrible as was the reality of its power, was not in fact Russian in origin, character, or purpose; and now it has been shaken off and the great, generous Russian people have been added in all their naïve majesty and might to the forces that are fighting for freedom in the world, for justice and for peace.

The embarrassing problem Wilson thought he'd just escaped, fighting on the side of one rigid autocracy against another, was to reappear in the next war on the Continent, with Stalin replacing Nicholas II in the role of autocrat and ally.

One side effect of the political crisis was the conversion of Wilson's cabinet meetings, until then dismissed by several secretaries as mere high-level storytelling sessions and a waste of time, into what "plump, amiable" secretary of the interior Franklin Lane later described as "real councils of war." The usual explanations for the meetings' lack of substance are Wilson's personal leadership style, and his conviction that the self-same Lane was a compulsive leaker, incapable of keeping the substance of cabinet discussions out of his gossip.

Wilson's request for a declaration of war against Germany was greeted with open satisfaction by critics of the president's earlier refusal to join the fight. One such critic was the enormously wealthy publisher and politician George

Harvey, since 1899 editor of New York City's prestigious *North American Review*, a former Wilson ally, and lapsed Democrat. Harvey spoke for the president's detractors in a lengthy *Review* editorial, "For Freedom and Democracy."

"The issue is in doubt no longer," he wrote on March 19 for the magazine's April 1917 issue, anticipating an American declaration of war. "We know now, if we have not known before, what this war is. It is the last of the great battles for Freedom and Democracy . . . We are for war, of course," Harvey announced, "we are; and for reasons good and plenty." First, "because we have reached and passed the limit of forbearance in trying to maintain amicable relations with a barbaric brute who has . . . incited all manner of treasonable activities and damnable outrages within our borders, has gloated over his avowed assassination of our innocent and harmless citizens of both sexes and all ages on the high seas."

Embedded in the two itemized reasons that followed ("to prove ourselves eager and fearless in support of free life and full liberty the world over," and "to complete the ring of democracies around the doomed autocracy and . . . infect all Germany, all Austria, and all Hungary with the new spirit of Russia") was Harvey's judgment that in the case of the coming test, "war is curative, not destructive; a blessing, not a curse." "Colonel" Harvey, fifty-three when he wrote this (the rank was an honorific), went on to become Harding's ambassador in London in April 1921. No trained diplomat, and apparently incapable of being circumspect, he played a prominent if confusing role in the talks preceding the three-power Washington Naval Conference of 1921–22 before leaving office in 1923, soon after Harding's death that August.

The American declaration of war followed, entirely coincidentally, by several days the launch of Germany's third great—and only successful—end-game gamble (seducing Mexico and again unleashing its submarines having been the other two): the introduction by train of Lenin and his claque into Russia, then writhing in violent confusion following the abdication of Tsar Nicholas II two weeks earlier. Lenin was supported by the provision of a German funding stream that by year-end allowed his Bolsheviks to defeat Alexander Kerensky and the provisional government, which had committed to continuing the war and terribly misjudged the threat from its left. On April 3, the day after Wilson delivered his historic war message, Lenin stepped off a train at the Finland Station in Petrograd (St. Petersburg) for the first time, ending his sixteen years of exile in Europe. His vision would make him, arguably, the most important political figure of his century. `

After months of bloody disorder in 1917, the revolution that ejected Nicholas II and led to Lenin—brilliantly described by Helen Rappaport in *Caught in the Revolution* (St. Martin's Press, 2016)—ended with the victory of the Bolsheviks, with a German-Russian armistice in early December, and with the Treaty of Brest-Litovsk near the end of the month that freed Germany to move its formations west. (Desertions from those units being redeployed to the western front suggests German morale was plummeting as the war moved into its fourth year and last phase.)

But first, on April 6, Congress responded to the president, saying he was "authorized and directed to employ the entire naval and military forces of the United States and the resources of the Government to carry on war against the Imperial German Government." The vote for war in the Senate was 82–6, in the House of Representatives a more reluctant 373–50. (Jeannette Rankin of Montana, the first woman to sit in the House, was one of the "nay" votes. She was to vote against going to war with Japan in 1941, too.) A similar declaration against what the *Ogden* [Utah] *Standard* styled as "two medieval governments," Austria-Hungary, didn't come for another eight months. And soon after that, Germany and Russia agreed to an armistice, withdrawing the Russians, their might and "naïve majesty," from the war entirely.

The American declaration of war surprised many in Berlin, not just German officialdom, where the expectation remained that the enormous population of immigrant German Americans in the country would act as an effective brake on any possible march toward war in Washington.

Not until the tenth and last chapter of the late John Keegan's *The First World War* (Alfred A. Knopf, 1999) and the book's final 50—of 427—pages did Keegan focus his attention on the United States. Keegan's tardy consideration reflects that when the United States entered the war, the other combatants had already been battling ferociously in Europe, the Middle East, Africa, and at sea for fully two and a half years.

Germany's bold, desperate gamble in February 1917 was that her submarines could defeat the British—whose countermeasures had been ineffective against submarines thus far, and who were dependent on imports to feed themselves and to continue the fight—before the United States had time to mobilize and deploy an expeditionary army that could shape the outcome of the war. In Berlin in early 1917 this looked like a very good bet. When Wilson finally renounced neutrality on April 2, the American army—then seventeenth in size in the world and lightly armed by the standards of the war being fought—was a trivial and inexperienced force as measured against the huge, veteran armies of the combatants in Europe. These few armed and trained Americans were, in any event, across the same contested waters that were making resupply of the British Isles so parlous. Further, the American merchant marine, never recovered since its collapse during the Civil War and constituting only 4 percent or so of global merchant ship tonnage in the summer the war began, was obviously incapable of moving an army of any size over the Atlantic swiftly and safely in the face of anything more threatening than bad weather.

In 1917 the US Army's authorized combat strength comprised 38 regiments of infantry, 17 of cavalry, and 9 of field artillery. Even including National Guardsmen, the members of state militias, and marines, American men in uniform and under arms in the spring of 1917 added up to no more than the Romanian Army's strength when it had lent its light weight to the Entente's allies in the fight against Austria-Hungary the previous August.[14] These relatively few American soldiers, outnumbered twenty to one by Germany's, included some who were members of the regiments with what passed for recent combat experience chasing Pancho Villa in Mexico under General John J. Pershing, along with many who had no field, never mind combat, experience at all. Their numbers would have to be multiplied exponentially. Then, together with their weapons, horses, and heavy equipment, the new divisions would have to be moved cross-country to East Coast embarkation ports and a further 3,600 nautical miles to reception ports in northern France, there to be trained some more, before the United States could play any meaningful military role on the ground in Europe.

Mindful of the draft's unhappy history on both sides of the Civil War, President Wilson had hoped that raising an army could be accomplished exclusively through recruiting volunteers. The early response to patriotic appeals, however, was tepid; through mid-May 1917 only 73,000 volunteers had come forward. That small number of men—equivalent to fleshing out something like a dozen typical European divisions, in a year that saw France and Great Britain field nearly 170 divisions and Germany almost 180—prompted passage in Congress of the Selective Service Act. Made law on May 18, 1917, the act authorized compulsory enlistment, first drawn from the 21-to-30-year-old cohort of men, but amended in August to include all men aged 18 to 45. (By comparison, in Germany the draft for either military service or compulsory labor in war industries had been recently extended to all men aged between 15 and 60.) Draft registration began a few weeks later, on June 5, and the first men inducted began to report before the end of the summer to training camps then under construction.

In its November 1917 issue (vol. 32, no. 5) *National Geographic* published a very long piece by William Showalter, one of two associate editors at the popular magazine, about the geographical and historical environment of the nation's thirty-two National Army and National Guard camps, entitled "America's New Soldier Cities." Their construction, the author wrote, "was an unprecedented task, executed in the face of unheard-of difficulties, with unrivalled speed and in an unparalleled spirit. It is America's answer to the world that has mistaken her natural love of peace for an unwillingness to go to war." *National Geographic*'s timing was good; interest in the subject on the home front was intense. Only a month earlier the first American troops had arrived on the front line and fired their opening shots of the war.

Showalter began his descriptive inventory of the camps with a flood of statistics, intended to dramatize the vast scope of the new construction and training programs that underlay the deployment of American divisions to the battlefields of Europe that had just begun.

Groping for a way to impart scale, Showalter quickly dismissed the obvious comparison with the effort behind the recent construction of the Panama Canal. Instead, to build the sixteen National Army cantonments (sixteen other bases supported the National Guard) he described material and supplies moving about the country metaphorically in "a string of [rail]cars stretching from Portland, Maine, to Portland, Oregon"; over four months 25,000 carpenters driving home 1,200 miles of nails a day, during 7-day, 65-hour-long work weeks; pounding those nails into enough sawed lumber to "make a boardwalk four feet wide—runners and all—from Palm Beach to Baghdad via the Bering Strait and the Arctic Circle"; and the kitchen waste from each camp (collected as part of a pioneering trash recycling effort) sufficient to feed fully 4,000 hogs, with every porker loyally gaining a pound per day on its economical diet.

Cooperation everywhere and on everything characterized the huge construction labor force, Showalter discovered. "Even the thousands of negro laborers at the Southern cantonments," he remarked, casually reflecting the usual prejudice of his times, "became imbued with enthusiasm for their work and heartily supported every effort to keep the camp sites up to the 100 per cent mark in sanitation, although sanitary science is well-nigh a sealed book to them." "Can you imagine several thousand Virginia negroes, in the midst of the watermelon season, with the Hanover crop in all its luscious luxuriance hard by, and not a rind to be found on a camp site thousands of acres in extent? It may have tried their souls to abstain, and yet the site of Camp Lee [near Petersburg, Virginia, and named after Robert E. Lee, the camp housed recruits from western Pennsylvania and both Virginias] was as free from watermelon rinds as it was from polar bears or African lions."

By the spring following publication, four American divisions were on the ground in France. About that time the first wave of "Spanish flu" appeared. A second, lethal wave erupted that autumn, soon revealing that the army's planning factor for training camp hospital beds (three per hundred men) was grossly inadequate to respond to a highly contagious disease that exploded through the crowded barracks of the camps, where young men from many places were pressed together.

The flip side of the German conviction that the United States couldn't go to war against Germany because, somehow, German and Austro-Hungarian immigrants and their American descendants would rally to prevent it was the no less powerful belief among American citizens that these same "hyphenated Americans" automatically posed a grave danger to homeland security and to the successful prosecution of the war once joined. (Similar fears one world war later would be behind the shameful incarceration of 100,500 Japanese Americans, more than two-thirds of whom were US citizens.)

Historic census data show that in 1910 resident immigrants in the United States born in Germany and Austria-Hungary, and first-generation Americans with their roots in these same places, represented roughly 16 percent of the US population—some 15 million, out of a total US population of just under 92 million. They were disproportionately concentrated in just five states—Pennsylvania, Illinois, New York, Ohio, and Wisconsin—where their political, economic, and cultural influence was substantial. (Among the 15 million were two-time immigrant from the kingdom of Bavaria, Friedrich Trump, ejected from the kingdom for having evaded military service, and his son, first-generation Frederick Trump, the grandfather and father, respectively, of former president Donald Trump.) Significant immigration from both Germany and Austria-Hungary continued until the start of the war, peaking at around 300,000 per year in 1913–14, and then collapsing after 1915 to a low of just 3,000 in 1917.

Before the United States joined the fight, both combatant sides had worked hard, openly and covertly, to stir up support among immigrants in America likely to be sympathetic to their cause. Thus, Germany saw the Irish in America as natural sympathizers, who could be enlisted to agitate locally for independence from Great Britain at home, and—importantly—for an end to American material support to the Triple Entente. For its part, the Triple Entente targeted propagandizing at Polish, Czech, and Slavic immigrants in the United States to serve its own goals. Hence, anxiety about political divisions at home and the threat that these divisions potentially posed to the preservation of American neutrality until April 1917, and in 1917–18 to the successful prosecution of the war, wasn't entirely irrational.

Oddly, in the innocent times between the Civil War and the Great War, federal statutes provided a very limited basis for action against political "intrigues" in the United States by foreigners. Stranger still, no federal statute addressed either sabotage or espionage in peacetime. Further, Wilson's insistence on neutrality and the initially cautious instincts of his attorney general, Thomas Gregory (who sharply reversed course later), worked at first to restrain any activism or improvisation on the part of the Justice Department to constrain foreign agents' activity.

By the end of 1915, however, as evidence of aggressive German propagandizing began to leak into the American press, the administration looked to Congress for authority to act against foreign agents, initially using the very modest investigative resources of the Departments of Justice and the Treasury. Months later, in July 1916, an explosion of more than a thousand tons of munitions stored on the powder piers at Black Tom Island in New York Harbor—supposedly heard in Philadelphia, and eventually determined to be sabotage by one Slovakian and two German saboteurs—provided a fillip to expansion of the Justice Department's seven-year-old Bureau of Investigation to a grand total of 300 agents. Justice's Bureau of Investigation and the Treasury's more established Secret Service then turned their attention to the threat, and also to internecine competition for control of the federal government's counterespionage portfolio. In this contest, in late March Justice began to draw on a new, remarkable citizens' auxiliary, the American Protective League.

The American Protective League, its first historian, Emerson Hough, explained imaginatively and ponderously in his *The Web: Authorized History of the American Protective League* (Chicago: Reilly and Lee Co., 1919), was "a silent, unknown army of more than a quarter million of the most loyal and intelligent citizens of America, who indeed did spring to arms overnight. It fought battles, saved lives, saved cities, saved treasures, defended the flag, apprehended countless traitors, did its own tremendous share in the winning of the war. It saved America. It did protect. It was a league."

Hough (1857–1923), *Saturday Evening Post* contributor, author of the 1902 bestseller *The Mississippi Bubble* and other popular Western fiction, and a hard-line nativist, went on to credit this "semi-vigilante" movement "with having brought to justice three million cases of disloyalty"—disloyalty manifested by "an organization comprising between 200,000 and 300,000 volunteers, in large part German-Americans, who were secret spies in this country and who reported regularly to German consuls and agents in widely scattered centers of the German spy system in the United States."[15]

Unsaid in this summary, but the subject of Hough's later chapters, was a different mission from sniffing out spies, that of unearthing draft dodgers by conducting "slacker raids." The largest of these dragnets came during several days in mid-July 1918 in Chicago, when reportedly 150,000 "suspects" were interrogated, 20,000 were seized, and 1,400 among them were inducted into the army as "willing or unwilling patriots." Two months later another such raid, in New York City, swept up 60,000 men, 199 (.3 percent) of whom were found to be draft dodgers.

The biggest of many volunteer vigilance organizations during the war—among them the colorfully named Boy Spies of America, the Anti-Yellow Dog League, the Sedition Slammers, and the Terrible Threateners—the APL was unique in that it alone could boast a loose official connection to the Department of Justice. The tie was substantial enough that APL's operatives were permitted to carry ID cards and to sport handsome badges identifying them as members of an auxiliary to that department. These now 100-year-old badges occasionally appear for sale on eBay.

Hough's book was published just after war's end (a year after French Strother's book from Doubleday, Page and Co., *Fighting Germany's Spies*, serialized in the *World's Work*, which included an admiring chapter about the APL), while American fears were shifting away from the threat posed by German sympathizers and toward that presented by Bolsheviks, the Industrial Workers of the World (IWW), the Non-Partisan League, and other leftists. In this anxious setting, it looked momentarily possible that the APL would find new life and vigor fighting the "Red Scare." For his part, Hough urged no pause in the remaking of America, to "purify the source of America's population and keep it pure . . . The old, polyglot, hubbub, hurdy-gurdy days of America are gone . . . The conviction is inevitable that we have too long been careless of our racial problems . . . We began to import work cattle, not citizens, for our so-called industrial captains."

More recent histories of the APL than Strother's and Hough's, such as Joan Jensen's *The Price of Vigilance* (1968) and Bill Mills's *The League: The True Story of Average Americans on the Hunt for WWI Spies* (2013), are much less enthusiastic about the work of the APL's largely untrained agents. A two-page appraisal strongly critical of the APL, Adam Hochschild's "All-American Vigilantes," appeared in the July 22, 2021, issue of the *New York Review of Books*. The reality seems to be that the league's amateur and self-important crimestoppers, in common with all other vigilante groups then and since, accomplished little more than harassing their neighbors and fellow citizens, and infringing on their civil rights.

The declaration of war was soon followed by legislation that reflected America's new status as a combatant (the Espionage, Trading with the Enemy, and Sedition Acts), by denying German Americans permission to live in the national capital and certain cities and ports, and by opening internment camps at army facilities in Georgia and Utah, where some five thousand Germans and even some conscientious objectors to the draft were held for the duration.

On November 14, 1917, the *New York Times* reported that former ambassador to Germany James W. Gerard had "flayed traitors" in a speech to an audience of two thousand the day before at a food conservation rally in Pittsburgh, one event in a yearlong speaking tour of the country and part of Gerard's continuing effort to stiffen resistance on the home front, and to monetize his abbreviated experience in Berlin. Later that month, in front of the Ladies

Aid Society of St. Mary's Hospital in New York City, Gerard delivered another scorcher. His message everywhere was the same: "the time for repentance of disloyal Americans and pro-German sympathizers has passed and the day is at hand when every person must decide whether he is for or against America," Gerard had trumpeted in Pittsburgh, continuing, "Americans are to be congratulated on their efforts to induce Germans in this country to be loyal, but there are still many under the protection of the American flag who are snakes in the grass." His solution: "we should 'hog-tie' every disloyal German-American, feed every pacifist raw meat, and hang every traitor to a lamp post to insure success in this war."

In anxious times, the audience for this kind of stimulation was huge. Broadway's 1,500-seat Knickerbocker Theater was the setting on March 10, 1918, for the premiere of a new silent film, *My Four Years in Germany*, based on Gerard's best-selling book of the same name published in New York City the year before, and serialized late in 1917 in the *Philadelphia Public Ledger* and also in Hearst's newspapers. Its producer, Warner Brothers, described it as "the whole inside story of Germany's diplomatic plots against America and the world . . . A tremendous production based on authentic facts, lavishly produced." Theater posters boasted it was "The Screen Classic That Has Put Pep in Our Patriotism."

In the heated, patriotic fervor approaching the end of America's first year in the war, the silent movie, 10 reels and 108 minutes long, garnered predictably enthusiastic reviews, among them one on March 23 from Peter Milne in the five-year-old trade paper, *Motion Picture News*.

> Last Sunday night at the Knickerbocker Theater when the film received its premier presentation, there was hardly a minute when the house did not ring with applause that turned into cheers. All the wily diplomacy with which the heads of the German nation sought to deceive the United States through its representative . . . all the atrocities witnessed by Mr. Gerard . . . these and a large assortment of views of Allied troops on the march make capital seeing for the man who goes to the theater ready to have his emotions stirred against the common enemy.
>
> "My Four Years in Germany" exposes the inner workings of the German political and military machine and lets its audience know why America is at war as clearly as did Mr. Gerard's book.

The four Warner brothers, Jewish immigrants from Germany, made their mark in an industry crowded with competitors, among them the still familiar names of Paramount, MGM, Universal, and Fox. All wanted to add movie production to the distribution businesses they were already competing for. *My Four Years in Germany* somehow became detached from Fox, which had bought it first, became the breakthrough piece of business for the Warners, and a model for the genre into the 1950s.

Gerard's book was, Harry Warner reportedly affirmed to Ambassador Gerard while trying to buy the title, "a stirring warning about the menace of the German military threat" that Americans and the world needed to hear in the fight for civilization, and that pitch seemed to seal the deal. (Nowhere, however, did the film visibly exhibit any connection to Warner Brothers, nor was its distribution under the company's aegis, and so even now its provenance is a little murky.)

My Four Years in Germany was pure propaganda, featuring superbly uniformed Germans behaving like Huns and punctually committing the requisite atrocities on film. It was, not surprisingly considering the times, a great commercial success. Never mind what Peter Milne wrote in 1918, the Warners' most recent biographer, David Thompson, described *My Four Years in Germany* in his *Warner Bros: The Making of an American Movie Studio* (Yale University Press, 2017) as "an awful, ambitious picture, stupid and noisy as only silent pictures could be, high-minded and low down, too long yet too short." It made the former ambassador a lot of money.

The New York Times reported the day after the premiere that Gerard had been in the opening night audience and had given a short speech afterward urging every patriotic American "to get behind the one man in the world who has the power to bring about the down fall of Prussianism, and that is the president of the United States." Reportedly the film grossed a then-huge $1.5 million; Gerard's deal had been $50,000 for the movie rights and 20 percent of the box office receipts. The same year that the film of *My Four Years* came out, Gerard, then back in private law practice (in 1913 he'd given up a seat as associate justice of New York State's Supreme Court to take the post in Berlin), published a second book, *Face to Face with Kaiserism* (George H. Doran Co., 1918), a lengthy sequel to his first. The film version of *My Four Years in Germany*, writes Thompson, might have stimulated a sequel, *Beware!* about which little is certain.[16]

Through the war years American hostility toward German Americans, their social and cultural groups, and their businesses swelled to encompass such contributions to homeland security as renaming sauerkraut ("liberty cabbage"), hamburgers ("Salisbury steak"), and German Shepherd dogs ("Alsatians"). The best of these might have been the transformation of German measles (rubella) into "Liberty measles."

Secretary Daniels had wanted Captain Henry Wilson Jr., USN, commanding officer of battleship *Pennsylvania*, to be the American liaison officer to the Admiralty in London, but Wilson declined, seeking duty at sea instead. So it was that at the end of March 1917, with a few days' notice, Rear Admiral William Sims (1858–1936, USNA '80), Daniels's next choice, left the Naval War College and soon sailed for Britain. He went with a single aide, both men traveling under aliases.[17] Their exciting Atlantic crossing accomplished (their ship, SS *City of New York*, hit a mine in the approaches to Liverpool's outer harbor on April 9), Sims slipped into London a day later and promptly began the work of coordinating operations and expectations with what he discovered to be a desperately hard-pressed Royal Navy.

That same work of coordination was going on simultaneously across the Atlantic. On April 10, the day Sims arrived in London, Admirals William Benson, Henry Mayo, and Clarence Williams met at the Chamberlin Hotel, Old Point Comfort, Virginia, with the senior British and French naval commanders in the Western Atlantic, Vice Admiral Montague Browning, RN, and Contre-Amiral Maurice Grasset, FN. The group moved the next day to Washington and joined in larger strategic cooperation discussions chaired by Secretary Daniels that also included some members of the General Board.

As Sims soon learned from Jellicoe (and later described to the public in his 1921 Pulitzer Prize-winning book *The Victory at Sea* [Doubleday, Page and Co., 1920]), these talks were being held against the backdrop of an imminent collapse of the British war effort under the pressure of a German submarine campaign that was "sweeping British commerce from the seas," even as additional U-boats were being built at the astonishing rate of a dozen per month. Meanwhile the campaign against U-boats deployed was being fatally impaired by a shortage of Royal Navy destroyers. Roughly half of the type were committed to escorting the battle fleet and unavailable to chase submarines.

FIGURE 8.2. Vice Admiral William S. Sims, USN.

This autographed photograph of the admiral appeared in Lieutenant Tracy Barrett Kittredge's *Naval Lessons of the Great War* (Doubleday, Page and Co., 1921). Sims's inscription reads: "in grateful remembrance of his efficient services as a member of my staff at the London Headquarters and, particularly, of his invaluable assistance in preparing the statements substantiating 'Certain Naval Lessons of the Great War' before the Senate Investigating Committee, March–May 1920 June 1920."

The reference is to the incendiary, lengthy (78 numbered paragraphs) letter Sims sent to Daniels on January 7, 1920, characterized as a "frank and fearless exposé" of blunders and mistakes in an article by Albert Fox published a week later on the front page of the *Washington Post*. That letter became the basis of the investigating committee's agenda.

Kittredge (1891–1957), a historian educated at University of California, Berkeley, and Oxford, was living in England at the start of the war. He became a navy reservist, served in the intelligence and historical sections of Sims's Grosvenor Gardens staff, and later joined the staff of the Naval War College. He subtitled his book, "A Review of the Senate Naval Investigation of the Criticisms by Admiral Sims of the Policies and Methods of Josephus Daniels." It was enthusiastically reviewed in the May 7, 1921, issue of *Scientific American* (vol. 124, no. 19), where editors Charles and Orson Munn—always interested in the navy—stood among Daniels's critics.

Source: Tracy Barnett Kittredge, *Naval Lessons of the
Great War* (Doubleday, Page and Co., 1921).

From these early talks, Secretary Daniels testified on May 10, 1920, in astonishingly acrimonious Senate subcommittee hearings on the conduct of the war chaired by Senator Hale, eight specific agreements emerged about how the burdens of defense and offense at sea would be shared.[18] The third of these provided that six destroyers would be "sent over in immediate future, based in British and French ports." The United States also accepted obligations to keep a naval presence off South America, off its own West Coast between Canada and Colombia, and off China, and to "supervise" the Gulf of Mexico. Nothing seems to have been said about Americans in the Mediterranean Sea, where a few powerful US Navy combatants had occasionally been sailing as neutrals since near the beginning of the war.

In time Sims's staff at its Grosvenor Gardens headquarters grew to 1,200, including 200 officers and 1,000 enlisted men. Much later, after he was back at home, Sims reflected on his long experience in England. That reflection appeared first as complaints about the distribution of awards to officers after the war in late 1919, then as an explosive letter sent to Secretary Daniels on January 7, 1920, and finally as testimony before a subcommittee of the Senate through that same spring. Sims charged that the navy afloat and in Washington had been grossly unprepared to join in the fight, and went on to blame its manifold failures directly on Daniels. The highly public squabble between the two provided the stuff of stories in American and British newspapers and periodicals for months.

But that spat was still three years off when Sims's first (April 14, 1917), short cable from London, addressed to Secretary Daniels through the State Department, reported that German submarine warfare was "very much more serious than the people realize in America," where thanks to censorship and British deception "reports of our press are greatly in error." In fact, resupply of and communications with allied forces on all fronts, he wrote the secretary, were "threatened and control of the sea actually imperiled." Sims recommended that the maximum possible number of American destroyers be immediately deployed to the United Kingdom, where from Queenstown they could join in antisubmarine patrols of the high seas west of Ireland.[19]

His second and much longer appraisal, drawing on candid conversations with a constellation of senior British government officials and navy officers, and dated five days later, was more frightening still. "The submarine campaign against merchant shipping of all Nations has resolved itself into the real issue of the war," Sims informed the secretary, "and, stated briefly, the Allied Governments have not been able to, and are not now effectively meeting the situation presented . . . 'Command of the Sea' is actually at stake."[20] In the critical area where the war would be decided, in the Eastern Atlantic "at the focus of all lines of communications," the allies had insufficient ships either to fight the submarines directly or to implement a long-delayed convoy system to better protect the literally vital commerce between North America and the British Isles. (That system wouldn't be implemented until June 19.) Unless success against the U-boats was somehow achieved over the summer of 1917, the grim arithmetic of ship sinkings versus new merchant ship construction meant, Sims warned, that defeat was certain that autumn, perhaps by November.

Sims's attack on Daniels was followed up by Lieutenant Tracy Barrett Kittredge, USNRF, whose *Naval Lessons of the Great War* was nothing less than an extraordinary, near 500-page assault on a sitting service secretary and cabinet officer in testimony and text by some seventeen of the secretary's senior subordinates, captains and admirals.[21] The tone of his book and the thrust of its accusations were anticipated in a very brief, four-paragraph foreword by Rear Admiral Bradley Fiske, USN (Ret.), that reads like a charge sheet against the navy secretary. Fiske (1854–1942, USNA 1874, and *Tennessee*'s commanding officer in 1908–10), a brilliant engineer and inventor, served while a junior rear admiral in 1913–15 as Secretary Daniels's aide for operations. (Established in 1909, the role became the precursor of the post of chief of naval operations.) He resigned in 1915. The assignment permanently soured him on Daniels, whose management of the navy Fiske described as "a menace to the national honor and safety," probably because the secretary had summarily rejected a Fiske reorganization plan that would have frozen the secretary entirely out of operations planning and execution. Daniels called it "Prussianism"; in a delayed riposte Fiske concluded his charges by accusing Daniels of gross incompetence and false testimony.

Fiske and Kittredge were echoing in print essentially what Sims had said to Hale's Senate subcommittee the year before, on March 10, 1920. Sims obviously couldn't argue that Daniels's leadership failures had lost the war, but he could and did argue that they'd greatly raised the terrible price of the ultimate triumph. He claimed that these failures had resulted in an additional 2.5 million tons of shipping lost, extended the war by several months, cost an extra $15 billion, squandered half a million lives, and possibly reduced AEF deployments to Europe in 1917 by two-thirds.

Secretary Josephus Daniels is largely remembered today not for his wartime role or these incendiary postwar disputes, but because in June 1914—two months before the war began—his General Order 99 shut down navy officer wine messes afloat, making the US Navy afloat fully dry, and some think lending his name, "Joe," to navy slang for "coffee." (He was less successful in keeping prostitutes away from navy bases, another of Daniels's campaigns.) The decision turned Daniels—one of two avowed prohibitionists in Wilson's cabinet, the other being William Jennings Bryan—into a punching bag.

Daniels explained and defended himself off Capitol Hill both ahead of Hale's hearings, in *The Navy and the Nation, War-time Addresses* (George H. Doran Co., 1919), and two years after the hearings, more explicitly in his memoir of his cabinet years, *Our Navy at War* (George H. Doran Co., 1922), the second of his four books. (Like Lincoln's navy secretary, Gideon Welles, Daniels was a compulsive diarist. His diaries, edited by E. David Cronon, were published by the University of Nebraska Press in 1963.)

Our Navy at War updated Daniels's collection of speeches with a cool, measured self-defense that persuasively described the navy's swift growth and great contribution to the eventual victory under his leadership. Chapter 25 began with the sunny title, "Sirs, All is Well with the Fleet," and went on to refute Daniels's critics in a storm of statistics by describing the great strength that the US Navy under his watch had brought to the war at sea. (That chapter title was lifted from the last line of a March 11, 1918, report to its parent committee by the House Subcommittee for Investigation of Conduct and Administration of Naval Affairs, chaired by Alabama Democrat William Oliver. Oliver's subcommittee members were clearly in the tank for Daniels: their report to the parent committee's chairman, Rep. Lemuel Padgett of Tennessee, lauded everything about and everybody connected to the wartime navy's first year, and criticized nothing and no one.)

In his "Sirs, All is Well with the Fleet" chapter, Daniels noted,

> With more than two thousand vessels in service and 533,000 officers and men, the largest personnel ever possessed by any Navy, our naval operations in the World War literally belted the globe. Operating with the Allies from the Arctic to the Adriatic, from Corfu to the Azores, we manned and operated the vast fleet of American transports carrying troops, munitions and supplies across the Atlantic, and furnished man-of-war escort to protect them.

FIGURE 8.3. "No Drink in the Navy, Says Daniels."

Josephus Daniels (1862–1948), a wealthy and politically powerful newspaper publisher from North Carolina and like most southern Democrats then a white supremacist, was an odd choice for Wilson to have made to join his cabinet. Not because of Daniels's profession—Hartford *Times* publisher Gideon Welles of Connecticut served Lincoln and Johnson brilliantly for eight years as their navy secretary, Lincoln's in wartime—but because of his perfect ignorance of the sea, his powerful temperance convictions, and his professed pacifism, which, even while the Europeans were at war, led him initially to view the American navy as a school for the social improvement of its men rather than a fighting force.

That said, Daniels wasn't Wilson's only odd choice for a service secretary. The president's second secretary of war, Newton Baker (1871–1937), confessed to knowing nothing about the army when he took office in March 1916, after the first secretary of war (Lindley Garrison) left in a spat with the president over the draft.

In May 1914, months before the war began, *Puck* was gleefully roasting Daniels in this centerfold cartoon, mocking the man the New York *Herald* and the *Tribune* were then ridiculing as "Sir Josephus, Admiral of USS Grapejuice Pinafore." An irreverent stanza of "The Armored Cruiser Squadron" had sailors singing about their secretary:

Josephus Daniels is a goose,
If he thinks he can induce
Us to drink his damn grape juice
In the Armored Cruiser Squadron.

This cartoon by German-born artist Henry "Hy" Mayer (1868–1954) appeared in *Puck*'s issue of May 9, 1914 (vol. 75, no. 1940): 10–11. Mayer joined *Puck* as a contributing editor that year after ten years as a political cartoonist at the *New York Times*.

Source: Library of Congress, Prints and Photographs Division.

Eight hundred and thirty-four vessels and two hundred thousand men of the United States Navy were either serving in European waters or engaged in transporting troops and supplies to Europe, before hostilities ended . . .

Four hundred vessels were assigned to the Naval Forces Operating in European Waters [Sims's command], 373 being present at the time of the armistice . . . [here followed an inventory by type and base, fourteen of them, including an obscure three Russian destroyers stationed at Murmansk, manned by USN crews].

Pages later, he concluded the chapter with an indirect, belated response to Sims: "the Navy performed successfully every task with which it was entrusted. In not one did it fail . . . If all the criticisms, of whatever kind or character, that have been made be lumped together, they would not tilt the scales one degree, if balanced against the Navy's achievements."

Secretary Daniels's persuasive and largely forgotten self-defense was strengthened in September 2009 in a scholarly paper, "Were They So Unprepared? Josephus Daniels and the United States Navy's Entry into World War I," presented by Naval History and Heritage Command historian Dennis Conrad at the US Naval Academy's annual Naval History Symposium that year. Conrad noted, among other proofs of the negative, that, prompted initially by the commander of the Atlantic Fleet's destroyers, preparation of US Navy destroyers for deployment overseas had actually begun in late February, and that the navy had in fact entered the war with a mobilization plan, prepared by the General Board in dialogue with the secretary. A much more detailed defense of the late secretary appeared four years later, in *Josephus Daniels, His Life and Times* (University of North Carolina Press, 2013), Lee Craig's well-reviewed and generally admiring biography of the man whom his own enormously ambitious, thirty-one-year-old assistant, FDR, first described as "the funniest looking hillbilly I had ever seen," but later came to appreciate.

Geoffrey Ward, author of Franklin Delano Roosevelt's 1905–28 biography, *A First Class Temperament* (HarperCollins, 1989), observed that "it would be hard to conjure up two men whose backgrounds and training for their shared task were more different than Franklin Roosevelt and Josephus Daniels." Daniels, countrified, idealistic, and fulfilled; Roosevelt, awkward in his new and unfamiliar status as anyone's subordinate, and consciously following his famous cousin's track to political power and fame.

Roosevelt apparently never resolved what he thought about this seven-year period of his life (1913–20) during which he served as assistant secretary of the navy, or at least never resolved it for public consumption. Although some bits of a book he contracted with Harper and Brothers in 1919 to write about his experience (working title: "The Work of the Navy Ashore") were set down by a ghostwriter under contract, Roosevelt never drafted any of his chapters himself. He'd immediately moved on to other, bigger things.

In contrast to the US Army, the US Navy was impressively large by global standards as 1917 began, and basking in satisfaction with the huge naval construction program that Congress had passed a year earlier. Fifty-nine of the program's sixty-six ships authorized were already under contract.

The US Navy experienced astonishing growth during the country's first year in the war: its approximately 300 ship fleet and its 15,000-strong officer corps both roughly tripled during 1917. The shore establishment nearly tripled as well, from 130 stations to 363, and enlisted strength quadrupled in the same year, to more than 250,000 men. Equally significantly, Secretary of the Navy Daniels boasted, to support the force, the department's disbursements had swelled from $8 million per month early in the year to $60 million per month at its end.[22]

Much of the growth in 1917 (and 1918, too) was a belated attempt at a course correction, reflecting the fact that the US Navy, in following the examples of the Royal Navy and recently its provocative competitor, the Kaiserliche Marine, had for nearly forty years been wresting from a very reluctant Congress money to build what would turn out to be in large part the wrong kind of fleet for the next big war. The model war at sea that turn-of-the-century Western naval powers and their strategists had anticipated was something very like the abbreviated one fought between Russia and Japan: the one that ended in May 1905, after a climactic clash between fleets of capital ships, with command of the sea in the hands of Japan, the victor in a final, decisive gun duel that saw 11 Russian ships sunk or scuttled and nearly 11,000 Russian sailors killed or captured in a few days' time. And that one, in turn, resembled the Battle of Trafalgar a century earlier.

That expectation explains why contemporary comparisons of rival fleets, in government assessments and the popular press alike, invariably focused on big ships and big guns. Size was thought to matter.

But the war that was in fact, not in theory, playing out on the Atlantic and around the British Isles a decade after Tsushima looked very different. The war at sea as it developed after the first few squadron-level engagements, turned out to be a contest between rival blockades. On one side, the Royal Navy's distant blockade and mine barrages closed off both entrances to the North Sea, while an intense effort was made to survey the movement of neutral shipping on trade routes terminating anywhere in Europe. And on the other side, a sporadic submarine campaign was mounted by the Germans but metered by the state of relations with the United States.

The service history of SM U-35, a German Type UB-II submarine, gives a good indication of the threat posed by U-boats to the survivability of Great Britain. In 17 patrols during the war under her four commanding officers, U-35 sank 224 ships totaling more than 500,000 tons—a singular record—this with just four torpedo tubes (and six torpedoes per cruise) and a single deck gun. U-35's most productive patrol, under the redoubtable Lieutenant (much later Vice Admiral) Lothar von Arnauld de la Perière, saw 54 ships sunk, almost all by gunfire.

The climax came unexpectedly with the renewal of unrestricted submarine predation against allied shipping in 1917. Not until the end of April did Washington (meaning the navy, Wilson's administration, and some in Congress) begin to comprehend the disconnect between the fleet the United States had, and the war that actually was being fought, and in very real danger of being lost, by Great Britain. At the start of spring 1917, some scary but not unrealistic projections suggested that the allied merchant fleet by year's end could be pared by something over 6.5 million tons, more than twice what available friendly shipyards could replace. If Britain were starved of imported war matériel, oil, and food, the inevitable defeat would come quickly, perhaps by winter. Sims, sharing with Washington what he learned during his first few days in London, warned that unless trends were reversed, the United Kingdom would be forced to sue for peace in six months. That's what the Germans thought, too.

Once the United States joined the war, pressure on the navy to reconfigure itself and its supporting industrial base on the fly—suddenly to emphasize series production of antisubmarine and convoy escort destroyers ahead of the usual handful of cruisers and battleships each year—quickly became ferocious.

The pendulum swung so far that 110 foot wooden submarine chasers and 50 foot harbor patrol boats were added to a mix of destroyers of several sizes (some displacing 750 tons, others 1,200) put on fast track for construction, if only shipyard facilities could be found.

After the first deployment orders were issued, the navy's initial contribution to the allied war effort at sea came reasonably quickly, but it was initially meager. On May 4, 1917, some four weeks after President Wilson had asked Congress for, and received, a declaration of war against the imperial German government, a division of six new US Navy *Tucker*-class destroyers, under Commander Joseph Taussig, USN, steamed into Queenstown (now Cobh), Ireland, behind an escort with a historic name, the British destroyer HMS *Mary Rose*. Their Atlantic crossing was not the first time that American destroyers had left home waters unaccompanied by larger combatant ships, but it was the first time they'd done so on the way to a fight.

Destroyer Division Eight—including *Conyngham* (Cramp's hull no. 419), *Davis*, *McDougal*, *Porter* (Cramp's no. 420), *Wainwright*, and *Wadsworth*—had left Boston ten days earlier, roughly a week after the second of Rear Admiral Sims's sobering strategic assessments arrived in Washington by coded cable from London. *Davis* and *McDougal*, from another destroyer division, were last-minute replacements for *Tucker* and *Jacob Jones*, which pair deployed with the next division that sailed east.

Chapter 3 of Admiral Sims's wartime memoir, describing Taussig's arrival at Queenstown, goes beyond liberal all the way to greasy in its admiration for all the allied players: for Taussig and his brother American officers, ready for sea on arrival; for their operational commander, Vice Admiral Sir Lewis Bayly, RN; for Miss Violet Voysey (his niece, official hostess, and companion until his death at age eighty-one), and their spaniel, Patrick; for Captain E. R. G. R. "Alphabet" Evans, RN, veteran of the recent Battle of Dover Strait and their Royal Navy liaison; even for King George V and his queen. His Majesty apparently especially enjoyed anecdotes about American colored troops, "the whole literature of Negro yarns" that spread rapidly throughout Europe.

Although the US Navy had moved to a war footing right after the rupture of US–German diplomatic relations, and notwithstanding Admiral Albert

IRELAND - SOUTH COAST
QUEENSTOWN
AND
PORT OF CORK
(OUTER SHEET)
SOUNDINGS IN FEET

Queenstown, now Cobh, would have been known to Commander Joseph Taussig, USN, even if he'd never been there before or wasn't familiar with its history as Ireland's principal emigration port during the great exodus of the nineteenth century. The city, at the head of Cork Harbor, had been RMS *Titanic*'s last port of call before she began her fatal, maiden Atlantic crossing in April 1912. Queenstown was also the place from which on May 7, three years later, the desperate search for survivors off RMS *Lusitania*, torpedoed and sunk in the approaches to the Irish Sea by SMS U-20, had been mounted.

After an Atlantic crossing into near constant half-gale winds off their forward, starboard quarters, the ships of Destroyer Division Eight sailed up the harbor in column behind *Mary Rose* between Dogsnose and Ram Points, passed through the gate in the submarine net, sailed by Spike Island, and then close aboard Queenstown's waterfront. *Wadsworth* and *Conyngham* tied up at the dockyard's oil jetty. The other four moored at buoys.

By war's end, some 85 American destroyers had served in the war zone, about 35 from Queenstown, which fast became the center of a major US Navy support complex that included docking for subchasers, a maintenance facility for patrol aircraft, a depot for spares, and barracks, hospital, and training buildings. The 8,000 or so deployed American sailors outnumbered Queenstown's citizens, perhaps by as many as 2,000.

Source: Library of Congress Geography and Map Division.

Gleaves's efforts in February to improve the readiness of the Atlantic Fleet's destroyers for future deployment, Destroyer Division Eight's departure from Virginia's James River fully ten weeks later and its progress along the East Coast through New York to Boston, and from there finally out into the Atlantic, had been a scramble everywhere, chivvied along by a stream of insistent messages and telephone calls from fleet headquarters to the squadron commander, and marked by herky-jerky preparations in each port for extended deployment and an as-yet-unidentified "special service" to come. The squadron left Virginia so hastily that its flagship, USS *Wadsworth* (DD-60), had left fifteen liberty men behind on shore when she sailed.

Just after midnight on April 24 Taussig, now at sea in *Wadsworth* and together with her squadron mates fifty miles east of Cape Cod, opened his sealed orders. Those "Secret and Confidential" orders, five paragraphs on a single undated page signed by Secretary of the Navy Josephus Daniels, informed Taussig that "the British Admiralty have requested the cooperation of a division of American destroyers in the protection of commerce near the coasts of Great Britain and France."

> Your mission is to assist naval operations of Entente Powers in every way possible.
>
> Proceed to Queenstown, Ireland. Report to Senior British Naval Officer present [Vice Admiral Sir Lewis Bayly, RN], and thereafter cooperate fully with the British Navy. Should it be decided that your force act in cooperation with French Naval Forces your mission and method of cooperating under French Admiralty authority remain unchanged . . .
>
> Base facilities will be furnished by the British Admiralty.
>
> Communicate your orders and operations to Rear Admiral [William S.] Sims [USN] at London and be guided by such instructions as he might give you.[23]

Taussig's orders from Secretary Daniels were remarkably openhanded, given the strong anti-British views of the US Navy's senior uniformed officer, Admiral William Benson, USN, (1855–1932, USNA '77), the first chief of naval operations. According to Sims's congressional testimony, as he prepared to take up his assignment in England, Benson had told him, "Don't let the British pull the wool over your eyes, we would as soon fight them as the Germans."

These half-dozen, four-stack "thousand tonners," each armed with four 4 inch/50 caliber guns and four 21 inch torpedo tubes, were the first American ships to join the fighting in Europe. Over the following six weeks, beginning with the ill-fated USS *Jacob Jones* on May 7, twenty-two other destroyers (and the destroyer tenders USS *Melville* and later *Dixie*) followed the first six. (*Jacob Jones*'s unhappy special distinction was to be the first American destroyer to be sunk in any war. She was torpedoed on December 6, 1917, by Kapitän-leutenant Rose in SM U-53, who until then had been known to Americans largely for his cheeky visit to Newport, Rhode Island, early the previous October. The wounded destroyer was quickly scuttled by her crew, some two-thirds of whom died.) The mission of the follow-on ships was the same that Daniels had assigned initially to Taussig's squadron: "the protection of commerce near the coasts of Great Britain and Ireland." Soon the destroyers were at sea for six days out of every eight, with a week in port each month for maintenance and crew rest.

Five years later, in December 1922 and January 1923, Taussig, then a captain, described his squadron's near-frantic preparations for deployment through a "thick fog of war," in a multipart article for the *US Naval Institute Proceedings*, "Destroyer Experiences during the Great War," and in a diary posthumously published by the Naval War College in 1996, *The Queenstown Patrol, 1917*.[24]

By the time of the armistice nineteen months later, Taussig's destroyers had been joined in European waters by 64 more, as well as by 8 battleships and 3 cruisers, some 12 submarines, and nearly 300 additional miscellaneous ships and craft. Among these last were mine sweepers and planters, transports and colliers, tenders and repair vessels, and 120 submarine chasers.

Married twice and the father of several children, Benton Decker had what his April 7, 1933, obituary in the *Lima* [New York] *Recorder* forthrightly described as "a stormy career" approaching the end of his thirty-six years in uniform.

Decker had been born in Lima, in New York State's Genesee Valley, in 1868, adding his bit to the small farm town's 2,900 residents. (Lima would not be as populous again for another century.) His death in Riverside, California, after what his distant hometown paper described as "a brief illness," shared an inside page in the *Recorder* with news of an ongoing milk strike that saw angry local dairymen dumping gallons into the street to keep prices up. Sadly, Decker's only other obituaries (in the *New York Times* and the *Army and Navy Register*, both published soon after his death in California on March 22, 1933) also focused on damaging professional missteps that seem to have begun ashore in Spain during the war and continued for the next half-dozen years, rather than on his successes at sea.

In retrospect, necessarily the perspective of obituaries, Decker's navy career had peaked nearly twenty years earlier, in 1914–16 ,while as a junior captain he was in command of USS *Tennessee*. Soon after he gave up command of *Tennessee* and continuing until he retired in December 1923, a series of developments relegated his career to slow and permanent eclipse, despite (or perhaps demonstrated by) a promotion to acting flag rank that to his public distress was never made permanent and that, when it expired on December 31, 1921, forced his reversion to captain.[25]

In early 1917, after American entry into the war, Decker very reluctantly became the US naval attaché in Madrid, serving there between April 25, 1917, and May 10, 1918. He'd been surprised by orders to Spain, a sideshow of the great conflict on the Continent, received while he was at the Naval War College during what seems to have been a months-long holding pattern in familiar surroundings immediately after his unusual back-to-back armored cruiser commands. The year in Madrid (at 2,100 feet atop a plateau in the center of Spain, cold and dry in the winter, hot and dry in the summer, and in no direction fewer than 200 miles from salt water) among nearly 650,000 Madrileños (Washington boasted a population in 1917 of a bit more than half that), and serving in an embassy with just eight other Americans, must have tested Decker's adaptability, but he wrote nothing about his life there, only about his work and local echoes from the war beyond its borders.

From twice recently commanding a crew of nearly four dozen officers and nine hundred men, Decker in Madrid was down to just a single subordinate, Lieutenant Commander Carlos Valerian Cusachs, USN, the assistant naval attaché, a fluent Spanish speaker (he was a graduate of the University of Barcelona) with an interesting past, but, as it would soon turn out, no future in the navy.

Cusachs (1874–1943), from New Orleans, had taught languages at Louisiana State University, Harvard, and the Naval Academy; sailed in USS *Wyoming* as a professor of mathematics; and had been married in 1903 to Marguerite

Porter, the granddaughter of the near-legendary admiral David Dixon Porter, USN, hero of New Orleans and Vicksburg. (The pair divorced in 1929.) In January 1918 Cusachs was suddenly recalled from his post in Madrid to Washington, and relieved by a naval reserve lieutenant. Three months later, near the end of April, Cusachs received orders as the naval attaché in Havana, from where after a year he again was fired; this despite later being credited with breaking up a German espionage ring run by the Upmann brothers, cigar and banking magnates in the Cuban capital. Cusachs's appearance before a congressional subcommittee in January 1920, to describe his service in Spain, defend his former career in uniform, and in passing persuasively accuse Ambassador Willard of manipulation and deceit in fabricating the case for his summary recall from Spain, was followed by a statement by Secretary Daniels that dismissed Cusachs as "a very bright, clever man, but impossible as an attaché . . . his judgment is not very good."

Once in Madrid in late April 1917, Decker, and perhaps only he and Cusachs among those on the Entente's side in the capital, persuaded himself there was a real chance that the kingdom would join in common cause with the Central Powers, and if Spain did that, then her military intervention would be significant and perhaps even decisive in shaping the war's outcome.

He suspected practically all Spaniards to be naturally sympathetic to Germany and Austria-Hungary. The many targets of Decker's suspicion included King Alfonso XIII, who in May 1902 at age sixteen assumed the powers of the monarchy (and who, Decker noted, was himself an Austrian archduke and the son of an Austrian archduchess); the clergy of the "Roman church in Spain," especially Jesuits, whose order had large investments in Germany; the Spanish nobility, which "in general approved of the autocracy of Germany, rather than the democracy of the Allied Cause"; and Spanish army officers. As for motives, there were plenty. "The Spaniard . . . hates England on account of Gibraltar. This rankles as an injury in the bosom of the Spaniard, and German propaganda has done much to unite the people against England." Moreover, "towards France, there was great bitterness on account of the attitude of France toward the Roman Church; and the acts of vandalism of soldiers during the Napoleonic Wars," bitterness apparently still virulent fully five generations later. And "towards Italy, there was a feeling . . . of antagonism, because of the treatment of the pope." Curiously, Decker claimed to find no such hostility toward the United States, despite a war less than a generation ago that had seen Spain humiliated at sea in two hemispheres, and stripped of her Caribbean and Pacific colonies by the Americans.

"In my opinion," Decker continued, recalling and defending his attaché tour in a long retrospective document now held in Stanford's Hoover Institution Archive, "Spain could enter the war with very serious results to the allies." He explained, "The position of Spain in the rear of the center of the Allied lines, was a position of tremendous danger to the Allies in this fight: that even though no active offensive was undertaken on the part of Spain, the mere fact of Spain lying behind the center of the Allied lines, with the north ports on the flanks of the line of communications to the United States, and the south ports flanking the Straits of Gibraltar, that Spain would control the destiny of the allies." Pressing his thesis further, Decker imagined a postmobilization Spanish army of 100,000 men boarding trains at Hendaye, in the Basque country, and also at Barcelona, in Catalonia, and riding these rails deep into the vulnerable French interior. "Such a diversion," Decker wrote, "would more than likely have resulted in the breaking through of the German forces, and the possibility of a crushing defeat for the allies." A month after his return from Spain, on June 7, during an appearance before the Navy's General Board (Rear Admiral Charles Badger, USN, presiding), Decker conjured up an even broader scary scenario. Considering the possibility of U-boats operating freely from Spanish bases at Cartagena, Cadiz, and Ferrol, he concluded that in that event any allied naval presence in the Mediterranean would have become "untenable." Thus, Spain flipped to the Central Powers' side constituted a mortal threat to the Triple Entente.

Decker's strategy to keep Spain out of the war and to ensure Madrid's true neutrality—compromised by Spain's very leaky controls on the access of German U-boats on subversive missions to Spanish ports—rested on two initiatives, both of which he later claimed were actively opposed by Ambassador Willard: preservation of a strategic materials embargo against Spain, and the elaboration of an aggressive newspaper and film "education" (read "propaganda") campaign in Spain, to impress Spaniards of all classes with the strength and vigor of the American society and economy. The first was intended to prevent any enhancement in Spain's war-fighting potential. The second was to discourage any misguided drift toward alignment with the Central Powers.

His expansive claim to having preserved Spanish neutrality, an achievement Decker thought superior to the contributions of many of his navy contemporaries in command at sea, had him taking credit personally for the delicate balance of domestic political, military, and economic factors that preserved Spanish neutrality during the war through four successive Spanish presidencies and despite the importuning of the warring alliances.

Spain's geographic position, however, connected across the Pyrenees to France but accessible by sea to anyone, argued for its neutrality, Decker's machinations entirely aside. So did its debility: an exhausted navy (not near to approaching its prewar 1898 strength despite a rebuilding program begun in 1908) and an army weakened by colonial campaigns in Morocco that absorbed fully half its formations. So, too, did the dynastic interests of King Alfonso XIII, who cast himself as the Continent's senior neutral, and now hoped for a larger personal and national role in shaping the order that would emerge in Europe after the war. Moreover, while most Spaniards were too uninformed or too poor to be engaged, what there was of Spanish public opinion divided over everything, pitting conservatives (the aristocracy, the church, and the army) against liberals (political reformers, professionals, and anticlericals) and guaranteeing stasis. Neutrality was, therefore, Madrid's default option, not Decker's handiwork.

Decker and his former VIP passenger in *Tennessee* and current boss, Ambassador Joseph Willard, appear to have agreed on none of this, in fact, on nothing at all. Spain's status and intentions aside, another source of friction between the two was the operations in Spain of George Creel's Committee on Public Information, peopled by propagandists who during wartime "carried the gospel of Americanism to every corner of the globe."[26] Originally chartered by Wilson in April 1917 to raise enthusiasm for the war at home (some believe, as the first structured American government effort to propagandize its citizens during wartime), over time the committee, thanks to Creel, its empire-building chief, expanded its domestic writ to include Spain and eight other countries before it was finally disestablished at war's end. Decker assisted Creel's men in Spain, Messrs. Marion and Harrell, enthusiastically, in the face of (according to Creel) obstructionists instructions from Willard to embassy staff "to refrain from assisting the Committee on Public Information in any way."

Given his and Ambassador Willard's profound differences, Decker managed to last in Madrid only several months longer than did his former assistant. In May 1918, after Decker returned home from Spain under a cloud, he wrote a long defense for the record of his duty in Madrid, an assignment that for him, too, eventually proved to be a yearlong career catastrophe. In that sixteen-page postmortem he revealed that "these orders were entirely unsought by me and I made every reasonable effort to be excused from this duty."[27] The new director of naval intelligence, Captain Roger Welles Jr., hadn't asked for him, nor had Ambassador Willard, and the source of and reasons for his nomination remain a mystery. His abrupt reassignment, Decker would soon argue, was in fact at his request in frustration, and only later characterized as disciplinary.

After Spain Decker served in New London, Connecticut, in 1918–19, as the commandant of the naval training station; in March 1919 he moved to Key West as the Seventh Naval District commandant, and simultaneously the commander of the headquarters' host naval station. A request for sea duty in the Mediterranean or elsewhere was denied by the secretary that same month on the grounds that no assignment suitable to his rank was available.

The March 1919 change of station began what turned out to be his last real assignment, eighteen months as commandant of the Seventh Naval District, where his responsibilities encompassed hosting several tenant activities based at the station at the southern end of the Keys. The navy's organization ashore in the late 1910s defies understanding. The Fifth, Sixth, and Seventh Districts all shared parts of the state of Florida, making coherent management of navy activities, especially of naval reserve personnel, in the state unworkable. Eventually Florida was consolidated into the Seventh District.

Rusticating on the Keys postwar, Admiral Decker had much to do and much to brood about. His tour there spanned the great hurricane of early September 1919, an enormously powerful storm (Category four by modern standards, almost up to the strength of "Irma" ninety-eight years later) that reached hurricane strength over the Bahamas and passed within forty miles south of Key West September 9–10 with near-150 mile per hour winds, before crossing the Gulf of Mexico and finally making landfall on September 14 at Baffin Bay, South Texas, with winds then down near one-third. The destruction at the naval station was horrific; nothing there—not the station's buildings, not the lighthouse and post office, not the hospital and the air station's hangars—had been built to standards to survive such a blow, the second most powerful in the past fifty years.

During the very wet year-end holidays of 1919–20 ("very wet" in this case describing not weather but anticipation of the imposition of Prohibition, just weeks away), on the last day of 1919, Secretary Daniels publicly revealed the embarrassing news that Decker had been "withdrawn from his post [as naval attaché] in Madrid" a year and a half ago "for insubordination against Ambassador Willard." Daniels's disclosure was clearly in reprisal for a letter from Decker to Daniels the admiral had leaked to the press two days earlier, laying out his case for high-level recognition for his wartime achievements "in spite of the opposition of the Ambassador."

Decker's explosive charge attracted immediate press attention. The *Times* noted in a front-page story on December 29, 1919, that "the allusion which Admiral Decker has made to the opposition of the Ambassador has developed the very keenest interest in official, diplomatic, and Congressional circles as to just how and why Ambassador Willard may have taken a course . . . in opposition to American naval officers who were trying to keep Spain from entering the war on the side of Germany."

In January, Secretary Daniels explained Decker's firing to Senator Hale and the several members of Hale's subcommittee as the solution to a management problem:

> We could not have a debating society in Spain. The ambassador was the representative of America. The naval attaché was there to obtain information for the Navy Department, not to fix the American policy; and when Admiral Decker and Mr. [Lieutenant Commander Carlos] Cusachs in their zeal, following the line, of course, that they thought best for the country insisted on policies that were contrary to the Government's, there was one of two things to do—have a new ambassador or have a new naval attaché. The ambassador was carrying out the policy of the Government. The attaché was dabbling in matters that did not concern the Navy. It took no time at all to say to the State Department, "Why certainly, these gentlemen are undoubtedly patriotic, but it is not our business to run the State Department."[28]

Decker's alleged insubordination at the embassy soon got caught up in a much larger dispute.

Although Decker wasn't among the seven senior naval officers who testified before or submitted statements about the navy's postwar distribution of awards to Senator Frederick Hale's subcommittee, which began hearings that month on Admiral Sims's and others' many complaints about the process, he soon would join them. The seven's testimony also sharpened interest in hearings in the House of Representatives chaired by Rep. Thomas Butler, Republican of

Pennsylvania, scheduled in the first week of January to begin looking into the medals brouhaha largely as a way to embarrass the secretary, surfing on the critiques of naval preparedness and headquarters organization that were also roiling Washington.

The hearings' nominal purpose was to evaluate the navy's distribution of these service awards, to ensure that the process as conducted had enhanced morale, and had been "beyond reach of patronage or of political or private influence." (The same issue of suitable recognition for outstanding service also came up for the army. The army's chief of staff, General Peyton March, was abused by Rep. James Gallivan of Massachusetts for having awarded more medals to "lounge lizards" in Washington than to officers on the front.)

The awards process had begun in March 1919, when the navy secretary convened a board named after its senior member, Admiral Austin Knight, to consider and make recommendations on the four thousand or so award nominations forwarded by commanders to the secretary after the armistice. Knight's board (retired, he was recalled to active duty for this purpose, as were its other members) reported its conclusions to the secretary in September, and he in turn announced his decisions in December, which prompted an immediate shower of complaints, the most vocal from Admiral Sims, now settled back at the war college in Newport and perhaps still decompressing from his challenging assignment. Sims's chief objection was the secretary's downgrade of awards for thirteen members of his London staff, of the thirty-two the admiral had proposed for recognition, but he and others noted that Daniels had often not followed the board's recommendations, and had treated captains who'd lost their ships in combat generously regardless of circumstances.

Hale, a Republican and the son and grandson of senators from Maine, was chairman of the Senate's Subcommittee on Naval Affairs considering the matter. (The counterpart subcommittee in the House of Representatives declined to participate in this hearing.) Its four other members included Republicans Joseph McCormick and Truman Newberry (the last for three months one of Teddy Roosevelt's secretaries of the navy) and Democrats Key Pittman and Park Trammell. As the proceedings progressed, the five split visibly along party lines, reflecting the fact that the subtext to the subcommittee's work was a critique of Daniels's and by extension the Democrats' management of the department and conduct of the war at sea. Pittman appended a personal statement to the committee's final, 700-page report, describing the dispute as "a tempest in a teapot," and "too ridiculous to be mentioned in connection with the morale of a fighting Navy."

While the hearings in Washington played out, Decker provoked another squabble, this one in the spring of 1920 over local school construction with members of the Monroe County, Florida, Board of Public Instruction. His charge that Superintendent Virgil Lowe (Decker: "one of the most contemptible public officials that has come under my observation") had committed graft in the acquisition of property for a new school so inflamed civil-military relations that the dispute swiftly reached members of Congress and, inevitably, the navy secretariat. An exchange of assorted accusations followed, slowed by the refusal of the editor of the *Key West Citizen* to publish Decker's in his paper, fearing a complaint of libel, but accelerated by the school board's formal filing of charges against the admiral for "having maliciously abused the County Su perintendent and the school board."

This brouhaha still visible behind him after formal chastisement by the Navy, at the end of May 1920, Decker applied to retire after thirty years' service. His letter, addressed to President Wilson (in his last year in office) via the chief of naval operations and the secretary of the navy (and filed with his papers in the Hoover Institution Archive), was vintage Decker:

> . . . I have been passed over in my promotion for the permanent rank of Rear Admiral . . .
>
> It is my opinion that the best interests of the service require that an officer of my rank be retired, who has been passed over for promotion.
>
> . . . The loss of prestige in the eyes of seniors and subordinates lowered his [meaning his own] efficiency; but of even greater importance in the supreme test of war is the loss of respect for his own ability, judgment and conduct of life that comes from a realization that group of high and respected officers, combining with his written record a knowledge of his actual service, have decided, under oath, that in the best interests of the service, he should be displaced by his juniors.

Decker was in the national news again a little later in the year. On June 17 (in the second year of his Key West assignment) Decker leaped publicly into the postwar flag officer assault on Secretary Daniels with an explosive letter addressed to Chairman Hale, accusing the navy secretary of gross and deliberate mismanagement of the Department of the Navy and with "intentionally and deliberately" misrepresenting the positions of Admirals Sims, Fullham, and Fiske.

"From my personal knowledge of Mr. Daniels' character," Decker stated, "I am led to believe that whatever is cited in his statements to the discredit of the officers is so perverted and twisted as to give the actual facts a false meaning . . . if these officers had bowed down and served the gods that Mr. Daniels worshipped, they would today have been fattened on the Navy as commanders of fleets on active duty or in pleasant jobs in Washington." A second letter to Hale, dated a day later, accused Assistant Secretary Franklin Delano Roosevelt of like but lesser failures, objecting in passing to Roosevelt's derisive characterization of the three admirals in opposition as "gold-laced gentlemen," after first charging that under its civilian leadership "the navy had been converted into a most perfect political machine, a machine where politics with its rewards and ways reign supreme." He ended that second letter: "in any reorganization of the navy today the navy needs, and the best interests of the country demand, that there shall be placed in the Navy Department a naval officer big enough and broad enough and of sufficient ability to maintain the standards of the navy against the encroachment of the civilian secretaries who seek to make the Navy a political organization."[29]

Decker next sent copies of both his Hale letters to the *Army and Navy Register* (five cents a copy, four dollars per year), where they appeared on June 26 (vol. 67, no. 2084) without editorial comment. The story was instantly picked up by dozens of civilian newspapers countrywide, often quoting Decker's letters extensively (and occasionally with obvious satisfaction), on their front pages. Even newspapers far inland, among them, the *Reno* [Nevada] *Evening Gazette*, copied the story.

This scandal peaked, perhaps not coincidentally, in late June and early July, while the Democratic Party was convened in San Francisco for the selection of its 1920 candidates for president (James Cox), and vice president (Franklin Roosevelt). Daniels was in San Francisco for the big event, berthed on board the fleet's flagship, USS *New Mexico*.

A month later, on August 5, Decker was relieved of district command. Despite his retirement request, he inexplicably remained on active duty in assignments that he later described as "humiliating." During the next several years Decker sat on general courts-martial (at the Fifth and First Naval Districts, in Hampton Roads and Boston) and on miscellaneous boards, including what seems to have been his last assignment, as the senior member of the Board of Inspection and Survey, meeting in San Francisco. In 1923 he finally retired, clearly having been sidelined by the navy some time ago. And a decade after that Benton Decker died, during his son's thirteenth year of navy service.

Josephus Daniels ended his government service as the American ambassador to Mexico for seven years during FDR's administrations. He died in 1948.

Le Petit Journal's almost comic cover illustration of American sailors departing France for home in what could have been either a *Kearsarge*-class or more probably a *Virginia*-class battleship (neither of the *Kearsarges* deployed to European waters, but the slightly newer *Virginia*s did late in the war, as convoy escorts) had none of the grand pageantry that swirled about Gribble's destroyers steaming toward Queenstown or his battleships entering Scapa Flow. But the newspaper supplement's cover, published six weeks after Battleship Division Nine had left the United Kingdom for home, suitably marked the end of the brief era whose beginning had been celebrated by Gribble's pair of arrival paintings heralding the historic first deployments of American men o'war to Europe not long before.

After the return to home waters of the American (and Japanese) combatants that had fought with allied navies against those of the Central Powers and soon after the end of the war, international attention turned soberly to negotiating an end to the great powers' naval construction competition fueled by Mahan, which many believed had been one of the chief triggers of the Great War. The future threat to peace and international stability inherent in such a contest was one motive for pursuing naval arms limitations (that motive lay behind US Senator William Borah's interest in opening negotiations, for example). But there were other considerations: American-British competition; the race's stunning costs, which if unconstrained threatened to beggar postwar recovery and other government programs; the subversive uncertainty that the past war had prompted among civilians about the cost effectiveness of major combatants, anyway; and American fears about Japan's ambitions in the Pacific. These also helped set the stage for the first of what eventually developed into a series of five international negotiations on naval force structure and limitations, extending between 1921 (in Washington) and 1935 (in London), and involving as many as nine nations around the table (but once as few as three).

FIGURE 8.4. *"L'adieu de l'équipage à la terre de France. Un navire de guerre des Etats-Unis quitte un de nos ports pour rentrer en Amérique."*

Most of the fifty-two color covers of *Le Petit Journal*'s illustrated Sunday supplement in 1919 (vol. 29) highlighted an aspect of the hard-fought and narrowly won victory over the Central Powers. The moment of triumph appeared on May 25, showing the German peace delegation being presented the allies' terms at Versailles (*"La Séance Historique de Versailles. Remis aux plénipotentaires allemands des conditions de paix des alliés."*) Other issues before and after that one celebrated revenge for the humiliation of 1871; one, a map, illustrated German territorial losses; several noted the courage of honored cities and towns, and of great French commanders. That of August 31 noted, in cartoon illustration style, the crushing weight of the costs of the wars since Napoleon, with the Great War in the center as a swollen bag of money marked "1.005 *millards*" (1 billion, 5 million French francs). A few other covers limned more complicated scenes, including one that showed a wedding being celebrated amid a ruin of the war.

The focus of the *Journal*'s covers was properly on France and the French, although the April 27 cover honored Admiral Beatty, "*Commandant en chef de la Grande Flotte britannique*," perhaps the first time that the Royal Navy's fleet commander received admiring recognition in France. The United States got two such grace notes, this one on January 12, 1919 (vol. 29, no. 1464), noting the departure of a US Navy heavy combatant ship from France for home at war's end, with a curiously disorderly crew on the foredeck, and one on March 9 honoring Herbert Hoover, identified as the "man who fed Europe," his head surrounded by US Food Administration propaganda posters.

The first American combatant ships, six tiny steam yachts and two tenders, had arrived in France on July 4, 1917, after a three-weeks-plus Atlantic crossing via Bermuda and the Azores. (The first troop transport convoy arrived at Saint-Nazaire several days earlier to deliver 14,000 troops.) The yachts were the leading edge of what became "US Patrol Squadrons Operating in European Waters," a command subordinate to Vice Admiral Henry Wilson, USN, the commander, US Naval Forces in France. At its peak his command included 35 destroyers, 5 torpedo boats, 18 yachts like the first six, 8 tugs, 9 minesweepers, and 8 auxiliaries, as well as substantial naval air forces based at nearly a dozen stations.

Source: Courtesy Bibliothèque Nationale, Paris.

Significantly, the first conference established parity in capital ship tonnage between the navies of the United Kingdom and the United States, formal recognition of new realities exposed by the war and an end to the thumb rule that had shaped British naval construction programs and spending.

The last several of these conferences, highly technical discussions treating with national geopolitical ambitions in the arcane language and arithmetic of ship types and tonnage, met against the backdrop of the Great Depression, a cataclysm that during the 1930s shattered public confidence in both capitalism and liberal democracy in many places, and firmly fastened powerful, amoral, and ambitious dictatorships atop more than 400 million of the world's citizens. From this poisonous environment, the next world war followed what was to have been the last world war by only a generation. The second war would couple science, engineering, industrial production, and the mobilization and control of populations in a way the horrors of the Great War had only hinted at. In its Pacific theater, World War II would also feature the enormous, decisive battles between ships at sea that the first had not, in forms that Mahan could not have imagined.

FIGURE E.I. USS *Tennessee*'s bow scroll at Centennial Park, Nashville, Tennessee.

Very little is left of the armored cruiser that began her service as USS *Tennessee* and ended it tragically and abruptly nearly a decade later as USS *Memphis*.

Some of the ship's artifacts were preserved by Annie Keith Frazier (1887–1978), who over the years kept up her connection to USS *Tennessee*. In 1907 at the Jamestown Tercentennial, Annie, just out of her teens, recalled "great fun taking in State parties, and dancing with the VMI and West Point cadets, and dining aboard my ship, the 'Tennessee,' which was part of the 'Great White Fleet' anchored in Hampton Roads, and brilliantly outlined in lights nightly." Almost ten years later and soon after *Memphis*'s destruction, Annie, now married and living in Mississippi, asked Secretary Daniels for a memento from the cruiser she had christened amid great ceremony years ago, her request boosted by coming to Daniels through Rep. Lemuel Padgett, representative in Congress for Tennessee's 7th District, and then the chairman of the House's committee on naval affairs.

After a search through the detritus that was left from the ship, in October Daniels volunteered an "airport," a bronze porthole fitting equipped with hinged glass and solid covers, from the salvaged items still in storage, if she would pay for shipment. Annie added the "prized" airport, suitably engraved, to another souvenir of her exciting day long ago, the neck of the champagne bottle she'd used to christen *Tennessee*, since mounted in silver and also engraved.

That airport and bottleneck aside, not much else remains of *Memphis* today: her bell (hanging above the Iglesia de Nuestra Señora de las Mercedes in the capital), miscellaneous small bits and pieces informally salvaged and collected by souvenir-hunting divers from the bottom near her last anchorage off Santo Domingo, and many volumes of deck logs, reports, and other official correspondence held by the National Archives and Records Administration in Washington, DC.

Memphis's forty-eight-star American flag (salvaged from her wreck by a junior quartermaster's mate and passed around among several crew petty officers for the next forty years) emerged in 1960 to ride around the globe submerged in USS *Triton* (SSRN-586), then on her shakedown cruise under the junior Captain Beach's command. *Memphis*'s flag's travels are described in an article by L. B. Kidwell in the December 1966 issue of *All Hands* magazine. In mid-2016 her flag was unearthed at the navy's headquarters in Millington, Tennessee, following a frantic search to locate it for an American Embassy Santo Domingo–sponsored centennial commemoration of the wreck on the capital's waterfront. The event had been prompted in Congress in June 2015 by HR 306, submitted by Tennessee's Steve Cohen, Democrat, representing the state's ninth congressional district, encompassing most of Memphis.

Several handsome descriptive placards stand today near the site of *Memphis*'s fatal grounding, installed in September 2016 as part of that embassy event. One panel highlights the heroic life-saving role of Sr. Emeterio Sánchez, a Dominican citizen who saved at least three *Memphis* crew members from their ship's boat, sinking off Matadoro Beach that afternoon. This was an act of acknowledged heroism for which his widow, Mercedes, waited into the 1930s for a solatium payment from the United States.

Tennessee's original $6,000 wardroom sterling silver service—when new, dozens of heavy, handsome pieces depicting state scenes cast in relief, designed by Nashville jeweler Heywood Norman and cast by Gorham in Pennsylvania—was presented to the ship at Hampton Roads on December 15, 1906, by then-Governor John Cox's only daughter Mary, with former Governor Frazier, now a US senator, and his daughter, Annie, looking on. The service was rescued from the wreck and held briefly for safekeeping in the local branch of the Royal Bank of Canada, and then returned to US custody. Some of its pieces are now on display at the State Museum in Nashville. Others rest at the state capitol.

Tennessee's elegant bow scroll had been removed from the ship in July 1909, when her glitzy white and buff paint job was replaced by a more utilitarian gray, the standard of navies throughout the world during the wars of the past century. An elaborate tracery of vines and leaves surrounds an oval centered on the bow, inside of which is a simplified version of the great seal of the United States in relief, originally painted in patriotic colors. By World War I such vestiges of romantic figureheads were generally gone from combatant ships, although surface ships of the Imperial Japanese Navy sailed through World War II behind an imperial golden chrysanthemum seal on the bow.

Acquired by the city of Nashville in March 1910, thanks to the efforts of Rear Admiral Albert Gleaves, USN, to honor his cousin, Rear Admiral Albert Gleaves Berry, USN (Ret.), in 1906 *Tennessee*'s first commanding officer, this scroll decorates an otherwise featureless 25-foot-long cement replica of the cruiser's bow that stands unidentified and unexplained near the southeastern gate of the city's lovely Centennial Park. According to stories in the March 29, 1910, issues of the *Nashville American* and *Nashville Tennessean*, however, the scroll on exhibition is actually the original master pattern from which *Tennessee*'s bow decoration was later cast, not an artifact from the ship.

Source: Photo by the author.

Epilogue

Inasmuch as the storm which occasioned the loss of Captain Beach's vessel was of volcanic origin and of such unusual severity that it may properly be considered an act of God which it was humanly impracticable to foresee and to make adequate preparation to meet, and [further] since the record of Captain E. L. Beach during the war has been most excellent . . . now is the time to remit the [five] numbers lost by Captain Beach as a result of the Court Martial.

—Josephus Daniels, June 27, 1919

Tennessee's bow scroll almost ended up instead in Franklin, Tennessee, Williamson County's chief city, some twenty miles south of Nashville and in the 1910s home to nearly three thousand people. (Twenty times that number live there today.) A request for the scroll from the activist regent of the town's resident "Old Glory" Chapter of the Daughters of the American Revolution, forwarded to the navy by the ever helpful Rep. Padgett, prompted an affirmative reply from the navy months later, explaining that this would be a loan and not a gift, and including the news that the decoration weighed nearly 4,100 pounds and the town of Franklin would have to pay its shipping costs from the navy yard in Bremerton, Washington, to middle Tennessee—in advance. That costly news squashed the DAR's initiative, one evidently not previously coordinated with the small city's government.

"Dear Sir," wrote E. M. Perkins, Franklin's embarrassed part-time mayor and a name partner of the local Campbell & Perkins fire insurance agency, to the navy on November 19:

We have received your [letters] of Oct. 16 & Nov. 9 of the present year, but as we had never made any request for the loan of the Figure-Head of the Good Ship Tenn. and as we had no funds appropriated for the purpose of paying freight on the same, we simply remained quiet. However, if the said

Figure-head is that of a beautiful Woman, we will take good care of her if she is sent free. But if it is something scary like a Mermaid or a Sea-Serpent, we dont want her at a discount even.

Trusting this meets with your approval.

Evidently it didn't. So it was that Nashville and not Franklin became the home for one of the biggest remaining bits of USS *Tennessee*, however unclear its provenance.

Secretary Daniels, too, is honored by a largely ignored memorial. His, an 8-foot-high bronze statue of the man in a frock coat and tie, left hand holding a hat and right hand raised (looking regrettably like he's hailing a taxi), stands in Nash Square in Raleigh, North Carolina. It was dedicated in September 1985, almost forty years after Daniels's death and twenty years after USS *Josephus Daniels*, the second *Belknap*-class guided missile cruiser, first went to sea. She was scrapped unceremoniously in 1999 in Texas. Daniels is honored, as well, by association with the University of North Carolina student stores complex, to which his name has been attached since 1967. Inevitably, given the *Raleigh News and Observer*'s role around the turn of the last century as "the militant voice of white supremacy" while he was the paper's editor, that now uncomfortable connection is under examination.

On Good Friday, March 29, 1918, Secretary Daniels spoke in Washington, DC, to the assembled membership of the National Geographic Society. His speech, "The Gem of the Ocean: Our American Navy," was notable for his obvious pride in the performance of the US Navy at sea during the past year of warfare, and also for his observation—drawn, he said, from history—that "every generation has its war," one usually lasting three years. He continued, in what sounds like a commentary on Jutland, "Great generals have won renown who were masters of the defensive, and there are times when Fabian methods on land spell victory. But at sea, the captain who depends on defense is lost. Offensive methods, daring attack, ability to maneuver so as to obtain the advantage, and to shoot quickly and to hit the enemy vessel—these are the essentials of high command afloat."

This bit of hard-nosed realism aside, Daniels then launched into something like an idyllic vision of a postwar world, one in which "all the peace-loving nations must enter into an international agreement neither to throw away their guns nor to tie up their ships, but to make them one common international peace police on land and sea, tendering to all nations great and small the High Court of arbitration for the settlement of all differences, ready to enforce the decrees of that tribunal and make this police force so strong that no war-lord will ever again dare resort to the sword to impose his will or his country's greed upon other nations."[1] As he spoke the beginning of the next world war on September 1, 1939, was barely more than a generation away.

Ignoring literally dozens of small sub chasers and scout patrol boats sunk by assorted causes, the US Navy suffered very few combatant ship losses at sea during the war, and none at all in the classical big-gun, ship-on-ship duel usually imagined to have been the essence of war at sea in that era. In October 1917 the destroyer USS *Cassin* was torpedoed by U-61 twenty miles off Ireland, but she was salvaged and saved with the loss of a single, very unfortunate sailor. (The official record of American ship casualties of World War I has this wrong. It identifies *Cassin* as "*Cousin*," and the victorious submarine as U-105.) The next month destroyer USS *Chauncey* sank on convoy escort duty, not due to hostile action but rammed in darkness by one of her charges, SS *Rose*, both steaming without lights to avoid detection. Twenty-one men died then. A month after that, in December, the last of the lost destroyers, USS *Jacob Jones* (the first of three ships with that name), was torpedoed and sunk by U-53 between Brest and Queenstown, losing two-thirds of her crew.

Because battleship USS *Minnesota* survived the explosion of the mine she struck off the Virginia Capes in September 1918, the biggest navy combatant ship lost during the war actually sank two months earlier, the *Pennsylvania*-class armored cruiser USS *San Diego* (ACR-6, former USS *California*). On July 19, 1918, she apparently hit a mine laid by U-156 ten miles off the Fire Island, New York, lightship (LV-68) and quickly went down, remarkably killing only six of the eleven hundred or so men on board, thanks to the rush of rescue vessels that soon congested the scene. *San Diego* was the third of the six *Pennsylvania*-class cruisers commissioned between 1905 and 1908, together the immediate forerunners of the four generally similar but better armed (and heavier by some 800 tons) *Tennessee*-class ships.

The sinking of *San Diego*, lightly gunned and armored for a modern cruiser, but by several times the largest warship lost by the US Navy during the war, underscores the gravity of the peacetime loss of *Memphis*, beached and destroyed some eight months before the US entered the fight. Had she been shoved aground months later, *Memphis*, not *San Diego*, would have been the principal American combatant lost during the Great War.

In 1923 the Navy Department's Historical Section completed its final review of "American Ship Casualties of the World War Including Naval Vessels, Merchant Ships Sailing Vessels and Fishing Craft" (Washington, DC: GPO, 1923). The historian's seventeen-page compendium itemized these many casualties under eleven headings, by ship type and by nature of casualty (for example, sunk or damaged by enemy torpedo, bombs, or gunfire; sunk or seriously damaged by fire or explosion, or in collision; and so forth). An exercise in statistics, not historical analysis.

Nearly 130 of the total lost were sailing vessels, schooners or barks, revealing that four generations after steam power first went to sea, world trade wasn't yet fully modernized—but this drew no commentary. Indeed, the great four- and five-masted, steel-hulled barks of Hamburg's Laeisz shipping company, its famous "flying P-liners," continued to move commercial cargoes across oceans well into the 1920s. Four of them are afloat today as museum or sail training ships.

By far the largest category of casualties included "merchant ships sunk or damaged by enemy torpedo, gunfire, or bombs." That list included fully 148 entries. The least of them, a covey of seven gas screw-powered fishing boats, none larger than 34 tons, were all shelled and sunk by U-117 150 miles east of Nantucket atop George's Bank, August 10, 1918. The biggest ship in this category, the tanker *O. B. Jennings*, 10,289 tons, had been sunk by U-140 the week earlier not far off Cape Hatteras.

But the *Jennings* wasn't the biggest support ship lost during the war. Several in-commission troop transports nearly twice her size, among them USS *President Lincoln*, were also sunk by submarines. (Happily, none had deploying troops on board.)

After transferring from the Pacific to the Atlantic Fleet in the summer of 1917, USS *San Diego* approached New York from Portsmouth, New Hampshire, near midday on July 19, 1918, to pick up what would have been her eighth convoy toward France when she was either torpedoed (as her commanding officer, Captain Harley Cristy, believed) or hit a submarine-laid mine (Secretary Daniels, the next day, and the consensus today). The eleven-year-old cruiser's watertight integrity fatally breached by the mystery blast, she sank in half an hour after first listing sharply and finally rolling over to port. Her collapsing funnels killed one of the crew, but otherwise the loss of life was remarkably small, a half-dozen, most of them men of the port engine room watch.

Here *San Diego*, still apparently making steam, is going down by the bow, with three ship's boats off her starboard side already pulling away with survivors, another boat hanging in the falls of a gaff boom, and a few swimmers visible. Her crew did manage put an assortment of the cruiser's smaller boats in the water (along with mess tables, kapok mattresses, and loose lumber for emergency flotation), but Muller's generic details of a disaster at sea are largely imaginary. An electrical failure had rendered *San Diego*'s boat cranes inoperable. Most men saved were pulled directly from the water by three ships quick to reach the scene, the steamers *Bussan*, *Malden*, and *E. P. Jones*.

Francis Muller, of Brooklyn, New York, is also credited with painting Dewey's flagship, USS *Olympia*, in the same style. Described in the contemporary Brooklyn borough press as a European-trained portrait painter and muralist, Muller taught at the Brooklyn Institute of Arts and Sciences, and later was the manager/director of the Brooklyn School of Art during the war years. In 1922 the school apparently suffered a blizzard of bad publicity about its debt collection practices, and might have closed in consequence. Little else is known about him.

Source: US Navy Art Collection.

The very largest of all ships lost, the collier USS *Cyclops* (Cramp's no. 355), 19,360 tons gross and carrying 11,000 tons of manganese ore, "mysteriously disappeared" in early March 1918 while steaming from Barbados to Baltimore in service with the Naval Overseas Transportation Service. All 309 on board, among them the US consul-general at Rio de Janeiro, went down with her—the largest single loss of American lives at sea during the war. For a while suspicions in the press of foul play focused on her captain, George Worley, born in Hanover, Germany, and suspected to be a German sympathizer, and also on the consul, Alfred Gottschalk.

The puzzle behind *Cyclops*'s disappearance was heightened later when two of her three *Proteus*-class mates, the colliers *Nereus* and *Proteus*, were quietly lost at sea in the same area decades later, suggesting that all three had fallen victim to a class structural problem, although mystics believed the common cause had something to do with the infamous "Bermuda Triangle."

At the conclusion of a ceremony on April 30, 1919, that echoed one at Cramp's fifteen years earlier, the red primer–painted hull of battleship *Tennessee* (BB-43) eased down the ways at Brooklyn's New York Navy Yard into the East River, to begin a months-long fitting out at the yard's Cob Dock before sea trials and, finally, commissioning in June 1920. Some 1,500 miles south the stripped, neglected hulk of her predecessor, ex-USS *Memphis* and formerly the armored cruiser *Tennessee*, still lay aground off Santo Domingo, just where the sudden big waves had left her nearly three years before.

This new *Tennessee*'s construction had been authorized and money appropriated on March 3, 1915. Congress capped the price for each of what it described as two "first-class battleships carrying as heavy armor and as powerful armament as any vessel of their class, [and having] the highest practicable speed and greatest desirable radius of action" at $7.8 million per ship, less armor and armament. That December the New York Navy Yard won the competition to construct one of the ships over four other yards, two navy and two private, but not until May 14, 1917, the month after the United States entered the war in Europe, was the new *Tennessee*'s keel actually laid down. The construction contract for the second of the pair, USS *California* (BB-44), was awarded to California's Mare Island Naval Shipyard, in Vallejo.

The nearly forty year-old Brooklyn Bridge is clearly visible in the background of the *New York Times*'s handsome, page-wide photogravure illustration of the big hull splashing into the river on the last day of April 1919, published the following Sunday. The photo's foreground is filled with well-dressed observers pressed shoulder to shoulder, backs to the camera, watching the excitement. Going into the water, *Tennessee* was cheered, the *Times* reported, by a crowd 25,000 strong, clustered together on the yard's grounds to witness the exciting event. A rival city paper, the *Evening World*, claimed a doubtful four times as many observers in its story that same night about the christening. Other newspapers guessed at audience numbers in between these two.

Like her namesake, the new *Tennessee* was launched with a flag-wrapped bottle of champagne by the home state governor's sixteen-year-old daughter, Helen, prettily "all dressed in white for the occasion, except for a bit of black fur at her neck." A year earlier her father, Governor Albert Roberts, had campaigned for the chief office in his bone-dry state on a prohibition platform; his objection to the use of a sparkling wine for this purpose was evidently ignored, but newspaper stories suggested that *Tennessee* marked the end of this tradition, and that from now on mineral water, and not champagne, would be used at navy ship christenings. And during the thirteen years the 19th Amendment remained in effect, navy ship christenings indeed featured water or cider.

Champagne aside, the midmorning ceremony must have been a career highlight for Governor Roberts. He stood watching proudly on the crowded platform among the fifteen Tennessee National Guard officers who constituted his staff for the occasion and a gaggle of other uniformed worthies, all of them sharing the crowded space with the Wilson administration's senior representative, Acting Secretary of the Navy Franklin D. Roosevelt, standing erect, patrician in a top hat, and still some two and a half years away from a diagnosis of polio that would force him into a wheelchair for the rest of his life.

During 1919–20 Governor Roberts would find himself on the wrong side of most political issues in the state, a stance that prompted the failure of his campaign for a second, two-year term. He never managed to hold elected office again. And a year after the christening, Roosevelt himself would absorb political defeat. But this would be on the national level in a contest that, oddly, saw both parties put up rival newspaper publishers from Ohio for the presidency, with Roosevelt paired with a forgettable loser, James Cox. A dozen years later, Roosevelt became president, one who arguably knew as much about naval issues as had a predecessor in office, his distant cousin, Teddy. And another dozen years after that, it became FDR's responsibility to lead the United States into history's greatest naval war, with flag officers he had known as lieutenants during the last war commanding this one's vast formations in the Pacific.

"THE SUPER-DREADNAUGHT *TENNESSEE*" was, the *Times* went on to explain proudly to its readers in an all-uppercase photo caption that spanned the page, "THE MOST POWERFUL NAVAL BATTLE UNIT BUILT IN THE HISTORY OF THE WORLD." As fitting out progressed, the nation's newspapers continued to watch developments closely and proudly. That July the *Grand Forks Herald* told its readers, more than 1,200 miles from the nearest salt water, that *Tennessee* was "BIGGER AND BETTER THAN ANY DREADNAUGHT AFLOAT! Uncle Sam's Powerful new Floating Fortress, the Giant USS *Tennessee*, Leads Navies of the World in Point of Size, Cost, Armaments and Ability to Inflict Punishment on a Foe." Six months later, the *Ogden* [Ogden City, Utah] *Standard*, no closer than Grand Forks to any coast, reported: "The Prize U.S. Superdreadnought Nears Completion."

On February 11, 1920, Wilson accepted from Secretary of War Newton Baker the original World War I Victory Medal, struck to commemorate America's participation in "the great war for civilization." Some 4 million similar medals were distributed to Americans who'd been in uniform during the war years. Many millions more (5.7 million alone to veterans of the United Kingdom and its colonies) featuring the same colored suspension ribbon, but different pendant medals, were presented to their own World War I veterans by the fourteen other nations that had, in one theater or another, at horrific cost in lives and treasure finally defeated the Central Powers.

Almost two years later, in midafternoon on November 9, 1921, another ritual of postwar closure began: Dewey's veteran former flagship, the protected cruiser USS *Olympia*, arrived in the rain at the Washington Navy Yard fifteen days steaming out of Le Havre. She was carrying the flag-draped casket of the war's Unknown Soldier, brought from France as the tired veteran ship's last wartime duty, and her last cruise. The casket lay in state in the Capitol rotunda until interment took place with great ceremony in Arlington National Cemetery two days later, on the third anniversary of the armistice. (That same day

Secretary of State Hughes welcomed the delegates of eight nations to the opening of the first conference on the limitation of naval armaments.)

Olympia, twenty-six years old in 1921, had seen deployed service during this, her second war, in the Atlantic and the Mediterranean. That westbound crossing in November was her last cruise in commission. The historic cruiser, the world's oldest steel combatant ship still afloat, now lies alongside a pier at the Independence Seaport Museum, on the Delaware River waterfront in Philadelphia (only a few miles downriver from the former site of Cramp's yard), in desperate need of costly restoration if she is to be preserved.

The new, 33,190 ton battleship *Tennessee* and her only classmate, *California*, boasted twelve 14 inch/50 caliber guns (compared to *Dreadnought*'s 12 inch/45s), mounted three to a turret, and at maximum elevation capable of firing "over the horizon," well beyond 30,000 yards. (Battleships at the Battle of Jutland had generally fought at ranges around 12,000 yards, although their shells—the largest as heavy as a Volkswagen "Beetle"—could reach out farther.) Her secondary battery included fourteen 5 inch/51s.

The great power and range of her main battery aside, the new *Tennessee*'s principal innovations included oil-fired boilers and turbine electric drive producing 26,800 horsepower and 21 knots, much improved armor and watertight compartmentation, and gun directors in her "fighting tops" on both cage masts. (Approaching twenty-five years later, her relatively slow speed kept *Tennessee* out of the fast aircraft carrier task forces that revolutionized war at sea in the Pacific, but she was one of six American battleships that fought the Battle of Surigao Strait in October 1944, the last big gun duel between ships of the line in history.)

All trials successfully completed, in mid-1921 the new *Tennessee* steamed through the Panama Canal for her home port, San Pedro, California, where, four years and one month since her keel had been laid down, she joined the Pacific Fleet's battleship force. Then followed nineteen years of more or less routine training exercises, readiness evaluations, deployed operations, and shipyard overhauls.

In August 1940 *Tennessee* and the rest of the Pacific Fleet's battleship force moved to Pearl Harbor, Hawaii, from always inadequate San Pedro, unsuccessfully attempting to lend sufficient heft to deter a Japanese thrust against European colonies in Southeast Asia. She was there on "Battleship Row" in the early morning of Sunday, December 7, 1941, moored on the southeast side of Ford Island at Quay Fox-6 in 40 feet of water, with boiler no. 1 on the line providing steam for auxiliary machinery; she was astern of *Maryland* and *Oklahoma*, and ahead of *Arizona* and the repair ship *Vestal*, with *West Virginia* alongside to port. At 7:58 a.m. *Tennessee* and the others came under surprise attack from Japanese naval aircraft.

And the rest, just like all that has gone before, is History.

Notes

CHAPTER 1

1. "Circular Defining Chief Characteristics of 2 Armored Cruisers Authorized by Act of Congress Approved July 1, 1902," CIS US Executive Branch Documents, 1789–1909; No. N-117–10.5.

2. "Plans for New Cruisers," *New York Times*, October 29, 1902.

3. James Dredge, *A Record of the Transportation Exhibits at the World's Columbian Exposition of 1893* (New York: John Wiley and Sons, 1894).

4. Cramp's SS *St. Louis* was not the ten-year-old, Bremen-built, Hapag Lloyd liner of the same name that infamously sailed in May 1939 from Hamburg for Havana with hundreds of desperate German Jewish refugees on board. All expected to find temporary sanctuary in Cuba from the crisis brewing in Germany. Cuba's subsequent refusal to let the refugees land (and America's and Canada's refusals to take them) forced *St. Louis* back to Europe, where as many as two-thirds of them perished in the war.

5. Promoted to rear admiral in 1909 after forty years in uniform and more than twenty-one years of service at sea, the durable Berry retired in 1910 and died twenty-eight years later. The Johnson appointment story is from Margaret M. Brearley, "Rear Admiral Albert Gleaves Berry 1848–1938," *Tennessee Historical Quarterly* 40, no. 1 (Spring 1981): 85–94, at 87. She cites the Catherine Berry Pilcher Avery papers at the Tennessee State Library as her source.

6. Annual Report of the Secretary of the Navy, November 28, 1881 (Washington, DC: GPO), 3.

7. Bent (1820–87) drew on his observations sailing in the Pacific as a naval officer to conclude that the Atlantic's Gulf Stream and the Pacific's Kuro-Siwo Current joined near the North Pole, together carrying enough heat between Iceland and Norway and through the "Behring" to ensure a wide expanse of open, ice-free water at the top of the globe, where the sun shone endlessly for part of the year. He believed these currents, styled "thermometric gateways," were the only "practicable avenues by which ships can reach" a postulated open polar sea.

Bent's theory was remarkably popular. Dr. Isaac Hayes believed it (*The Open Polar Sea* [Hurd and Houghton, 1867]); so for a time did Lieutenant Adolphus W. Greely, USA (*Handbook of Arctic Discoveries* [Roberts Bros., 1896]), as did many others, among them Matthew Maury, Elisha Kane, and Louis Agassiz.

8. HR 653, "Construction of Vessels of War for the Navy," 190–214.

9. Among the pretenders to the title of "father of the modern navy," the best claimant might be engineer John Neidermair (1893–1982), who beginning in 1928 at the Bureau of Ships led the preliminary design branch, responsible over the next thirty years for literally hundreds of ships, including the ungainly, superb Landing Ship, Tank (LST), mainstay of amphibious operations in both World War II oceans.

10. F. T. Bowles, "Our New Cruisers," *Proceedings Magazine* 9, no. 4 (September 1883): 595–626. Bowles's long article contains an excellent, plain-language description of the technical specification of all four ABCD ships. Assistant naval constructor Francis Bowles, USN, went on as a rear admiral to become the navy's chief constructor after the turn of the century.

11. Arthur might have had special interest in the navy. His late wife and the mother of his two children, Ellen Lewis Herndon, was the daughter of the late Commander William Herndon, USN, who in 1850–51 famously explored the Amazon River Basin by dugout canoe, beginning at the river's headwaters in Peru, a mission conceived by Lieutenant Matthew Fontaine Maury, USN, chief of the navy's Depot of Charts and Instruments. Herndon (on her bridge in dress uniform), and many others on board, died in September 1857 in a hurricane off Cape Hatteras while he was on leave from the navy and master of the merchant steamer SS *Central America*, carrying a cargo of gold from California. Gary Kinder's *Ship of Gold in the Deep Blue Sea* (Atlantic Monthly Press, 1998) tells that story.

CHAPTER 2

1. The "czar" in question was Tsar Nicholas II, who ruled Russia from 1894 until 1917. He was the beneficiary of American affection for his grandfather, Alexander II, who freed the serfs—thus prompting awkward comparisons to Lincoln—and who sent Russian navy squadrons to San Francisco and New York during the Civil War. Their unexpected arrival and presence in Union ports was wrongly assumed to reflect Russian political and potential naval support for the North.

2. Volker Schult, "Revolutionaries and Admirals: The German East Asia Squadron in Manila Bay," *Philippine Studies* 50, no. 4 (2002): 496–511.

3. "Armored" meaning the ship's hull was armor plated as protection against the flat trajectory of naval guns. "Protected" meaning an armored maindeck, meant to protect against attack from above.

4. "Official Records of the Union and Confederate Navies in the War of the Rebellion, Series 1, Vol. 7, North Atlantic Blockading Squadron, March 8–September 4, 1862," 55th Cong., 2nd Sess., Doc. 559 (Washington, DC: GPO, 1898), 410–13, 482–85.

5. SMS *Königsberg*'s story is told in Robert Gaudi's *African Kaiser: General Paul von Lettow-Vorbeck and the Great War in Africa, 1914–1918* (New York: Caliber, 2017).

6. The magazine, subtitled "A History of Our Time," was published between 1900 and 1932, when it was absorbed into the *Review of Reviews*, itself absorbed into a rival monthly five years later. *Time*'s July 25, 1932, obituary of the *World's Work* described it as a "heavy review," as compared to other monthlies that featured "high-grade fiction & belles lettres." The *World's Work*'s first publisher was Walter Hines Page, later Woodrow Wilson's ambassador in London.

7. Oliver, "Shall We Control the Pacific?" *World's Work* 28, no. 1 (May 1914): 64–74.

8. St. Paul *Globe*, Sunday, September 19, 1897, 17.

CHAPTER 3

1. President James Monroe, Seventh Annual Message to Congress, in *Milestone Documents in the National Archives* (Washington, DC: NARA, 1995), 26–29.

2. January 1, 1823–June 14, 1824, with gaps.

3. In the collection of the Library of Congress, https://lccn.loc.gove/98511150.

4. Murray G. Lawson, "Canada and the Articles of Confederation," *American Historical Review* 58, no. 1 (October 1952): 39–54.

5. House Executive Documents, 33rd Cong., 2nd Sess., Vol. 10, Doc. 93, 127–36.

6. Hamilton Fish, January 16, 1871, in 41st Cong., 3rd Sess., Senate Executive Document No. 17, "Message of the President of the United States Communicating . . . Information Relative to the Proposed Annexation of the Dominican Portion of the Island of Santo Domingo," 8.

7. *Index to Executive Documents*, 41st Cong., 3rd Sess., 1870–71, 2 vols. (Washington, DC: GPO, 1871).

8. *Personal Memoirs of U. S. Grant* (New York: Charles L. Webster and Co., 1885), 2:550.

9. McCullough, *The Path Between the Seas* (New York: Simon & Schuster, 1977), 492.

10. Vol. 17, no. 5 (1907): 479–96. The same story also appeared in newspapers at about the same time, among them the Sunday, May 5, 1907, issue of Honolulu's *Pacific Commercial Advertiser*.

11. 59th Cong., 2nd Sess., Senate Doc. 242, "International Maritime Exposition at Bordeaux, France," US Congressional Serial Set No. 5072.

12. See Seward W. Livermore, "The American Navy as a Factor in World Politics," *American Historical Review* 63, no. 4 (July 1958): 863–79.

13. *Los Angeles Herald*, October 7, 1907, 1.

14. "America Ahead in Fighting Strength. A Comparison of the Two Fleets . . . ," *New York Times*, July 7, 1907, SM7.

15. Incorporated in New York City in 1884 by a group of retired and serving army officers, the American Military Service Institution was modeled after a British Army professional interest organization, and shared some purposes, features, and programs with the roughly contemporary, but much longer lived, US Naval Institute. The Military Service Institution dissolved around the end of World War I.

16. This snippet of a quote and the ones that follow are from chapter 29 of Captain Fiske's autobiography, *From Midshipman to Rear-Admiral* (New York: Center Co., 1919). Fiske served as USS *Tennessee*'s commanding officer from July 1908 through August 1910.

17. Good contemporary descriptions of the challenges of an early twentieth-century passage through the Strait of Magellan are found in the sailing directions in H. O. Publication 89, *West Coast of South America* (Washington, DC: GPO, 1905), chap. 2, "Magellan Strait," 43–127; and in the later H. O. Publication No. 173, *South American Pilot*, vol. 2, 1st ed. (Washington, DC: GPO, 1916), 271–387.

18. Ambassador Rockhill to the Secretary of State, October 31, 1912, File No. 767.70/75, "Turkey, War Between Montenegro, Serbia, Bulgaria, and Greece—Protection of American Interests—Good Offices of Neutral Powers," in *Papers Relating to the Foreign Relations of the United States* (Washington, DC: GPO, 1919), 1341–54.

19. Ten years later these retreads from civilian service were aging out of the fleet, prompting construction of eight navy-designed, purpose-built replacements in three classes, beginning with *Vestal* (6,400 tons of coal) and *Prometheus*, then *Mars*, *Vulcan*, and *Hector*, and finally the much larger *Cyclops* (Cramp's no. 347), *Jupiter*, and *Neptune* (12,500 tons). They were commissioned between 1909 and 1913. Out of Barbados in early March 1918, USS *Cyclops* disappeared in the Bermuda Triangle with all hands. Two later navy colliers, *Proteus* and *Nereus*, Nos. 9 and 10, in Canadian merchant service in 1941 were both also lost at sea mysteriously. "The Eight New Fleet Oilers," *Navy*, March 1910, 24–25.

20. "Uncle Sam Ordered Two Cruisers Home from Turkish Seas . . . Navy Acts Quickly upon Learning Japan Will Receive New Battleship," *Cairo* [Illinois] *Bulletin*, May 10, 1913, 1.

CHAPTER 4

1. Henry J. Hendrix, *Theodore Roosevelt's Naval Diplomacy: The U.S. Navy and the Birth of the American Century* (Annapolis, MD: Naval Institute Press, 2009), xiii.

2. Charles Bonaparte, "Experiences of a Cabinet Officer under Roosevelt," *Century Magazine* 79 (March 1910): 752–58.

3. For more, see Nicholas J. Danby, "The Roots of Roosevelt's Navalism," *Naval History* 35, no. 1 (February 2021): 33–39.

4. The description is by assistant naval constructor F. T. Bowles in "Our New Cruisers," *Proceedings Magazine* 9, no. 4 (1883): 595–623.

5. Roosevelt to Dr. Albert Shaw, from Oyster Bay, September 3, 1907, Raab Collection, Ardmore, PA. The term "yellow press" described newspapers and magazines that relied on sensational or lurid reporting of poorly researched events to boost circulation. The allusion was to the "Yellow Kid" cartoon strip that ran in the New York *World* from 1895 to 1898.

6. *Information Relative to the Voyage of the United States Atlantic Fleet around the World* (Washington, DC: GPO, 1910), 16.

7. C. S. Forbes, "Captain Charles E. Clark, U.S.N.," *Vermonter* 7, no. 7 (February 1902): 39.

8. James and Mary Ford, eds., *Every Day in the Year, A Poetical Epitome of the World's History* (New York: Dodd, Mead and Co., 1902). The Fords offered a second poem for the same day, March 19, "Battle-Song of the Oregon," by Wallace Rice.

9. [San Francisco] *Call* 104, no. 34 (July 4, 1908).

CHAPTER 5

1. Christopher Clark, *The Sleepwalkers, How Europe Went to War in 1914* (New York: Harper Collins, 2012); Charles Emmerson, *1913: In Search of the World before the Great War* (New York: Public Affairs, 2014); Max Hastings, *Catastrophe 1914: Europe Goes to War* (New York: Knopf Doubleday, 2014); Margaret MacMillan, *The War That Ended Peace: The Road to 1914* (New York: Random House, 2014); Dominic Lieven, *Towards the*

Flame: Empire, War and the End of Tsarist Russia (London: Allen Lane, 2015); and Sean McMeekin, *The Russian Origins of the First World War* (Cambridge, MA: Belknap Press of Harvard University Press, 2011). See also titles by Gordon Martel, T. G. Otte, and Geoffrey Wawro.

2. Angell (1872–1967) was an enormously fecund author, averaging an astonishing book a year for several decades. In 1934 he was awarded the Nobel Peace Prize for 1933; by then he'd written twenty-seven books since his first, published under a pseudonym, *Patriotism under Three Flags: A Plea for Rationalism in Politics* (London, 1903).

3. General John "Black Jack" Pershing, USA, the commanding general of the American Expeditionary Force on the western front in 1917–18, subscribed to a similar aggressive strategy. Only the very late entry of the United States into the fighting spared American infantry the horrific losses suffered by France and Great Britain that Robert Service had described in his verse. Even so, under Pershing's leadership some 26,000 doughboys were lost in little more than a month, with a like number killed during the other five months of serious fighting that included Americans.

4. Mahan, "The Great Illusion," *North American Review* 195, no. 676 (March 1912): 322. Angell prompted the fight. In both his 1909 pamphlet-length exposition of his thesis and in the full-length book that followed a year later (*The Great Illusion: A Study of The Relation of Military Power in Nations to Their Economic and Social Advantage* [W. Heinemann, 1910]) Angell repeatedly cited Mahan's thesis as an example of fundamentally flawed theorizing.

5. Theodore Roosevelt, review, *Political Science Quarterly* 9, no. 1 (March 1894): 171–73. Roosevelt, thirty-six then, was in Washington in 1894, serving as a civil service commissioner, from where he would move to New York City the next year to become its police commissioner. His explosion onto the national political scene was still five years away. Roosevelt's interest in naval history came naturally from his maternal uncles James and Irving, who'd served with distinction in the Confederate States Navy. That interest was reflected in his excellent history of the War of 1812, published in 1882, years before Mahan's seminal books.

6. "Many divisions were ready for transport a week or more before railways could accept them. After the railways reached their mobilization readiness they were expected to work at full capacity only for a few days" (J. N. Westwood, *A History of Russian Railways* [London: George Allen and Unwin, Ltd., 1964], 171–72).

7. Mine is the usual narrative of the Schlieffen Plan, as reflected, for example, in Dennis Showalter's *Instrument of War: The German Army 1914–18* (Oxford: Osprey Publishing, 2016), or Walter Goerlitz's much older *The German General Staff, 1657–1945* (New York: Praeger, 1953). There is another: Terence Zuber has since 1999 argued that no such plan existed or could have shaped German operations at the outset of the war. His interesting, controversial thesis is presented in *Inventing the Schlieffen Plan: German War Planning 1871–1914* (New York: Oxford University Press, 2002).

8. Initial German plans aside, Verdun—the most modern fortress in Europe—drew battle like a magnet. The idea of the frustrated, second wartime chief of the German general staff,

Eric von Falkenhayn, who in February 1916 launched the German Fifth Army's attack on the fortifications, was that Verdun would fast become a sump down which the blood of France would drain to exhaustion—an expectation that by this point in the war passed for high strategy. The ensuing campaign cost some 300,000 men their lives and von Falkenhayn his job on August 29. He died in retirement in 1922 at age sixty. See Peter D. Eicher, ed., *"Emperor Dead" and Other Historic American Diplomatic Dispatches* (Bloomington, IN: Universe, 2012), 347.

9. "The Question of Coast Defense," *Collier's Weekly* 20, no. 25 (March 26, 1898): 2–3.

10. World War I Document Archive, Brigham Young University Library, https://wwi.lib.byu.edu/.

11. Jay Winter, "How to Commemorate Catastrophe, Remembering World War I, 100 Years After," *Yale Alumni Magazine* 80, no. 4 (March–April 2017): 59.

12. "Few Americans had taken the precaution of travelling with passports, and passports had become a necessity," explained Ambassador Gerard at the start of his memoir's second chapter, about "The Americans at the Outbreak of Hostilities" (James W. Gerard, *My Four Years in Germany* (New York: George H. Doran Co., 1917), 143).

13. Soon Hoover expanded his volunteer humanitarian efforts to chair the Commission for Relief in Belgium. He did an outstanding job, successfully feeding the small nation under almost impossible conditions. Fifteen years later he became the thirty-first president of the United States—his first elective office, and the first time a president had been elected with no prior experience in office. Hoover's hapless response to the Great Depression made his a one-term presidency and delivered the White House to the Democrats for the next two decades.

14. Henry Breckinridge, *Report on Operations of the United States Relief Commission in Europe* (Washington, DC: GPO, 1914).

15. *New York Times*, September 12, 1914.

16. The big liner's sinking prompted outraged newspaper reporting, soon echoed in a poignant June 1915 recruiting poster, "Enlist," by artist Fred Spears, that featured a drowning mother and child. The most unusual commemoration of *Lusitania*'s loss came in July 1918, in an eleven-minute animated film of the submarine attack on the ship by *New York Herald* cartoonist Winsor McCay. McCay's fascinating movie, the product of 25,000 hand-drawn images, can be viewed online.

17. Impelled, perhaps, by lurid scenarios posed by authors of genre fiction or by the fears of the Royal Defense Corps, the government in London prepared for an invasion of the home islands by, among other things, moving the gold reserves of the United Kingdom to North America. Beach wrote that when *Tennessee* finally returned home, she surreptitiously brought with her to North America the gold reserves of the United Kingdom, where they could lie safely in Canadian vaults while the war raged on. Edward L. Beach, *The Wreck of the Memphis* (Annapolis: Naval Institute Press, 1998), 18.

Possibly, but almost certainly not. Under a headline that read "Seven Carloads of English Gold Reach New York," on August 11, 1915, the *New York Times* reported that $52 million in gold and securities from the Bank of England had arrived in the city after a transatlantic passage in a Royal Navy battle cruiser and a ride in an armored train from Halifax. British reserves were moved to Canada again during World War II, this second time also in His Majesty's ships.

18. Caperton described his role during these years in his *History of U.S. Naval Operations under Command of Rear Admiral W. B. Caperton, USN, Commencing January 5, 1915 ending April 30, 1919*, NARA RG 45, Subject File ZN (1911–27), Boxes 936–37.

19. Ernest Bicknell, the national director of the American Red Cross, riding to Europe in *Tennessee*, later said the kegs weighed 200 pounds each and contained $50,000 in gold coin.

20. Douglas R. Burgess Jr., *Engines of Empire: Steamships and the Victorian Imagination* (Stanford: Stanford University Press, 2016), 254.

21. "Tennessee off with $5,867,000," *New York Times*, August 7, 1914. The *Times's* digital archive for 1914–15 contains substantial reporting on *Tennessee's* European cruise. USS *Tennessee's* deck logs for 1914–15 are held at the National Archives in Record Group (RG) 24.

22. *Regulations for the Government of the United States Navy (Navy Regulations) 1913* (Washington, DC: GPO, 1913), 151R–52R.

23. Decker to Secretary of the Navy (Aide for Operations), January 26, 1915, NARA, RG 80, Box 1505.

24. From William G. Cassard, ed., *Battleship Indiana and Her Part in the Spanish-American War* (New York: Indiana Ship's Company, 1898).

25. *Yavuz Sultan Selim* remained in commission with the Ottoman Navy and later the navy of the Turkish Republic until 1950. She was finally scrapped in 1973, the last surviving ship of the Imperial German Navy. *Midilli's* remaining service life was decades shorter. Sailing in company with *Yavuz Sultan Selim* on January 20, 1918, after sinking two Royal Navy monitors in Kusu Bay, Imbros Island, in the Aegean, *Midilli* hit some mines and quickly sank, drowning two-thirds of her crew.

26. *Papers Relating to the Foreign Relations of the United States* (1914), supplement, *The World War* (File No. 867.00/643) (Washington, DC: GPO, 1928).

27. *Papers Relating to the Foreign Relations of the United States* (1914), supplement, *The World War* (File No. 867.00/644).

CHAPTER 6

1. "Remarkable Details from American Consul on Palestine Locust Plague," *New York Times*, November 21, 1915.

2. "The attack on the Canal was of interest," Decker said in a speech he gave about *Tennessee's* surprise Mediterranean cruise, "because we were able to get glimpses from both sides. When it was over the English reported the results of the attack and by marching the prisoners through Cairo to the encampment, the natives [Egyptians, who conspicuously failed to rally to their fellow Muslims' side] were convinced of the truth. The Turks, on the other hand, held many celebrations of the great victory at the Canal in which the British were so badly defeated that there was nothing left for the Turkish Army to do, so it had to return to Palestine."

3. Morgenthau to Secretary of State, No. 374, July 27, 1915, FRUS 955–58, Doc. 1350, Office of the Historian.

4. Decker Papers, Hoover Institution Archive.

CHAPTER 7

1. Marrion Wilcox, *Harper's History of the War in the Philippines* (New York: Harper and Brothers, 1900), 312–14.

2. Edward L. Beach Sr., with Edward L. Beach Jr., *From Annapolis to Scapa Flow: The Autobiography of Edward L. Beach Sr.* (Annapolis: Naval Institute Press, 2003), 234.

3. Lieutenant Commander Thomas Withers, "The Wreck of the USS *Memphis*," *Naval Institute Proceedings* 44, no. 7 (July 1918): 1459–63. Lieutenant Withers, a ship's company officer, was on the sick list and not on the watch bill the day *Memphis* went aground. Promoted to flag rank in 1941, Rear Admiral Withers commanded Pacific Fleet submarines at the beginning of World War II. He retired at the end of the war.

4. *Army Navy Register* 60, no. 1895 (November 11, 1916): 579.

5. Edward L. Beach Jr., *The Wreck of the Memphis* (Annapolis: Naval Institute Press, 1998), 285–86.

6. De Booy (1882–1919) died of influenza in February 1919, one of the many millions who fell in the epidemic. An admiring summary of his short life is in Marshall H. Saville, "Theodore De Booy," *American Anthropologist* 21, no. 2 (April–June 1919): 182–85.

7. "Chronicling America," the Library of Congress's newspaper digital database, has 308 entries for a search for "cruiser Memphis" in 1916.

8. Anthony F. Sarcone and Lawrence S. Rines, *A History of Shipbuilding at Fore River* (Quincy, MA: Thomas Crane Public Library, n.d.), chap. 3.

CHAPTER 8

1. "War Is Noise, Jonathan Raban on the Anzio Landings," *London Review of Books* (December 2020), 40–43. Raban, age seventy-nine, is a British travel writer and prolific, prize-winning author of fiction.

2. Kitchener (1850–1916), then secretary of state for war but no longer exercising much formal authority, had died six months earlier, on June 5, 1916, when HMS *Hampshire*, the cruiser that he was riding to Arkhangelsk, Russia, from Scapa Flow hit a submarine-laid mine west of the Orkney Islands and swiftly sank, drowning him and 736 others. Only 12 of her crew survived.

3. "Memorandum in Regard to the Present Progress of the Blockade, January 1st, 1917," British National Archives, CAB 1/22, January 1, 1917.

4. David A. Janicki, "The British Blockade during World War I: The Weapon of Deprivation," *Inquiries Journal/Student Pulse* 6, no. 6 (2014).

Quoted material is from Charles D. Horne, ed., *Source Records of the Great War* (New York: National Alumni, 1923), 5:2–8. The verbatim records were accompanied by extensive annotation.

5. In his review in the *London Review of Books* of Hennessy and Jinks's *The Silent Deep:*

The Royal Navy Submarine Service since 1945 (Allen Lane, 2016), British maritime historian N. A. M. Rodger objected to the phrase, arguing that "'unrestricted submarine warfare' implies the rejection of legal restraints that did not really exist, for international law as yet had taken almost no note of the existence of submarines." The realities of international and Admiralty law aside, most people understood the phrase then (and do now) to mean an open season on ocean shipping of any type, including passenger liners, sailing under any flag, without prior inspection for contraband or even warning. That's what the Germans meant by it, too.

6. *Papers Relating to the Foreign Relations of the United States* (1917), supplement 1, *The World War*, File No. 763.72/3179.

7. *Papers Relating to the Foreign Relations of the United States* (Lansing Papers, 1914–20), 1:623–26.

8. Captain Greg Williams, a World War II merchant marine veteran, found that 383 ships crossed the Atlantic during World War I with a navy armed guard on board after the first, SS *Manchuria*, did so on March 16 (*The United States Merchant Marine in World War I* [McFarland and Co., 2017], 74). These vessels averaged almost five crossings each, 1,832 all told. Nearly 60 percent (227) encountered a U-boat during a crossing; 33 were torpedoed, 3 were sunk otherwise, but half (113) managed to drive off their attackers with gunfire, presumably saving themselves. Perhaps ignorant of these numbers, but likely not, Sims described the worth of these guns as a "minor measure" Rear Admiral William Snowden Sims, USN, with Burton J. Hendrick, *The Victory at Sea* (Garden City, NY: Doubleday, Page and Co., 1920), 33–34, and app. 3.

9. Rodney Carlisle, "The Attacks on U.S. Shipping That Precipitated American Entry into World War I," *Northern Mariner/Le marin du nord* 17, no. 3 (July 2007): 41–66.

10. On March 24, 1916, Captain Pustkuchen in his submarine, SM UB-29, torpedoed the cross-Channel ferry *Sussex*, formerly of British registry but then sailing between Folkestone and Dieppe under French colors. Some fifty passengers were killed, and several Americans numbered among the injured. *Sussex* then limped into Boulogne under tow with most of her bow gone. The following May Germany pledged to provide for the safety of passengers should a merchant ship be sunk following confirmation that arms or munitions were on board.

11. Its author was actually Hans von Kemnitz, age forty-six, an obscure official in the ministry. His telegram's core idea—territorial ambitions satisfied in exchange for alliance—wasn't original. In August 1914 Von Moltke had mused that perhaps the United States might be persuaded to become a German ally if promised Canada in any postwar settlement as a reward. Lamar Cecil, *Wilhelm II, Vol. 2: Emperor and Exile, 1900–1941* (Chapel Hill: University of North Carolina Press, 1996), 208. Encrypted and decrypted copies of the telegram are held by the National Archives in RG 59, General Records of the Department of State, Nos. 302022 and 302025.

12. Henry Morgenthau, *Ambassador Morgenthau's Story* (Garden City, NY: Doubleday, Page and Co., 1918), 401. Morgenthau's ambassadorial memoir was also serialized in nine issues of *World's Work* from May 1918 through June 1919.

13. Dozens of munitions plants fell victim to successful sabotage efforts, and impounded German ships almost inevitably had their propulsion plants mysteriously disabled, forcing costly repairs before they could be diverted into American service, but the most notorious German sabotage might have been the effort to introduce fatal equine diseases into the American breeding stock of cavalry and draft horses. See Robert Koenig, *The Fourth Horseman: One Man's Mission to Wage the Great War in America* (New York: Public Affairs, 2006).

14. Oddly, this comparison would also be true one war later. "When the United States entered [World War II]," Andrew Roberts reported in his *The Storm of War* (HarperCollins, 2011), "she had the world's seventeenth largest army, numbering 269,023, smaller than that of Romania" (214).

15. Emerson Hough, *The Web: A Revelation of Patriotism* (Chicago: Reilly and Lee Co., 1919), 88.

16. Deliberately aping the route to fame and wealth pioneered by Gerard in 1917–18, in 1941 the second American ambassador to the Soviet Union, Joseph Davies (he served in Moscow just before the war, during 1936–38) wrote—had ghost-written, actually—a best-selling memoir of his service, *Mission to Moscow*, which in 1943, with a lot of prodding, was made into its own Warner Brothers movie. This one starred Walter Huston as the ambassador, character actor Manart Kippen as Stalin, and the unknown Dudley Malone as Churchill. Posters touted the new film, a deliberate propaganda piece that echoed the wartime alliance-building themes in the government-sponsored "Why We Fight" film series by Frank Capra, as "One American's Journey into the Truth!" Not long after the release it was described in the *New York Times* as "totalitarian propaganda for mass consumption" by no less a light than philosopher John Dewey. Reportedly, under this kind of critique, the film never recovered its expenses. Not long thereafter, the entire doubtful enterprise came under the lens of the notorious House Un-American Activities Committee.

17. "Sims Sailed Abroad under Assumed Name," *New York Times*, April 8, 1919.

18. *Hearings before the Subcommittee of the Committee on Naval Affairs, US Senate, 66th Cong., 2nd Sess.* (Washington, DC: GPO, 1921), 1981–3179.

19. Sims, *The Victory at Sea*, 374–86.

20. Sims, *The Victory at Sea*, 376–84.

21. Lieutenant Tracy Barrett Kittredge, USNRF, *Naval Lessons of the Great War: A Review of the Senate Naval Investigations of the Criticisms by Admiral Sims of the Policies and Methods of Josephus Daniels* (Garden City, NY: Doubleday, Page and Co., 1921).

22. *Annual Reports of the Navy Department for Fiscal Year 1917* (Washington, DC: GPO, 1918).

23. Sims, *The Victory at Sea*, 53.

24. Captain J. K. Taussig, USN, "Destroyer Experiences during the Great War," *US Naval Institute Proceedings* 48, no. 12 (December 1922): 2015–40; 49, no. 1 (January 1923): 39–69; 49, no. 2 (February 1923): 221–48; 49, no. 3 (March 1923): 383–408.

25. The 1920 *Register of Commissioned Officers of the United States Navy and Marine Corps* had then-Rear Admiral Decker 47th on the lineal list among 69 rear admirals; in the

1921 register he was 41st, among 63. Then came the passover and the pain of watching eight junior contemporaries be advanced over his head. The January 1, 1922, edition of the register shows Decker as the senior captain of all 176 in grade, no. 61 on the navy's lineal list, and junior only to all 60 admirals above him on the list.

26. See George Creel, *How We Advertised America* (New York: Harper & Brothers, 1920).

27. Not so Decker's relief in the Spanish capital, Captain (ten years later Rear Admiral) Walter Crosley, USN (1871–1939, USNA '93), who was delighted to find himself in Madrid in Decker's place. Crosley arrived in Spain following an aborted tour as the attaché in Berlin (diplomatic relations with Germany had been broken after he was detached from command of the Cramp's-built transport USS *Prairie* off Santo Domingo but before he reported to Berlin), and a thrilling one subsequently as naval attaché in Petrograd, Russia. That tour of duty was climaxed by a desperate escape by rail north from Petrograd, in upheaval under the Bolsheviks in late winter 1918, shepherding for two months a party of sixteen civilian countrymen and -women through the cold wastes of Finland and Sweden. Madrid must have been as welcome to Crosley as it was unwelcome to Decker. See Fredrick M. Corse, "An American's Escape from Russia," *World's Work* 36 (May–October 1918): 553–60.

28. "Awarding of Medals in the Naval Service," Friday, January 16, 1920, Senate Subcommittee on Naval Affairs (Washington, DC: GPO, 1920).

29. The quotations are from the *Richmond* [Virginia] *Times-Dispatch* of Sunday, June 27, 1920, "Admiral Decker Bitter in Assailing Secretary," 1–3.

EPILOGUE

1. Daniels's fantasy of "an international peace police on land and sea" soon collided with reality. The American resumption of capital ship construction two years later found its reflection in a British commitment to matching the growth of the American navy (the so-called "one power standard"), and in a new construction program of sixteen battleships and cruisers announced by Japan in autumn of 1920. It was this evidence of another hugely expensive and dangerously destabilizing naval construction competition that prompted President Harding to sponsor in November 1921 the first of the several Great Powers naval arms limitations conferences that followed.

Bibliography

Items marked with an asterisk (*) are available online.

Primary Sources

Papers

Edward L. **Beach** Jr. (1918–2002) Papers, 1951–99. Nimitz Library, US Naval Academy. No. MS 422, Record Series 3.

Albert Gleaves **Berry** (1848–1938) Papers, 1865–1910. Tennessee State Library and Archives. III-K-6.

Josephus **Daniels** (1863–1947) Papers. Southern Historical Collection, Wilson Library, UNC University Libraries, Chapel Hill. No. 203.

Benton Clark **Decker** (1867–1933) Papers, 1914–21. Hoover Institution Archives. No. 74078.

Annie **Keith Frazier Somerville** (1887–1977) Papers. Genealogical Collection, Mississippi Department of Archives and History. No. Z2103.000, Box 1, Folder 1.

Keith-McHenry-Pond Family Papers, 1841–1961. Bancroft Library Archives, University of California, Berkeley. BANC MSS C-B 595.

Tracy Barrett **Kittredge** (1891–1957) Papers, 1910–57. Hoover Institution Archives. No. 60017.

William Sowden **Sims** (1856–1939) Papers, 1856–1951. Library of Congress. No. MSS 53645, Boxes 53, 54.

National Archives and Records Administration (NARA)

RG 19, Records of the Bureau of Ships.

Records Relating to Weights, Performances, Tests, Repairs, and Alterations of Ships' Machinery. Engineering Trial Data Reports and Performance Data of Vessels 1886–1939. Steam Engineering reports 1886–1930. Box 61.

Engineering Performance Reports 1886–1939. Box 70.

RG 24, Records of the Bureau of Naval Personnel. Deck Logs, USS Tennessee, 7-17-1906 to 3-13-1907, part of entry 118.

RG 26, Logs of Revenue Cutters and Coast Guard Vessels. Vol. 639, NC-31, 159-A.*

RG 45, Records Collection of the Office of Naval Records and Library, 1911–27. US Naval Vessels OS-Memphis to Menhaden, Entry 520, Box 1222 of 1630.

RG 45, Records of the Office of the Chief of Naval Operations, 1887–1945. Register of

the Movements of Naval Vessels, January 1, 1900–June 30, 1941, E217 1–18, Vol. 13 of 42.

RG 80, General Records of the Navy Department.
General Correspondence, 1897–1915, Box Nos. 764 and 1505.
Secretary of the Navy, General Correspondence, 1916–26, Box Nos. 828, 1704, 2204, 2610, and 2611.

RG 84, Records of the Foreign Service, Posts of the Department of State.

RG 125, Records of the Office of the JAG (Navy). Proceedings of General Courts Martial 1866–1942, 33164 through 33229, Box Nos. 301–2.

DOCUMENTS

"Addresses of President Wilson, January 27–February 3, 1916, 64th Cong., 1st Sess., HR Doc. 803." Washington, DC: GPO, 1916.

British Hydrographic Office. *The Mediterranean Pilot, Vol. IV, Comprising the Archipelago, with the Adjacent Coasts of Greece and Turkey: Including Also the Island of Crete or Candia.* 4th ed. London: Taylor, Garrett, Evans and Co., Ltd., 1908.

Caperton, William B. *History of U.S. Naval Operations under Command of Rear Admiral W. B. Caperton, USN, Commencing January 5, 1915 ending April 30, 1919.* NARA, RG 45, Subject file ZN (1911–27), Boxes 936–37.

———. *Regulations for the Government of the Navy of the United States (Navy Regulations) 1913.* Washington, DC: Government Printing Office (GPO), 1913.*

"Circular Defining Chief Characteristics of 2 Armored Cruisers Authorized by Act of Congress Approved July 1, 1902." Congressional Information Service, US Executive Branch Documents, 1789–1909, No. N-117–10.5.

William Cramp and Sons Ship and Engine Building Company Records (1876–1910). Temple University Special Collections Research Center, RG MSS031.

"Hearing before a Subcommittee on Naval Affairs, US Senate, 66th Cong., 2nd Sess., on S. Res. 285, 'Awarding of Medals in the Naval Service.'" Washington, DC: GPO, 1920.

"Hearings before the Subcommittee of the Committee on Naval Affairs, United States Senate, 66th Cong., 2nd Sess." 2 vols. Washington, DC: GPO, 1921.*

Hexamer General Insurance Surveys. Vol. 9, pls. 771, 772 (1874). Vol. 18, pls. 1685, 1686 (1882). Vol. 22, pls. 2140, 2141 (1887). Vol. 26, pls. 2503, 2504 (1891). Vol. 28, pls. 2688, 2690 (1893).*

Hydrographic Office. Chart No. 5978, "Island of Khios and Gulf of Smyrna, from British Surveys between 1835 and 1837, with Additions and Corrections to 1898." Washington, DC: Hydrographic Office, March 1915.

"Island of Haiti, West Coast of Santo Domingo, Santo Domingo Harbor, from a Survey by USS *Castine* in 1914 and USS *Nashville* in 1912."

Secondary Sources

Alden, John D., CDR, USN (Ret.) .*The American Steel Navy.* Annapolis: Naval Institute Press, 1972.

Anderson, Scott. *Lawrence in Arabia: War, Deceit, Imperial Folly and the Making of the Modern Middle East*. New York: Doubleday, 2013.

Bax, E. "The American Embassy, August 4, 1914." *Atlantic Monthly*, October 1930, 503–11.

Beach, Edward L., Jr. *The Wreck of the Memphis*. Annapolis: Naval Institute Press, 1998.

Beach, Edward L., Sr., with Edward L. Beach Jr. *From Annapolis to Scapa Flow: the Autobiography of Edward L. Beach Sr.* Annapolis: Naval Institute Press, 2003.

Bernstorff, Count [Johann Heinrich graf von]. *My Three Years in America*. New York: Charles Scribner's Sons, 1920.*

Bicknell, Ernest P. "Relief of Americans in Europe." *American Red Cross Bulletin* 9, no. 4 (October 1914): 232–36.*

Bonner, Kermit. *USS New York (BB-34): The Old Lady of the Sea*. Paducah, KY: Turner Publishing, 2002.*

Bowen, Harold G. *Ships, Machinery and Mossbacks: The Autobiography of a Naval Engineer*. Princeton: Princeton University Press, 1954.

Brearley, Margaret M. "Rear-Admiral Albert Gleaves Berry 1848–1938." *Tennessee Historical Quarterly* 40, no. 1 (Spring 1981): 85–94.*

Buell, Augustus C. *The Memoirs of Charles H. Cramp*. Philadelphia: J. B. Lippencott Co., 1906.*

Clark, Christopher. *The Sleepwalkers: How Europe Went to War in 1914*. New York: Harper Collins, 2012.

Collin, Richard H. "The 1904 Detroit Compact: U.S. Naval Diplomacy and the Dominican Revolutions." *Historian* 52, no. 3 (May 1990): 432–52.

Conrad, Dennis M. "Were They So Unprepared? Josephus Daniels and the United States Navy's Entry into World War I." *U.S. Military History Review* 3, no.1 (December 2016): 5–20.*

Copeland, Clem A. "Boiler Tube Explosion on USS *Tennessee*." *Journal of Electricity, Power, and Gas* 20, no. 25 (June 20, 1908): 385–87.*

Craig, Lee A. *Josephus Daniels, His Life and Times*. Chapel Hill: University of North Carolina Press, 2013.

Crawford, Michael J., ed. *The World Cruise of the Great White Fleet*. Washington, DC: Naval Historical Center, 2008.

Creel, R. H., F. M. Faget, and W. D. Wrightson. "Hydrocyanic Gas, Its Practical Use as a Routine Fumigant." *Public Health Reports* 30, no. 39 (December 3, 1915): 3537–50.*

Cummings, Lindsey. "Economic Warfare and the Evolution of the Allied Blockade of the Eastern Mediterranean: August 1914–April 1917." Master's thesis, Georgetown University, 2015.*

Decker, Lieutenant Benton C., USN. "The Consolidated Mess of the Crew of USS Indiana." *US Naval Institute Proceedings* 23, no. 3 (1897): 463–67.*

De Long, Emma, ed. *The Voyage of the* Jeannette, *the Ship and Ice Journals of George W. De Long*. 2 vols. Boston: Houghton, Mifflin and Co., 1883.*

Dredge, James. *A Record of the Transportation Exhibits at the World's Columbian Exposition of 1893*. New York: John Wiley and Sons, 1894.

Evans, Rear Admiral Robley D., USN. *An Admiral's Log, Being Continued Recollections of Naval Life*. New York: D. Appleton and Co., 1910.*

———. *A Sailor's Log, Recollections of Forty Years of Naval Life*. New York: D. Appleton and Co., 1901.*

Everett, Marshall, ed. [pseud.]. *Exciting Experiences in Our War with Spain and the Filipinos*. Chicago: Book Publishers Union, 1899.*

Farr, Gail E., and Brett F. Bostwick. *Shipbuilding at Cramp and Sons: A History and Guide to Collections of the William Cramp and Sons Ship and Engine Building company (1830–1927) and the Cramp Shipbuilding Company (1941–46) of Philadelphia*. Philadelphia: Philadelphia Maritime Museum, 1991.*

Fiske, Rear Admiral Bradley A., USN. *From Midshipman to Rear-Admiral*. New York: Center Co., 1919.*

Forbes, C. S. "Captain Charles E. Clark, U.S.N." *Vermonter* 7. no. 7 (February 1902): 39–43.*

Friedman, Norman. "The Fleet's Ambiguous, Versatile Warships." *Naval History* 29, no. 5 (October 2015): 16–23.

———. *U.S. Cruisers: An Illustrated History*. Annapolis: Naval Institute Press, 1984.

Gatewood, James Duncan, M.D. *Naval Hygiene*. Philadelphia: P. Blakiston's Son and Co., 1909.*

Gerard, James W. *Face to Face with Kaiserism*. New York: Geo. H. Doran Co., 1918.*

———. *My Four Years in Germany*. New York: George H. Doran Co., 1917.*

Glasgow, W. J. "The Commissioned Strength of the Regular Army in War." *Journal of the Military Service Institution of the United States* 40, no. 197 (May–June 1907): 321–25.

Gleaves, Vice Admiral Albert, USN. *A History of the Transport Service: Adventures and Experiences of United States Transports and Cruisers in the World War*. New York: George H. Doran Co., 1921.*

Grenfell, Commander Russell. *Sea Power in the Next War*. London: Geoffrey Bles, 1938.*

Hahn, Steven. *A Nation without Borders: The United States and Its World in an Age of Civil Wars, 1830–1910*. New York: Viking, 2016.

Heinrich, Thomas R. *Ships for the Seven Seas: Philadelphia Shipbuilding in the Age of Industrial Capitalism*. Baltimore: Johns Hopkins University Press, 1997.

Hendrick, Burton J. *The Life and Letters of Walter J. Page*. Garden City, NY: Doubleday, Page and Co., 1923.*

Hendrix, Henry J. *Theodore Roosevelt's Naval Diplomacy: The U.S. Navy and the Birth of the American Century*. Annapolis: Naval Institute Press, 2009.

Hough, Emerson. *The Web: A Revelation of Patriotism*. Chicago: Reilly and Lee Co., 1919.

Hunt, Thomas. *The Life of William H. Hunt*. Brattleboro, VT: E. L. Hildreth and Co., 1922.*

Jensen, Joan M. *The Price of Vigilance*. New York: Rand McNally and Co., 1968.

Kazin, Michael. *War against War: The American Fight for Peace, 1914–1918*. New York: Simon and Schuster, 2017.

Keiley, Charles Russel, ed. *The Official Blue Book of the Jamestown Centennial Exposition*. Norfolk: Colonial Publishing Co., 1907.*

Kennedy, Brian M. *Over Here: The First World War and American Society.* Oxford: Oxford University Press, 2004.

Kidwell, L. B. "Crews Muster Again: Memphis Reunion Fifty Years After." *All Hands* 599 (December 1966): 20–21.

Kinzer, Stephen. *The True Flag: Theodore Roosevelt, Mark Twain, and the Birth of American Empire.* New York: Henry Holt and Co., 2017.

Kipling, Rudyard. *Sea Warfare.* New York: Doubleday, Page and Co., 1917.*

Kittridge, Lieutenant Tracy Barrett, USNRF. *Naval Lessons of the Great War: A Review of the Senate Naval Investigations of the Criticisms by Admiral Sims of the Policies and Methods of Josephus Daniels.* Garden City, NY: Doubleday, Page and Co., 1921.*

Lawrence, W. J. *The United States Navy Illustrated, a New Series of over Fifty Reproductions from Original Photographs.* New York: Continent Publishing Co., 1898.

Leighton, John Langdon. *SIMSADUS London, the American Navy in Europe.* New York: Henry Holt Co., 1921.

Lincoln, W. Bruce. *Sunlight at Midnight: St. Petersburg and the Rise of Modern Russia.* New York: Basic Books, 2002.

Long, John D. *The New American Navy.* 2 vols. New York: Outlook Co., 1903.*

Mahan, A. T. *Naval Administration and Warfare: Some General Principles, with Other Essays.* Boston: Little, Brown, and Co., 1908.

Massey, Robert K. *Castles of Steel: Britain, Germany and the Winning of the Great War at Sea.* New York: Random House, 2003.

Matthews, Franklin. *Back to Hampton Roads: Cruise of the U.S. Atlantic Fleet from San Francisco to Hampton Roads, July 7, 1908–February 22, 1909.* New York: B. W. Huebsch, 1907.*

———. *With the Battle Fleet: Cruise of the Sixteen Battleships of the United States Atlantic Fleet from Hampton Roads to the Golden Gate, December, 1907–May, 1908.* New York: B. W. Heubsch, 1908.*

McClintock, Robert. "The End of Ex-USS *Memphis.*" *US Naval Institute Proceedings* 64, no. 427 (September 1938).

Miller, Edward S. *War Plan Orange: The U.S. Strategy to Defeat Japan, 1897–1945.* Annapolis: Naval Institute Press, 1991.

Morgenthau, Henry. *Ambassador Morgenthau's Story.* Garden City, NY: Doubleday, Page and Co., 1918.*

Musicant, Ivan. *Empire by Default: The Spanish-American War and the Dawn of the American Century.* New York: Henry Holt and Co., 1998.

———. *U.S. Armored Cruisers: A Design and Operational History.* Annapolis: Naval Institute Press, 1985.*

Oren, Michael B. *Power, Faith and Fantasy: America in the Middle East 1776 to the Present.* New York: W. W. Norton, 2007.

Pedisich, Paul D. *Congress Buys a Navy: Politics, Economics, and the Rise of American Naval Power, 1881–1921.* Annapolis: Naval Institute Press, 2016.

Ridgely, Frank E., and Gershom Bradford. *The West Indies Pilot, Vol. 1: Bermuda Islands, the Bahama Islands, and the Greater Antilles.* Washington, DC: GPO, 1913.*

Rose, Lisle A. *America's Sailors in the Great War: Seas, Skies, and Submarines.* Columbia: University of Missouri Press, 2017.

Schmidt, Carl H. *Navy Yearbook, Embracing All Acts Authorizing the Construction of Ships of the "New Navy" and a Resume of Annual Naval Appropriation Laws from 1883 to 1920, inclusive, with tables showing present naval strength, in ships and personnel, and cost of maintaining the navy of the United States, also statistics of foreign navies.* 66th Cong., 2nd Sess. Sen. Doc. 302. Washington, DC: GPO, 1921. *

Schult, Volker. "Revolutionaries and Admirals: The German East Asia Squadron in Manila Bay." *Philippine Studies* 50, no. 4 (2002): 496–511.*

Shaw, Stanford J. *The Jews of the Ottoman Empire and the Turkish Republic.* New York: New York University Press, 1991.

Showalter, Dennis. *Instrument of War: The German Army 1914–18.* Oxford: Osprey Publishing, 2016.

Simpson, Rear-Admiral Edward, USN. "The Navy and Its Prospects of Rehabilitation." *Proceedings of the United States Naval Institute* 12, no. 1 (December 1886).

Sims, Rear Admiral William Snowden, USN, with Burton J. Hendrick. *The Victory at Sea.* Garden City, NY: Doubleday, Page and Co., 1920.* [Also serialized in *The World's Work, a History of Our Time.*]

Stein, Stephen K. "The Greely Relief Expedition and the New Navy." *International Journal of Naval History* 5, no. 3 (December 1906).

Stephenson, Michael. *The Last Full Measure: How Soldiers Die in Battle.* New York: Crown Publishers, 2012.

Still, William N., Jr., ed. *The Queenstown Patrol, 1917: The Diary of Commander Joseph Knefler Taussig, U.S. Navy.* Newport, RI: Naval War College Press, 1996.

———. *Victory without Peace: The United States Navy in European Waters, 1919–1924.* Annapolis: Naval Institute Press, 2017.

Swann, Leonard A., Jr. *John Roach, Maritime Entrepreneur: The Years as Naval Contractor, 1862–1886.* Annapolis: Naval Institute Press, 1965.

Tyler, David B. *The American Clyde: A History of Iron and Steel Shipbuilding on the Delaware from 1840 to World War I.* Newark: University of Delaware Press, 1958.

Vego, Milan. *Naval Classical Thinkers and Operational Art.* NWC 1005. Newport, RI: Naval War College Press, 2009.

Westwood, J. N. *A History of Russian Railways.* London: George Allen and Unwin, Ltd., 1964.

Williams, Greg H. *The U.S. Merchant Marine in World War I: Ships, Crews, Shipbuilders and Operators.* Jefferson, NC: McFarland and Co., 2017.

Williams, William J. "Josephus Daniels and the U.S. Navy's Shipbuilding Program during World War I." *Journal of Military History* 60, no. 1 (January 1996): 7–38.

Withers, Lieutenant Commander T., Jr., USN. *Cramp's Shipyard Founded by William Cramp, 1830.* Philadelphia: William Cramp and Sons Ship and Engine Building Co., 1902.*

———. *Information Relative to the Voyage of the U.S. Atlantic Fleet around the World December 16, 1907 to February 22, 1909.* Washington, DC: GPO, 1910.*

———. *Investigation by the Committee on Naval Affairs of the U.S. Senate in Relation to Prices Paid for Armor for Vessels of the Navy*. Washington, DC: GPO, 1896.*

———. *Report on Operations of the United States Relief Commission in Europe*. Washington, DC: GPO, 1914.*

———. "The Sims-Daniels Row." *Literary Digest* 65, no. 9 (May 29, 1920): 20–21.*

———. "The Wreck of the USS *Memphis*." *Naval Institute Proceedings* 44, no. 185 (July 1918): 1459–65.*

Wohlforth, William C. "The Perception of Power: Russia in the Pre-1914 Balance." *World Politics* 30, no. 3 (April 1987): 353–81.

Wüstenbecker, Katja. "German-Americans during World War I." In Giles R. Hoyt, ed., Immigrant Entrepreneurship: German-American Business Biographies, 1720 to the Present, vol. 3. Washington, DC: German Historical Institute, 2014.

Index